WAKE UP

WAKE UP

What are your emotions really telling you?

Chris Partridge

3-Heads Publishing

ISBN-13: 978-1-8381456-2-0

Cover design by: Nicolas Bowley
Cover formatting by: Emanuel Carballo
Editor: Leslie Williams
Branding and promotions: Mark Showler

Printed in the United Kingdom

For all those currently contemplating their 'new normal'

"Only you and you alone know what it's like to be you. From the rich colour palette of our deepest pain to our heartfelt joy, we can all become artists ...."

CHRIS PARTRIDGE

CONTENTS

FOREWORD

By Professor Gerard Egan

This is an appropriate book for our unprecedented times. Filled with fresh insight, it goes a long way in bridging the gap between established psychology and modern awakening spirituality. Chris Partridge's writing is innovative, intuitive and, in many ways, uplifting. If you are a 'traditional thinker', prepare to be challenged. His message is that 'truth seekers' welcome, and even look for, challenge.

Chris, in his own gentle yet bold way, unravels the complexities of the human psyche. The reader's psyche. Your psyche! On a chapter by chapter basis he unlocks what he sees to be the deeper messages of our emotions, reframing them as messages whose hidden meanings help us to discover our own truth and inner potential. In doing this he delves into, what I would call, the 'shadow side' of human nature and behaviour.

Through interactive exercises, focused on reflective questioning and real-life examples drawn from his own holistic therapy practice, Chris helps the reader shine a challenging light on the difference between everyday suffering and spiritual growth.

The book is a unique literary journey of hope, meaning and

purpose. It is both an enlightening and a provocative read. It will make you think differently about yourself, others and the world.

Professor Gerard Egan.

Professor Emeritus at Loyola University, Chicago. Consultant, coach and counsellor.

Author of the internationally acclaimed book: 'The Skilled Helper', now in its 11th edition, and other works including 'Working the Shadow Side' and 'Interpersonal Living'.

PREFACE - THE 'NEW NORMAL?'

After much personal research, soul-searching contemplation, thinking, typing, tinkering and testing, this book is written. As I sit and write these last finishing touch words in August of 2020, the whole world is still responding, and adapting, to the effects of the latest coronavirus health crisis.

Rarely in our history as a species have we faced such a common global challenge together. Rarely have the boundaries we normally use to focus on where we are different, fallen away so rapidly. Rarely do we say as a human race, 'we are all in this together'.

The anxiety that this enforced shift in worldview has created brings out the best and worst in human nature. We are witnessing how the fear leads some into egocentricity, hoarding and howling 'who will help me?' While others are prepared to bravely peer into the abyss beyond their immediate selves and declare 'how can I help?'

But let's not be too quick to judge either of these voices. They coexist within every one of us. We do need to love and take care of ourselves to be able to love and care for others. If we try to do one without the other we become out of balance. We forget to nurture the spirit within ourselves so that we might be able to better connect with the spirit of others.

Is this what the coronavirus has come to remind us? To redress the balance of our extremes? To show us that when we remain in fear and solely self-serving, our planet suffers and our humanity flounders?

Many of us around the world are having to self-isolate. The physical 'going within' presents us with a deeper spiritual opportunity to go within too. To meet our true selves as we may never have done so before.

Necessity, as they say, is the mother of invention. During these times we have witnessed the hidden potential within the human spirit shining through ego-centred fear and anxiety. People on their balconies singing and applauding together. Setting up on-line support groups. Working from home and reducing their carbon footprint. Home schooling their children. Having more time to follow true passions. Being more creative with less. Forging a greater empathic connection with others who are not 'like' themselves.

None of us particularly looks forward to that early morning alarm going off when we are in our deepest slumber. Yet this virus, and the deeper implications of it, seem to be acting as that wake-up call. Rousing the unifying humanity within us all.

As I observe the unfolding world response, I'm struck by how many parallels have emerged reflecting the themes I have written about in this book: discovering who we really are, and what we are capable of, when our ego is no longer king; working on our spiritual growth and embracing the current potential for a planetary shift in our consciousness.

That is why I am trusting that the timing of the release of 'Wake Up - What are your emotions really telling you?' will help you reflect on the going within opportunity that now lies before us all.

I believe the wake-up call is happening now. Our time to change is now. Mother Nature, the planet, and our deepest self, are urgently imploring us to do so....

If you would like to stay in touch, leave comments, receive newsletters, blog updates and more please join me at:

www.thenewnormalmovement.net

PART ONE

WHAT'S IT ALL ABOUT?

Now who said this was going to be easy? This crazy roller-coaster of life which takes us up and down, through twists and turns. Showing us the greatest panoramic vistas, before seemingly plunging us downwards at great speed, forcing us to shut our eyes when it all gets too much....

But, what if there were some sort of purpose to it all? What if being spun around, and seeing the world from all angles, actually helped us to discover who we *really* are. To better understand what we are supposed to be doing here?

Through these pages I am going to explore just that possibility. I want to shine a new light on what your emotions may really be trying to tell you. To explore how to use that light to better understand just where your life's roller coaster may be trying to take you. Are you merely surviving the ride or thriving from it? Suffering it or living it?

I invite you to use this book as an opportunity to take a step back from your life right now. To begin to view it from a different perspective. To resist just seeking answers. To contemplate the bigger questions:

- ❑ Why does the same thing keep happening to me?

- ❑ What is life trying to show me about who I *really* am?

- ❑ Is *my* treatment of *my* problems benefitting me or destroying me?

Having been a counsellor and therapist for more than 25 years, I have had the privilege of sitting for many hours with many people who have asked themselves these very questions. The longer I have done this work, the more I have come to realise that it is not what happens to us that determines who we are and how we come to understand the world, it's what we *do* with what happens to us. This is what ultimately defines the sort of human being we believe ourselves to be. And the one we wish to strive to become.

If we want to develop a better, fitter physical body we go to the gym. We work against resistance or lift weights to challenge ourselves, so that our bodies grow muscle and lose unnecessary fat. This is exactly what happens if we begin to understand the deeper messages in our everyday emotional and psychological challenges. We let go of the parts of ourselves that no longer serve us. We build up our spiritual 'muscle'.

Unlike physical muscle, spiritual muscle may not be visible in a mirror. Yet, once we become aware of its true strength, we see more of the 'why' of what happens. Our lives take on a new meaning. A greater purpose.

The subject matter of each of the following chapters could probably warrant a whole book in themselves. But, by viewing our emotional complexities through the clarifying lens of our spiritual self, I aim to make the material concise, easily digestible and personally meaningful to you. My hope is that you will be stirred beyond simply reading the words. That you will start to see yourself as something more than just your currently known 'ego self'.

I will explore the hidden power that is contained within our emotions and how we use that power to either build ourselves up or bring ourselves down. I look at how we can better respond to the emotional pain that arises when we allow ourselves to fully feel whatever's troubling us. And understand why we develop unhelpful coping mechanisms to block this pain: addictions, compulsions, manipulations, denial, blame, victimhood.

I also devote chapters to the various feeling states that we enter into when we over-rely on these coping strategies: anger, sadness, stuck grief, low self-esteem, fear, depression, shame, guilt, anxiety, stress.

By separating out our differing emotional states, coping mechanisms and spiritual endeavours into a natural evolutionary flow, there is a connective thread running through this book from beginning to end. Whilst you may wish to hang onto this thread to help navigate your journey, each chapter does also stand alone in its own right.

I suggest that you read all of Part One - which sets out my spiritually inspired philosophy - as a foundational springboard off which to jump into any chapter in Part Two. So, if you wish, you can also think of Part Two as a quick reference section and refer easily to a particular emotional theme which may be relevant for you currently.

To work out your spiritual muscle at regular intervals, I will hold up a psychological mirror in the form of soul-searching questions, personal reflections and interactive exercises. To help these stand out, they will be written in *italics*. For those of you who want specific suggestions as to how to put into immediate practice the ideas I discuss, I highlight these in ***bold italics.***

At these points you will have the opportunity to stop and reflect on how the material relates to you personally. I encourage you to pause. To contemplate the questions, exercises, visualisations and suggestions and to listen to what your deeper spiritual self may be saying to you as you read. You may want to write down these inner thoughts and feelings, so you can later reflect back on your self-awareness journey.

To add some different thought flavours into the mix I'll sprinkle in quotes from counsellors, healers, philosophers, New Age thinkers, authors, poets, playwrights, spiritual teachers, theologians and inspirational speakers from around the world.

And finally, to breathe in some everyday life, I'll share some counselling clients' therapeutic journeys who have passed through my doors over the years. With thanks to them for allowing their enlightening stories to be shared, I have changed their names to ensure their anonymity.

From the outset, my hope is to encourage you to start to think about where you inhibit or restrict yourself. When you fear to look into the psychological mirror at the reflection of who you really are.

As I write these words, I am aware of the times in my life when this was difficult for me. And where, and when, this is still difficult. Increasingly, I've come to realise that I refuse to look when there is something about myself that I have difficulty in accepting or loving. The moments when I fear to know myself fully.

For more on my own inner work of spiritual growth and awakening, please join me via the blog page of my website at www.chrisjpartridge.com.

It is by no coincidence that 'know thyself' are the words inscribed at the entrance to the sacred oracle of the Temple of Apollo at Delphi in Ancient Greece: the birthplace of western culture. But do we take enough time to really get to know ourselves? Or do we spend too much time trying to work out, and understand, others?

The great Greek philosopher Plato claimed that, 'the essence of knowledge is self-knowledge'. He suggested that we can better understand our experience of the world by becoming more knowledgeable of, and about, ourselves. Buddhist philosophy professes that self-knowledge is the key that unlocks the place within us where true joy and bliss reside. Yet we convince ourselves that we are anything but the key. That it lies somewhere outside, waiting for us to discover it.

The last paragraph sums up my motivation for wanting to write this book. I want to stress that it is not intended to diagnose, or treat, any specific mental health issue. My intention is that you can use it as an interactive guide to help navigate your emotions. As a tool for unravelling the complex world of feelings.

The material I cover here is what I have personally learnt about the nature of human nature, as I have come to understand it, through my therapy work with clients over the years.

My hope is that by sharing it in the pages that follow it will help you to illuminate your own true nature. To discover that *you* hold the key. Somewhere inside. The key to your own greater understanding. Come on let's get cracking:

> "Your vision will become clear only when you can look into your own heart. Who looks outside, dreams; who looks inside, awakes."
>
> Carl Jung (Swiss founder of analytical psychology, psychoanalyst and psychiatrist)

THE DIFFERENCE BETWEEN EMOTIONS AND FEELINGS

Fortunately, Mother Nature has provided us with a unique range of biofeedback mechanisms that act as our personal navigation system. They are designed to help guide us on the journey of self-awareness. Our emotions and feelings. Like them or loathe them, they are nature's way of inviting us to make our own personal sense of what happens. Of the events and experiences of our lives.

Life presents us with a context, a stage. Upon it we have the chance to play out the person we wish to be. As we act out our part, the joys, challenges and obstacles that appear on that stage serve to help or hinder the original plan we had for ourselves. For how things were 'supposed' to be. It is our feeling response that helps us decipher the difference between what we want, or expect should happen, and what actually happens to us.

Our emotions, however, are physically sensed states arising from our body's reactions to external stimuli, events and experiences. Thus they are largely universal across our human condition.

So, before an important exam or test, the vast majority of us will experience a natural level of nervous tension as our body releases the stress hormones cortisol and adrenaline. These bodily chemicals are designed to energise, prime and prepare us for the mental and/or physical challenges ahead.

If we break down the word 'E-Motions' we literally see that, when experienced in our bodies, they become E-nergy in Motion. And, potentially, our E-nergetic Motivators. The modern word for emotion derives, in part, from the old French 12th century word 'emouvoir' meaning 'to stir up'.

Our feelings are our *individual* mental assessments and perceptions of our emotional bodily states. They represent our unique interpretations of those states. When we experience hormonal tension before an exam, some will interpret this as a sign to constructively channel the release of bodily energy to perform at their best. Others will use this same heightened state to berate themselves, turning the potential energy inward in a self-doubting fashion.

Our feeling response to these emotional states is revealed through the sorts of internal dialogue we have with ourselves. Dialogue which, in this case, can range from: 'You are ready and primed for this, let's give it our best shot!' Through to: 'You are no good at exams, why are you here? You know you are going to flunk this!'

Our feelings reveal the relationship we are currently having with ourselves. Our emotions inform us as to how we are relating to others and to the world around us.

We all hear a scream, we all emote fear. But I feel apprehensive. He feels shocked. She feels concerned....

The reason we all feel differently is because the bodily energy, created from the experiencing of external emotional triggers, has to pass through our personality 'filters'. These filters are partly made up of our environmental influences including our family of origin, our caregiver's parenting style, our education, culture, religion, nationality and so on. Yet, even though siblings in the same family are subject to virtually identical upbringings, they are still unique. Different from one another.

What helps to make us unique is how we personally interpret what happens to us. Where we place our attention. What we 'want' to see.

Ask any parent and they will say they believe in the influence of 'nurture' in defining the character of their first born. They think the way they parent, and the values they share, will result in similarly behaved and motivated siblings. That theory soon changes when they witness what different wills and characters their subsequent children have!

It seems we all have a singular 'blueprint'. Our own nature. A core character program we are born with. While our environment may influence how this program runs, it doesn't change it fundamentally. It appears we are designed to process the world, and find meaning in it, in our own one-off way from the day we are born.

Do you believe that you are meant to interpret the world as you do?

Does that imply that you are here to learn specific things about yourself?

So, recalling our previous example, if we perceive being tested by life as a chance to shine, we will interpret an exam as an opportunity to see what we are capable of. However, if we tend to perceive being tested by life as merely threatening, that same exam will be regarded as an obstacle. A hindrance to our sense of psychological safety and well-being.

How do you currently perceive being 'tested' by life?

Our perceptions, the way we filter life, function like a pair of coloured sunglasses. If yours are coloured orange then everything you experience in the world will have an orange hue. And if they are green you will see green things much more readily than you see orange. But you will have no real sense of what colour your sunglass filters are until someone wearing blue sunglasses lets you know how they see the world:

"We don't see things as they are, we see them as we are."

Anais Nin (French-Cuban diarist, essayist and novelist)

This explains why we do not always understand why we feel what we do. We just know that we feel that way. When this is different to how someone else feels, we often wonder whether our feelings are 'valid'. Whether we deserve to feel them. But they are always valid. Because only we know how we perceive experience *as us.*

The aspiration of counselling therapy, any self-awareness activity or spiritual practice, and of this book, is to help to bring more of what is unknown about ourselves into the light of our awareness. Only then can we begin to understand the 'why' of the motivation for many of our thoughts, feelings and behaviours. If we never undertake this inner exploration, we may never really know what drives us to repeatedly think, or behave, as we do.

Why we do what we do with the energy that emotions create in our bodily systems gives us clues as to how our core character expresses itself. Of what our principal 'life motivators' are.

For example, the energy that arises from anger in the face of a great social injustice will encourage some to feel empathy with another's plight and motivate them to help. For others, to feel hate or disdain for a specific group. Blaming them for having caused the injustice in the first place.

Do you tend to focus first on the anger of a perceived injustice or on compassion for those affected?

Consider how you might feel if you see an old friend on the other side of a busy street. You wave hello, but they appear to look through you and don't wave back.

Would you immediately feel annoyed or hurt, assuming that your friend had deliberately ignored you?

Or would you feel concerned that they looked worried and drop them a message later to see if they were okay?

What might these different reactions, to what are identical scenarios, say about how your personality filters, and so effectively creates, your everyday reality?

Our feelings give us the opportunity to listen to ourselves. To look within. To understand how we are personally filtering and interpreting our life experience. They help us to see how we regard ourselves in relation to a given situation. When fully acknowledged, they act as the medium through which the voice of our everyday ego self can be heard by our deeper spiritual self.

Imagine for a moment a world without emotions or feelings. Would we still feel compelled to contemplate the hitherto unexplored parts of ourselves? Would we ever have a sense of our depth and breadth as human beings? Of our deepest sadness to our greatest joy?

Can you know the true height and magnificence of a mountain unless you have stood within the depth of the valley that lies alongside it?

> "We have no right to ask when sorrow comes, 'Why did this happen to me?' unless we ask the same question for every moment of happiness that comes our way."
>
> Author unknown

Emotional stimulus from the outside world initiates a hormonal energy flow in our bodies. It stirs, awakens and challenges us. We determine a unique meaning from this energy as it passes through the influencing filters of our personality and combines with the core of our character. Of the 'nature' we were born with. It is our feelings which inform us how we are perceiving our emotions. How we see ourselves. What the relationship with ourself is currently like.

How much influence do you feel you can have over your ongoing mood, as you become aware of how your personality filters and interprets external emotional triggers?

Does this normally initiate positive or negative conversations that you have with yourself?

If more negative, then how could you instead use this awareness to improve your inner dialogue? To be more gentle with yourself?

After all, it is only you that talks to 'you' inside your own head!

JUDGING HOW WE FEEL

All too often we allow feeling states to totally define us: 'I am happy.' 'I am sad.' How strange would it be to hear someone say: 'I am currently relating to something happy or sad.' Yet this is more accurate. It is more indicative of the continuing consistency of our innate nature, despite it being washed with the energetic waves of life's emotional waters. Emotions and feelings are meant to help us to discover our true nature. Not to define it.

Instead of viewing emotional states as personal relationships with events, we come to believe we *are* the events. We might define our whole existence as 'sad', rather than seeing ourselves as currently processing a sad experience.

Stuck in this mindset, we remain enslaved. The primary purpose of emotions and feelings is to increase our awareness of self. To let us know whether we are aligning with our internal valuing system. So experience doesn't happen *to* us, it happens *for* us. It acts as the bridge which links the tangible parts of ourselves to the non-tangible. The physical outer to the spiritual inner.

So often this endeavour of connection gets frustrated when emotions become blocked. When we allow them to act as barriers through which it seems impossible to pass. If we felt ashamed at school when our classmates laughed as we muddled our words reading aloud, that harboured emotional anxiety can feel like a perpetual threat. Inhibiting us from doing any form of public speaking in later life.

By allowing this kind of threat-based fear to take hold, we are telling ourselves that we don't want to feel those same emotions again. Our anxiety 'protects' us from the risk of being shamed once more. The sad consequence is we then restrict ourselves, inhibit our psychological growth and sabotage our latent potentials.

What events have happened in your past which now make you feel frightened, embarrassed or not confident to have a go at in the future?

Does that mean that you have allowed a single previous feeling state to predetermine many of your future ones?

Sometimes we give our feelings the power to decide whether life is worth living or not. Before we give them a chance to inform us, we judge them as either good or bad. Some become familiar sought friends. Others feared enemies.

Instead of *relating* to, what is, a transient feeling, we can identify with it so strongly that it becomes part of us. Affecting us not just mentally, but physically too. We literally embody it. Notice how when we feel very sad, or insecure, we tend to look down to the ground. And raising any form of a smile seems like hard work.

Over time our repetitive or stuck feelings can affect our physiology and, finally, our very biology. Our spiritual essence is a constant. A state of open, conscious awareness. Yet we judge and resist more painful emotions and feelings *as if* they have the capacity to change who we actually are.

We reject sadness, deny jealousy, avoid shame, run from fear and push down anger. When we refuse to feel these difficult emotions we have little hope of finding the true, authentic 'us' on the other side of them. *All* our feelings are data sources. They are all trying to communicate something of ourselves back to ourselves.

If you are constantly stressed at work, is it simply because you get too many emails every day? Or because you are suppressing a deeper sense that you might actually be in the wrong job?

If you find yourself being resentful much of the time, is it because you solely blame others for treating you poorly? Or can you use the deeper message within the resentment to question how you treat yourself? Inside your own mind.

If you get angry with others easily, is it because they really are that irritating? Or are you irritated that you are not living the life that you want. One that fulfils your real aspirations?

We need to fully *feel to heal*. To know, accept and successfully navigate, our *whole* self. Only then, once our feelings have 'done their job', do we have the choice to let them go or to change their form. Once something has served its purpose, it doesn't need to hang around forever in its exact same state.

If you are worried about a friend's poor health, acknowledge that worried feeling. Even say to yourself, 'I'm aware that I'm feeling really worried about my friend right now.' Fully embrace it. Don't run from it or try to water it down. Then allow the deeper message to emerge, perhaps: 'This reminds me how much I love him and all that he stands for.' Notice how much more peace is inherent within this deeper contemplation.

Be aware of not blocking the deeper emotional message. Of creating an 'identity' of worry that then becomes part of your personal identity. If you consistently define yourself through a feeling of worry, the net result is two people whose wellbeing is compromised. Ironically, this makes it more difficult to remain in a position of positive emotional support and empathic understanding.

Resisting difficult emotions requires mental energy. One of the primary reasons people seek counselling support is that they are simply exhausted trying to keep them inside. Yet, so often their life experiences appear to conspire to bring them back to face, and feel, these suppressed emotions fully.

Until we begin to face our fears we unconsciously seek out, draw in or perceive situations in ways which continue to frighten us. When we resist a healthy expression of our own anger, we either meet anger in others or are drawn into situations to be angry at. If we refuse to forgive ourselves for something, the guilt we harbour will act like an unconscious beacon, seeming to encourage others to unjustly displace blame upon us. I will return to these central themes throughout the book.

What emotions and feelings do you judge harshly and therefore tend to repress?

Do they still find a way of manifesting in your life? Either through the actions of other people or similar repetitive circumstances?

Can you allow yourself to name and feel any now?

As difficult as that might seem, does that give you a sense of what emotional data, what deeper message, might be within them?

> "Unexpressed emotions will never die. They are buried alive and will come forth later in uglier ways."
>
> Sigmund Freud (Austrian founder of psychoanalysis and neurologist)

THE PURSUIT OF HAPPINESS

Hopefully, a principle emotion we do not judge harshly is happiness. The great philosopher, Aristotle, 2300 years ago proclaimed that happiness is the only possible purpose and aim of life. Because it is the only goal that is an end in itself. Everything else we aim for: success, power, love, relationships, achievement, recognition, money, we strive for but *in order* to be finally happy.

So why do we complicate what seems to be a simple enough aspiration and try to find it through so many other means? As babies and young children - as long as our immediate survival needs are met - we seem happy and content simply living in the present moment. Exploring and experiencing our new world.

Yet, as we mature, this natural default emotional setting is compromised. It becomes buried beneath layers of restrictive fear-based thoughts, beliefs and attitudes. This changes the potential for happiness within thriving to a struggle of merely 'surviving'.

In which areas of your life do you feel you thrive and in which do you just survive? What sort of thoughts and feelings would you want to experience, if you were to visualise yourself as thriving?

Is it the world, or you, that prevents you from feeling these feelings?

Through this inner questioning we become more aware as to whether we view life as only a struggle for survival or as a joyful opportunity for personal growth and expanding awareness. Depending on how we filter and perceive experience our inner voice can, in one moment, encourage and motivate us and, in the next, seemingly sabotage our ability to be happy.

Take a moment to listen to what your inner voice is saying to you now. As you read these words, is it generally kind to you, encouraging and positive .... a friend?

Or is it, as is so often the case, more punitive, disparaging and tough on you? Perhaps telling you that you do not have time for all this indulgent, self-awareness stuff?!

Whilst allowing this voice to have its say for a moment, let's take a closer look at H-A-P-P-I-N-E-S-S, and attempt to define it through its acronym.

The first:

Hoping **A**ll **P**ainful **P**roblems **I**dentified **N**ever **E**voke **S**uperficial **S**adness

And the second:

Harvesting **A**ll **P**ersonal **P**otentials **I**n **N**early **E**very **S**tressful **S**ituation

As these succinct definitions might suggest, our happiness potential ranges from merely seeking satisfaction and pleasure through the avoidance of the pain, to trying to be the best person we can be by growing and learning from difficult life experiences.

Do you currently see life problems and challenges as pains that need to be avoided or solved?

Or do you see them as opportunities to stop and see something from a different perspective. Maybe because they appear to be asking you to stop and see yourself from a different perspective?

Where do you currently fall between these two polarities? The answer will give you some insight into whether you exercise your physical muscle or your spiritual muscle when it comes to the perception of life's challenges. How much of their emotional data you are ready to download.

When first coming into counselling therapy, many clients express a natural desire to be happier in their life. They see this as a state to be achieved. Moving towards some fantastical point in their life which will have certain things and experiences in it: success, power, achievement, money, fame.

What they cannot see is that the constant pursuit of these false happiness 'gods' is ultimately an avoidance. An attempt to anaesthetise some unresolved emotional pain. Some unbearable present reality.

Is the pursuit of happiness and the avoidance of pain the whole point to your life?

If your answer to this question is largely yes, then is it your principal motivator? Your ultimate life goal?

But what happens to us if, and when, we ever get 'there?' To this elusive happiness place? Do we suddenly change forever? Is it a nebulous apparition designed to motivate and evolve us as human beings?

> "When I was five years old, my Mother always told me that happiness was the key to life. When I went to school, they asked me what I wanted to be when I grew up. I wrote down 'happy'. They told me I didn't understand the assignment and I told them they didn't understand life."
>
> John Lennon (British songwriter and singer)

Perhaps John Lennon puts it more succinctly and simply than most. Despite his material wealth he was known for living a simple, but incredibly creative, life. Whatever inner state of happiness and peace he managed to realise, it clearly liberated him to be one of the most original and innovative songwriters the world has ever known.

Yet, in our modern, connected and technological society, have we somehow become persuaded to think that happiness is more complex than this 'simple' concept of inner peace? Of self-acceptance? That maybe it has to be fought for? And involves achieving, maintaining and controlling some complex set of external life circumstances. Of constantly pursuing something outside of us?

> "If you're in a bad situation, don't worry, it'll change. If you're in a good situation, don't worry, it'll change."

John A Simone Sr (American author)

How do you choose to perceive this quote?

Does it make you happier or sadder about life? More optimistic or more pessimistic?

Can you use the deeper message in this quote to accept both the highs and lows of life, without attaching to the highs and fearing the lows?

To accept that all experience is a spiritual opportunity for self contemplation and exploration?

When we start to detach from specific ego-centred expectations, we allow life experience to flow through us without resisting or prejudging it. Our overthinking acts as a resistance to our direct experiencing. When our mind works overtime it takes us away from being fully in the present moment. From being fully alive to the present.

If I were to suggest that you take a moment to pause and listen to your mind right <u>now</u>, what happens?

Inner silence? Did your incessant thinking take a break for a while?

Our overthinking leads us to create false stories about who we think we are, according to what happens to us. It is the mind that plays old familiar records that keep us reliving the past. Or fearing the future.

Catch yourself next time you are aware that you are overthinking. Defining who you are as a result of what is happening around you.

When you do not create a false story about yourself, notice what this allows you to be. More fully present to both joy and pain?

When we free ourselves to be more present to our moment to moment experiencing, we are less likely to seek refuge in the diversionary false gods of happiness. We liberate ourselves to learn from, as opposed to be defined by, what happens to us.

Imagine yourself to be like an unfinished block of wood when you first enter this world. The action of life's experience over time acts like a sandpaper. Smoothing your rough edges and honing you into a shape.

Yet we need not be a victim to the action of this sandpaper. We always have a choice in how we turn to face it. By maintaining a trust in the evolutionary flow of life, we can determine what kind of inner carving to reveal of ourselves through it. We ultimately have the choice to decide how we want to evolve.

It's important to remember, whatever the action of life, we are made of the same stuff at the end as we were at the beginning. Experience may shape us, but it cannot change our raw material. Our essence.

We are here to evolve, to learn, to discover. Making the occasional 'mistake' and taking the odd detour along the way is part of that journey. In fact, it is essential if we are to maintain the free-flowing, happy present state we enjoyed when we were very young. At this tender age too we had little sense of being a separate self. Us and our playground teaching world were one.

In this state of oneness, of connectedness, our emotional resonance was more highly attuned. If we heard other babies in distress, we too became distressed. If they laughed, we laughed also. In this connected free-flow, emotional energy passed through us unhindered. Uniting us with others. The same sense of blissful unification we get as adults when we fall in love.

Can you recall a time you felt in this contented flow state. Maybe a moment when you did not want to be anywhere else, doing anything else?

Do you remember feelings of connectedness, timelessness, happiness? A sense that you were 'harvesting all personal potentials?' Fully immersed in, and surrendered to, the wisdom inherent in life's evolutionary flow.

As babies we remain content simply exploring our new world, happily experiencing ourselves fully through it. But what happens to this universal default setting? Where, when and how does it all go wrong?

CONDITIONING

Our perception is everything. What we experience in life has a direct affect on how we feel, according to how we perceive what happens to us. When we listen to our inner voice telling us what to make of something this helps us to conclude what it means for us, *as us*.

Yet, when we are young and impressionable, our inner voice is small and weak compared to the opinions and perspectives of influential people around us. The outer voice of our parents, carers, elder siblings, teachers, cultural and religious leaders, colour and influence how clearly we can listen to our own. When these other voices are loud, domineering or threatening, they affect how we would otherwise freely perceive. In turn this impacts how we feel.

Can you ever really know yourself when your inner voice is drowned out among the beliefs and opinions of others?

When we cannot freely know, and trust, our own mind fully we cannot help but succumb to the wider group mindset. Our approval and acceptance within, and from, this 'tribal' mindset becomes the dictator of how we think we *should* be. Of how we *should* feel about ourselves.

Our most influential tribe is, most commonly, our family. The relationships we had with our parents, caregivers, grandparents and siblings form the foundational templates of how we come to understand, and conduct, relationships later on.

Sadly, an optimal functioning family unit, or indeed 'perfect' parenting, rarely exists. We are all human, so how could they? However we interpreted the love of our caregivers, however complex or fraught that might have been, we automatically seek the same in adult partnerships because it feels familiar. We have grown used to it, quite literally. That is what we feel we deserve to have. That's all we know about relating, all we were taught. Until, that is, we do the inner work of reconciling with our childhoods. Of healing our own 'inner child'. Of loving ourselves for *ourselves*. (See Our Life Scripts.)

How have your family conditioning and experiences influenced your ideas about love within adult relationships?

Can you use your awareness of the 'imperfections' to improve your personal relationships today?

No matter how old we are. Whether we feel able to admit it to ourselves or not, and whether our parents or caregivers are still alive or not, there is a Mother Nature inspired programming within us which seeks out and yearns for their continued approval. And little wonder. We relied on their love, attention and an emotionally secure attachment to ensure we were physically nurtured as babies. Much of this inherent need for approval shaped how we acted and behaved. It is what continues, often out of our awareness, to drive a good deal of our behaviour as adults.

How do you remember being when you were young in order to win your parents' or caregiver's love and approval?

If this love seemed elusive or absent, did you try even harder to impress them?

Or did you just rebel against the whole idea and become disruptive and mischievous in an attempt to at least get some sort of attention. Even if it was 'negative?'

Whether we comply with it, or rebel against it, our familial conditioning remains the foundation stone which shapes our forming personalities. As we grow, this primary conditioning is influenced by other tribal groups too: social, religious, political, career, cultural, gender, sexuality, race, nationality.

Remember when you were young and learned to speak by copying the words of those around you? This was our way of showing interest in, and to, the world. To try to ensure that it loved and accepted us back. Later, we do the same thing with our attitudes and behaviours. Complying with, and mirroring, others to ensure a sense of belonging. Of fitting in.

Think of how safe you feel when you can identify with, and be approved by, a familiar tribe. Or of how unsafe you feel when you are not.

Do these feelings arise from a primal need to want to belong somewhere, anywhere, in order to feel lovable?

As we mature our mirroring behaviours and attitudes can become habitual. Sometimes even unquestioned doctrine. We blindly follow role models and idols. Without being aware that we are simply mimicking their own conditioned attitudes and reactions which they have, in turn, inherited in the same way. Unsurprisingly, as they appear to have 'worked' for them, we naturally assume they will work for us too.

Through this universal survival tendency to observe, copy and gain approval, we all develop behaviours, attitudes and beliefs we think are just our own. In reality, they have merely been filtered down from, and through, our tribal mindset. The group personality filter of our tribe.

This sums up both the opportunity, and the threat, inherent within our conditioning programming. The opportunity being a sense of belonging. Of safety and acceptance in our tribe. But the threat is the price we pay for this acceptance. As we try to be like, and liked by, others we betray our authentic self. Our unique uniqueness.

Subsequently, we develop a latent mistrust in, and disconnect from, the world around. It becomes increasingly difficult to gauge who we really want to be, and to find personal meaning, within it. To clearly hear our 'inner calling'.

Try to recall the last time that you went along with your tribe group just to keep the peace?

What stopped you from disclosing your own unique perspective?

What do you really fear may have happened if you did?

> "To be nobody but yourself in a world doing its best to make you everybody else, means to fight the hardest battle any human can ever fight and never stop fighting."
>
> E E Cummins (American poet, author, artist and playwright)

Let's explore how subtle, continual conditioning manifests in our everyday lives, without us even being particularly aware of it. Imagine for a moment how we feel when someone emotionally close to us dies. We're likely to feel lost, confused, perhaps angry, sometimes even relieved, but nearly always sad.

Our group mind so often dictates that we are *only* supposed to feel sad. Of course, this is part of the natural, healthy, heartfelt response. Yet we are conditioned to think that when someone is 'taken away' from us, we must solely focus on the loss of what we once had. And less on the love and joy that the person brought into our lives. Rather than being free to feel grateful and appreciative for the good times, we are conditioned to feel cheated and aggrieved by the loss. Indeed, frequently *expected* to feel cheated and aggrieved.

I'm not suggesting for a moment that we should exclusively feel grateful when we are faced with loss. What I want to gently highlight is, in that sadness and pain, we are generally taught not to feel any joy or gratitude. We are conditioned to see sadness as 'bad' and joy as 'good'. As we judge bad and good to be opposites, it becomes very hard to see, and feel, both at the same time.

Being unable to feel joy and sadness together, we have little choice but to be in either one state or the other. Either happy or sad. It becomes hard to accept or process an experience holistically, due to our programming to seek pleasure and to avoid pain. (Recalling our first definition of happiness.) Even so, there is always pleasure and pain in the experience of relating to another living thing. At some point, that other living thing is going to change in a way which affects how we relate to it. As we will to it. The ultimate change being death. An ending of the physical level of relating as we know it.

So the experience of loss becomes a confused fragmentation of feelings. Expected sadness and suffering because of the pain of the loss versus, and often in conflict with, gratitude for the joy of having known the person who has departed.

Try to recall your own life experiences which triggered apparent opposing feelings. Perhaps it did involve loss, and a subsequent feeling of both gratitude and pain?

Or a mix of guilt and liberation, when you decided to end an unsatisfactory relationship?

How about inner pride after facing a personal fear?

Notice which of these feelings may have arisen from your more superficial conditioning and which from your deeper authentic self.

Tracey's Story

Tracey was a kind, caring person. She enjoyed her work as a nurse immensely. She came from a family of nurses and doctors. Having been raised in a family culture of being there for others, nursing seemed the natural role for her. The perfect vocation to express her innate care and compassion.

When she first came for counselling Tracey seemed broken. Racked with guilt. She had recently split from her dominating partner after 11 years of marriage. She had not been happy for many of those years. Following a recent illness, she decided that life was too precious. She had to listen to her heart. It took a lot of bravery for Tracey to act upon its calling and finally decide to leave her husband.

Stepping away from years of family inspired selflessness proved the biggest challenge for Tracey. She knew that she was worthy of happiness. Now this inner knowing was in conflict with the outer expectation she had placed on herself. On the way she had always been 'seen'.

It was inevitable there would be a fall out of guilt. For years Tracey had validated herself solely through her familial conditioning of being of service to others. She recounted the numerous times in her life when she had permitted herself a degree of 'freedom'. Of self interest. They had always been tainted with guilt.

Now, having summoned the courage to act on her heart, Tracey felt free. She was relieved and proud of herself, but the guilt came back in waves. How would her ex-husband be without her? Without her to take care of him?

Having an exclusive therapeutic space where Tracey could just be with her own feelings, without filtering them through the lens of another, enabled her to connect with her own self care. With her own exclusive value. A safe sanctuary for her to contemplate and to be. To see herself more clearly in the mirror I held up as her therapist.

This was the first time in her life that Tracey had ever been offered this unconditional holding space. When she was young her elder brother had been quite poorly for many years. Tracey remembered having to share a room with him when the family moved to temporary accommodation to be near a specialist hospital. Even then her 'space' was shared with another. To have her own through the therapeutic encounter was an important part of her self realisation. Of her burgeoning self respect. An important part of her healing process:

> "It is a universal law that any difficulties that can come to you at any time, no matter what they are, must be exactly what you need most at the moment, to enable you to take the next step forward by overcoming them. The only misfortune, the only real tragedy, comes when we suffer without learning the lesson."

> Emmet Fox (Irish new thought spiritual leader and writer)

When feelings are confused and fragmented we tend to make less sense of them. In separate pieces they do make less sense. Entering therapy, Tracey was confused. She could not reconcile her positive feelings of freedom alongside her destructive pangs of guilt. (See Mistakes and Guilt.)

When we see something in pieces we remain confused. We are conditioned not to see any joy in what appears incomplete. Yet, to truly know and sense what something is made of, we must contemplate and experience its component parts. Its fragments. Tracey had to fully face her innate guilt to be able to understand that it did not come from her. It came from her conditioning. The expectations that she had placed on herself as a result of her interpretation of the expectations from others.

◆ ◆ ◆

From a spiritual perspective, it is only through an endeavour to understand the pieces that we can genuinely gain a sense of the power of the whole. To see the self-awareness 'data' that is hidden in the crevices of our emotions.

'He's in pieces following the loss of his job.' 'She's totally broken since she left.' 'He was shattered to hear the news.' Everyday examples of how the very language we use to describe such experiences reflects the potential for greater self-awareness. Sometimes things have to get a bit worse, to break down, before we get to see the diamond hidden in the rock.

Do you ever remember as a child taking the back off the clock to see how it works? Or opening the washing machine door to check who was actually doing the washing?!

As children we are hardwired to be curious. To question. To wonder how life works. It is a pity that we subdue this natural propensity as adults. We rarely ask: 'What makes my clock of self tick?'

For you, right now, is this the conditioned need for acceptance from others or the spiritual dedication to follow your own pathway?

Can you identify the emotional energy of acceptance that you normally seek from others and generate it for yourself, from within?

With the courage to remove the blinkers of our conditioning we benefit from the full panorama of our emotions. We get to tap into their data sources. Their enlightening messages. The gift of existential freedom through the portal of short term pain. The gratitude for a loved one's life waiting on the other side of heartbreaking grief.

Before the effects of our environmental conditioning, in our default newborn state, we are open and curious to fully experiencing life. We have less compulsion, and less developed psychological defences, to filter out the 'bad' bits. That's why the emotional events of our childhoods remain powerfully anchored in our psyches. The joy and the pain.

In this infantile phase we are like open experiencing channels. Our pure consciousness becomes more aware of its breadth by experiencing events wholly and completely. We realise holistically.

By 'real-ise' in the last sentence, I literally mean to 'make real'. When you allow yourself a free, unfettered exposure to life, you feel the full range of your emotional repertoire. Meaning reveals itself. Spiritual truth transpires.

FINDING MEANING

We are naturally meaning seeking creatures. We find meaning in an experience if there is potential to discover something new about ourselves from it. To learn something different. Life can be more meaningful, more growthful, with an awareness of how we're *choosing* to relate to it.

Recall a recent experience which was painful or left you feeling angry. Did these emotions block you from looking within yourself? Of having a complete 'realisation?'

Visualise yourself working through the deeper implications of the experience now. Were there any potential lessons in it for you? Fresh self-awareness gained?

Consider this acronym of M-E-A-N:

Meeting **E**veryone **A**s **N**avigators.

This potentially 'means' that everyone we meet, and everything that happens between us, has the potential to evoke something different within us. A different side to our character. A new colour of our personality. With this open attitude, everyone is a potential 'navigator' on our life journey. Some seem to help us along. Others to block our way. Perhaps the ones that make us take the odd detour show us scenery we may not otherwise have passed:

> "Everything that irritates us about others can lead us to an understanding of ourselves."

> Carl Jung (Swiss founder of analytical psychology, psychoanalyst and psychiatrist)

What kind of person really makes you think about who you are and how you normally 'operate'. Is it the one who challenges, annoys and frustrates you? Or someone that you find easy and comfortable to be with?

Compare your mind for a moment to a sealed jam jar full of water, with mud which has sunk and settled at the bottom. The mud represents the unquestioned beliefs, judgements and assumptions that we carry around, formed as a result of our external conditioning.

When we are agitated by something, or someone, the mud in our mind jars gets shaken up. The water becomes cloudy and unclear. Eventually it settles again at the bottom. Yet had we not been shaken up in some way, we would have no real sense of just how much mud we were carrying around.

Following the shake-up, any shake-up, we are left with a choice. Do we contemplate the source of our mud? Do we devote time to see what pushes our buttons? Or do we just avoid being similarly provoked again in the future?

One way to avoid being continually stirred when we least expect it is to choose when to be agitated by life. To have the courage to step outside of our normal comfort zone. To risk a certain level of uncertainty by thinking more independently of the group mind:

> "The quest for certainty blocks the search for meaning. Uncertainty is the very condition to impel man to unfold his powers."
>
> Erich Fromm (German social psychologist, psychoanalyst and humanistic philosopher)

Where we find new meaning in life by varying our experiences, and remaining curious of how we relate to those experiences, we cannot help but develop our spiritual muscle.

The muscle that raises us up out of the mud in our mind jars. Sees meaning. And with new awareness, stops us going around in the same pointless cycle of repetitive, meaningless experience.

Dion's Story

On paper, Dion's life appeared to be going relatively well. He was in his early twenties, dating, and in the fortunate position of contemplating a promotion. He worked in marketing for a large multinational pharmaceutical company.

Dion described his job as his 'dream career'. His whole family were immensely proud of him. Rationally, it made sense to accept the promotion on offer to him, to further his career in the dynamic world of pharmaceuticals.

However, the recent death of a friend meant that Dion began to question this incessant climbing of the corporate ladder. He struggled with a nagging unease. A sense of pointlessness. Everything on the surface was happening as he had dreamed of, yet he questioned the meaning of it all. His life seemed full, but he felt empty inside.

When we sense an inner emptiness there is a great temptation to want to fill it with prescriptive meaning. Something we are told will make us feel better. Dion had tried to fill his emptiness with what society said should help, only to find that he still questioned. His doubt seemed unhelpful. His angst confusing.

Dion had endured psoriasis, a chronic skin condition, for many years. He noticed that his skin became more irritated when he was particularly stressed. The shocking news of the death of his friend had caused a major flare-up. He had always treated his condition with steroid creams, as prescribed by his doctor. Ironically, the company he worked for produced the creams used to treat his psoriasis. Yet he often wondered whether that was the best course of treatment for him to continue to obediently follow.

It was hard for Dion to delve deep into the complexity of his emotions. With everything going so well on the outside, he hoped this would automatically defuse his internal quandary. Fill his inner emptiness. He teetered nervously on the edge of it.

As our therapy progressed Dion noticed that sharing his feelings, being able to cry, tapping gently into his emotional void, seemed to reduce the severity of his skin flare-ups. This sparked a latent interest in the connection between his own mind and his body. It seemed the more he risked finding words for his inner struggle, the less his body felt compelled to do it for him.

Something about this new focus ignited Dion's enthusiasm. His passion. A passion that found little expression in his current position in marketing for a large multinational. He wanted to take more time to explore it. His body appeared to be asking him to focus on that. His inner emptiness a sign that he had not been following his gut.

A few months after ending therapy Dion decided to leave his 'dream' job. In the end the decision was not as difficult as he had expected. His skin spoke to him more than a large paycheck. Now he is following his new dream and recently completed a course in complementary medicine. Using his own healing journey as the subject for his first case study.

Life, its lessons and its meaning, involve a two-way relationship. Both from the apparently opposing points of what happens to us and how we 'happen' to life. (It is probably no coincidence that the word happen and happ-i-ness come from the same root.)

Some happen to life, some observe things happening, others have life happen to them.

Where do you see yourself right now?

What sorts of difficult feelings would you be facing, and actions taking, to move into the 'happen to life' zone?

Does this all mean that we have a choice in how we relate to life events? Maybe the bigger question is, are we free to define who we are in any given situation by choosing how we respond? Or do we continually allow that to be dictated to us by outside influences and historic conditioning?

Happiness implies having a sense of freedom. Freedom to respond according to how we see and relate to ourself in any given moment. If we respond in a way which originates from our judgements and assumptions mind jar mud, we *react* rather than respond. We react from our primitive, conditioned self. Less so from our present awareness.

There is limitation and rigidity in a reaction. Qualities representing fear. There is choice and freedom in an authentically self-aware sourced response. Qualities of peace and joy:

> "Between stimulus and response there is a space. In that space is our power to choose our response. In our response lies our growth and our freedom."
>
> Victor E Frankl (Austrian neurologist, psychiatrist and holocaust survivor)

What else can go wrong with this freedom of choice in how we relate to experience? Why, after our relationship with an experience is over, do its muddy, judgemental remnants often stay with us? Tainting our future outlook? Affecting how we approach much of the rest of our life?

On a physical level our psyche - both the conscious and unconscious mind - learns from situations that may cause us actual danger or harm. It uses this learning to help us avoid similar experiences in the future. From many perspectives, a healthy response.

If we run across the road narrowly missing a car or put our finger into a flame, the fear and pain of this experience will remind us not to try to do something similar again in the future.

The more primitive area of our brain - the limbic system - is responsible for these types of primal survival instincts and reactions. It records and stores frightening, threatening or anger-evoking life experiences as highly emotionally-charged thoughts. This allows them to later become easily recallable memories. The limbic system, specifically the amygdala, is the control centre of the well known 'fight or flight' reaction. This is triggered when we perceive external danger. (For more on fight or flight see Defences.)

Being programmed to help us survive, the amygdala also allocates a high degree of emotional investment into life-sustaining pleasurable activities: eating, sex and love. Consequently, when we react only from this more primitive part of our brain, we tend to seek happiness through the avoidance of psychological pain and the pursuit of pleasure.

This explains why when we react, we do so impulsively, reflexively. We don't leave any space for a pause before responding. The pause which allows us to bring the prefrontal cortex part of our more recently evolved brain online. This facilitates higher levels of reasoning. Of wondering. Of what something may mean for us spiritually.

Next time you notice yourself automatically judging someone or something, try to create a pause in your reactive thinking. Consider that:

❑ Anything that annoys you is teaching you patience.

❑ Anyone that outwardly disempowers you is shining a light on your innate spiritual power.

❑ Anyone that rejects you is encouraging you to reflect on your own self-love and acceptance.

❑ Anything that you fear is calling you to move through it in order to dissolve it.

❑ Anything you can't control is teaching you how to let go and accept what is.

❑ Anyone who emotionally hurts you is exhibiting the degree of their own pain and teaching you greater understanding.

❑ Anyone you dislike is teaching you about unconditional love.

❑ Anyone who loves you is creating an opportunity to see how much you truly love yourself.

The limbic brain categorises memories of life enhancing, or life threatening, experiences so they become grouped together in our minds. That is why when we feel happy we easily remember previous happy experiences. And when we feel sad other sad events readily come to mind.

Do you find that when you feel down about something in the present moment, your mind immediately replays previous sad life events?

This is particularly apparent when previous sad or painful emotions have not been fully acknowledged. If we delegate the job of feeling a painful, or sad, experience to our more primitive brain, it will seek a more defensive 'solution'. Anger and/or fear.

Unfortunately, anger and fear are blocking type emotional reactions. They prevent the higher level consciousness of the prefrontal cortex from integrating, learning and appropriately *responding*.

Our limbic brain assumes that sad or painful experiences are nothing more than a threat to our physical sense of well-being. The resulting blocking emotional energy it produces causes stress and rigidity in the body, eventually leading to disease. That is a 'dis-ease' within our energetic bodily system.

Recall the last time you watched, witnessed or felt something that moved or saddened you greatly. Did you get that familiar lump in your throat, ache in your heart or perhaps tightness in your abdomen?

This is a real, tangible indication of how, and where, emotional energy can build up and is felt, like a momentary block, within our physical bodies. If we continue to be aware of this kind of energy block, it suggests there is an emotion that we don't want to explore. To articulate in a feelings sense.

We are more than just our physical bodies. We have emotional 'bodies' as well. Our overall health being depends on how well our physical and emotional selves interact. How much we nurture the relationship between mind and body. How much we listen to our body, when our mind tries to block us from feeling.

If you become aware of emotional blocks or heaviness within your physical body try to bring your 'highest conscious attention' to those areas. By this, I mean engage your more evolved prefrontal cortex brain function. The part that doesn't feel compelled to want to try to solve the problem with anger or to hide it away behind fear. Allow it to contemplate the 'what if' questions:

What if I really begin to see and wonder who I am behind my protective cloak of anger and/or fear?

What is this current difficult feeling trying to communicate to me or protect me from?

The problem with the tendency of our limbic brain to store and record old, painful feelings is we develop fear-based beliefs which effectively restrict us from being open to new emotional experiences. 'He will never marry again' or 'she lives in the past'. Phrases we often hear when someone becomes victim to their fear-based primitive mind sets.

Take a moment to reflect on how much anger, arising from a past challenging or painful event in your life, you continue to hold onto. What personal benefit do you derive from holding onto this anger?

Is it possible to also sense any, more insightful, awareness whilst in this defensive emotional state?

If you can let, or imagine, the anger and any associated pain energy start to pass through, and out of, your body now.

Who can you become when you are not defined by your anger?

Our personal feelings make us all different. Yet the journey of understanding them, and therefore ourselves, is the same journey that unites us all. Through differing, challenging and painful, life experiences we have an opportunity to better understand our complete and unique personhood. That which lies just beyond our primitive brain's defensive reactions.

The act of seeking meaning in life's events cannot help but increase our awareness of self. This very endeavour, in and of itself, necessitates seeing life from a broader and higher perspective. Of appreciating the bigger unfolding picture.

Somewhere, within this greater awareness, we come to realise that we are actually the creators and architects of our own lives. It is us that happens to life. Not the other way around. In this place we can begin to trust that *every* experience and *every* person, no matter how difficult, has the capacity to enlighten, to enrich, to inform us. To add meaningful signposts to our self-awareness journeys. Should we care to look up:

> "Your pain is the breaking of the shell that encloses your understanding."
>
> Khalil Gibran (Lebanese writer, poet, philosopher and artist)

EGO AND DEEPER SELF - THE INNER RELATIONSHIP

Let's take a moment to listen more closely to our inner dialogue. The voice in our head. Our own internal relationship. The one that exists between our ego and our deeper self. Our worldly face and our inner feelings. But what do we really mean by the terms ego and deeper self?

Our ego is designed to give us our sense of 'I-ness'. Of knowing where we are different. Unique from the rest of the world. It has a vital role in our development as it gives us a sense of individuality. Of identity. Of self importance. Only then do we know how best to assess, care for and value ourselves in this physical world.

Ego could be crudely defined as all the ways we would prefer to think and feel about ourselves, combined with how we want or need others to think and feel about us. As a way in to questioning how your own ego operates, ask yourself:

What do I want others to see and to know about me?

What does that allow me to feel about myself, that I might otherwise have difficulty in feeling?

Ego is like our preferred sense of self-image. The window through which we initially see the world and how we want, or need, the world to see us. When operating solely from our ego self we go from one life event to another, following its innate drive - seeking pleasure and avoiding pain. This reflects our first definition of happiness (see The Pursuit of Happiness), and also parallels the typical reactions of our more primitive limbic brain.

Our deeper spiritual self is less concerned with outer form and impression. It prefers to focus on celebrating our individuality in terms of our creative passions and natural talents in life. Of remaining curious as to why we are here.

It helps us to develop a personal philosophy giving meaning and purpose to our lives. Our deeper self's quest is to answer our unique calling in the world. And to realise and share our unique potential within it.

This aligns with our second basic definition of happiness. Being able to see meaning in, to build our spiritual muscle from, and to realise our personal potential through, life experience.

In order to gain a quick sense of your felt, knowable deeper self, try to recall a recent experience when you remember time passing really quickly. Of being lost or totally immersed in an activity.

It may have been during a pleasurable pastime such as relaxing on a beach, reading a good book, playing a sport, communing with nature, watching a stirring movie, doing a yoga class, getting a massage, listening to a piece of music, meditating, singing, playing an instrument, painting or creating something.

The sense of timelessness indicates that we are living from the deepest realms of ourselves. Linear time does not exist. We feel like we're 'in the zone', having a fundamentally positive, profound connection with the world.

Here our separate sense of self dissolves. We feel we are conjoined with the natural flow of life. After such an experience there is often a sense of well-being. Of having been recharged and personally nourished. Not by chance, it was these very qualities that I also discussed in the concluding paragraphs of 'The Pursuit of Happiness'.

This deep, profound place within us may be referred to by many names or labels. Real, genuine, authentic, spiritual, metaphysical, transpersonal, soul, higher self are a few examples of what may be more familiar to you. For the purposes of this book I shall use the term 'deeper self'. Please feel free to substitute whatever terminology, label or concept feels right for you.

Our deeper self focuses on the questions around the point, potential and opportunity of our existence. While ego focuses on satisfying personal and material needs from, and through, it. Both, then, have important functions to fulfill.

Let's return briefly to what ego tries to achieve. It is primarily concerned with supporting, affirming and safeguarding our physical selves, to ensure we survive in the world, *as it perceives it.* This is a vitally important mechanism when we are young babies. We need all of these things from our primary caregivers. Initially to survive physically and then to develop psychologically.

Envisage (or remember) being the first born child in a family, enjoying the sole love and attention of your parents. Until, one day, it was unexpectedly disrupted because of the birth of a new sibling. Imagine how threatened you might, or did, feel. The moment when your parent's undivided love and attention was suddenly split between you and another human being.

As you contemplate this scenario, be aware of what emotions may rise up in your body now. Is it a sense of anger, fear or both?

Being associated with the limbic area of our brain, the natural survival mechanism of ego rises when we are psychologically - but experienced as physically - threatened by the arrival of a new sibling.

Ego can therefore make us behave and act in ways we never knew we were capable of. When we perceive our external environment as changing from one of relative safety, to one of threat, insecurity and apparently divided loyalties, we employ all sorts of primitive mechanisms to combat this. As a child we may cry more, rebel more and become more needy. All to try to win back the vital attention ego craves for its sense of security.

Any of you who have had a dog will no doubt recall times when you showed affection to another animal or person, just how quickly your pet would become jealous and insecure. The ego-survival tendency of an animal acts in a similar way to ours to ensure it gets enough love, attention and, of course, a continued supply of food!

For all of us in our early development ego will, at some point, perceive our immediate environment as threatening. Even the most perfect, or theoretically perfect, of childhoods and upbringing contain elements of insecurity. The classic, but unavoidable, 'growing pains'.

As we mature, once we can start to be able to look after, clothe, feed and sustain ourselves physically, ego's drive rarely diminishes. If it has proven it helped us to survive physically when we were young, it makes sense to continue to employ its services. All to ensure our ongoing psychological well-being.

The sad consequence of ego's blinkered perspectives is that the world becomes rather one-dimensional: competitive and threatening. Lost in it, we feel compelled to compare and contrast ourselves with others. Seduced, and reduced, into the need to continually prove ourselves. To be better than, and to achieve more than, the 'competition'.

We judge and assess ourselves purely based on physical or material status. Money, fame, beauty, property and status take on the utmost importance. All the tangible, measurable things that ego persuades us will make others perceive us in the way that it needs them to.

Recall a time when you felt very proud of something you had achieved. It may have been buying something that you had always wanted, winning an award, passing an exam, making a speech, getting a pay rise, losing weight....

Remember the feeling of pride that you felt on reaching this achievement or milestone. As much as you can, try to go back into the feeling within that memory.

Was the felt sense of your pride solely sourced from an acceptance or affirmation from others, or did it also come from a place somewhere deep within you?

If it was from both sources which felt, or currently feels, the most important?

Part of ego's make up is that it only really knows, or is capable of knowing, two distinct states. They are either survival or death. Although ego 'death' as an adult doesn't lead to the same outcome as the lack of care, attention and food would have on a vulnerable baby. Nevertheless, as we grow, it still experiences a lack of societal acceptance as a form of death. With similar fearful consequences:

'I was so embarrassed I could have died.' 'When the teacher ignored me I felt like I didn't even exist.' 'It felt like I was crucified when I forgot my lines.'

These are natural expressions of ego struggling to maintain itself in a threatening world. Being driven largely driven by comparison, this world becomes a more fearful place. Ego perceives within it a finite, limited amount of affirming acceptance and loving approval.

Remember the last time your ego felt dented. It may have been when you were overlooked for a promotion at work, let down by a partner, snubbed by a friend, failed a test or were simply unable to maintain an unrealistically high expectation of yourself.

Afterwards, how did you support yourself to move forwards again?

Did you beat yourself up and chastise yourself? Or philosophically accept that you did your best and 'put it down to experience?'

It is our ego that chastises and rejects us in these moments. Our deeper self accepts and grows from such experiences. It knows they can't 'kill' us:

> "There are no failures - just experiences and your re-actions to them."
>
> Tom Krause (American author and motivational speaker)

Within ego's fearful resistance to reflect on a difficult experience, the opportunity for the deeper self to adapt, and grow, is restricted. Ego's job is to keep things static and stable. Predictable and manipulable. Through a desire to control its environment and, frequently, the people within it.

Whilst needing to be accepted and feel part of the crowd, perhaps paradoxically, ego also enjoys the attention of standing out from it. It craves this stand alone attention as an opportunity to win more affirmation. More adulation.

Our deeper self also wants us to celebrate our uniqueness. But in such a way that we feel encouraged to share our gifts and talents to make a positive difference to the lives of others. Not merely in service of the separate self.

Ego plays a vital role in recognising ourselves as a separate being in the world. Yet problems occur when it runs riot. When it dominates. Then we, and it, feels disconnected from the deeper self out of which it was born.

Ironically, in a vain attempt to soothe the pain of this isolation, we seek more affirmation from others. Where, and when, we cannot achieve this adequately from our environment, ego employs more 'negative' emotional feeling states: fear, anger, blame, jealousy. All in an attempt to protect us from the underlying existential angst that our sense of disconnection brings.

How does your ego attempt to nourish itself on a day to day basis?

How do you feel when you don't get the acknowledgement you think you need to feel good about yourself?

Perhaps it shows up when you don't get enough likes on social media, get less attention than your friends or insufficient recognition for what you do.

Take a moment to close your eyes now and turn your focus inwards toward your heart centre. Try to connect with a sense of your own internal validation mechanism.

Does this greater internal connection change what affirmation you might normally seek from the outside world?

By listening to the internal dialogue of our feelings we understand if ego drives us through fear or inadequacy or our deeper self motivates us through loving encouragement. Which one are you currently backing?

OUR QUEST TO BE OUR BEST

Everything living on this planet is undergoing a process of growth. Of maturation. Of development. Including, of course, ourselves. The signs of outer growth we see form into the lines on our faces. Some when we smile, others when we frown.

They are all lines of the expression of emotional experience. Indicating a life lived of triumph to tribulation and of joy to sorrow. The outer manifestations of physical growth are, to a large extent, outside of our control. We grow old and look older. But our inner growth is something we are able to have a greater participation in. A greater control over.

Just as surely as acorns have the potential to grow into great oak trees, we all have the innate ability to flourish. Whether it be to create, compose, teach, help, sing, heal, write, paint, design, build, invent, play, inspire, we all, like the acorn, have the *unique* blueprint of a gift. A passion. A talent within. I emphasise unique here because, just as each person's fingerprint is different in the world, so too is the role we can play in the contribution to, and betterment of, it.

Our deeper purpose is to discover, to develop and, most importantly, to trust the existence of this inner potential. The outward expression of our intrinsic life purpose manifests when we finally wake up to the very nature of our deeper self. Every one of us has the capability and natural propensity to grow in our own way, at our own pace and in our own one-off style. That is part of our birthright, our human potential and our group evolutionary process:

"The purpose of life is to discover your gift. The work of life is to develop it. The meaning of life is to give your gift away."

David Viscott (American psychiatrist, author and radio talk show counsellor)

Yet, in this quest to discover our innate blueprint we have to face many trials and tribulations. As if to test our resolve and commitment to find, and follow, our real passions. The metaphorical internal treasure chest we unearth, following much searching and digging, feels all the more valuable than were it simply to be handed over to us on a plate.

The spiritual muscle we grow as we tirelessly search for our treasure helps us to share its value with the world. If we hadn't fully experienced the ego-breaking pain of the struggle, we would likely just keep it for ourselves.

Unearthing our inner treasure is rarely an easy task. It involves both an outer and inner journey. We need to adopt the mindset of an explorer - a spiritual warrior - being prepared to go to places that we have not been before. Or perhaps could never even have envisaged ourselves going to.

How many times in your life have you stood back and said to yourself: 'How on earth did I end up here, doing this, right now?!'

The explorer part of us is hungry for fresh experiences, new paradigms, undiscovered worlds. It reminds us to stay open. Faithful to our journeying. Learning. Trusting that challenge is good for our spiritual muscle.

Take the real life example of one of the greatest ever global explorers, Christopher Columbus. When he sailed off on his first voyage he set his sights on making landfall on, what is today, Japan.

However, he 'accidentally' landed in the Caribbean islands, eventually discovering the New World, further west. Although he had planned on landing somewhere completely different, Columbus trusted that his ultimate destiny was to take him somewhere else. Notably, this apparent error of judgement did not deter him from going on to become one of the most foremost explorers in history.

When we have a positive explorer mentality there are no wrong turns, diversions or wasted effort. Every discovery is important and valuable. Every experience trusted. Even if the learning is about how *not* best to get somewhere!

Unbridled ego can make us lose our spiritual trust in our treasure hunting journey. It already has a fixed idea of what it judges we need to derive satisfaction from life. It wants specifics. Nothing else will do. We can become very blinkered and rigid in both our aspirations and our expectations.

Then, when we hit the inevitable dead end, detour or 'wrong' destination, disillusionment and disappointment abound. We tell ourselves we have failed. We dislike the world. Lose our trust in fate and blame something convenient for thwarting the only goals that could possibly bring us happiness.

I wonder what would have happened if Columbus had adopted this attitude? It would, no doubt, have taken a lot longer for the Americas to be discovered. Explorers, by their nature, are up for a challenge. They see it as part of their territory:

> "We are all inventors, each sailing out on a voyage of discovery, guided each by a private chart, of which there is no duplicate. The world is all gates, all opportunities."

> Ralph Waldo Emerson (American philosopher, essayist and poet)

We've all had occasions where fixed expectations of how something is going to turn out, only to be disappointed with how things actually do. But, the person we get chatting to on the train following the rejection at the audition or the understanding words of a colleague following the break-up of a relationship, can often affect the course of our lives. If we are prepared to be less attached to the outcome that our ego had originally planned for us.

Recall a time where you metaphorically took a 'wrong' life turn and ended up somewhere completely different from where you had originally planned. Did you discover a new quality about yourself as a result?

Ego sparks the blocking emotions of frustration and resentment when we, at first, do not get what we want. Compare that with how much gratitude and appreciation we can eventually feel, when we allow ourselves to trust in the bigger unfolding picture. The picture trying to show us what we really need for our spiritual growth.

With this in mind, let's develop the earlier metaphor of the acorn and the oak tree. Those trees that impress us the most are not necessarily the ones growing obediently side by side with others in the lush forest. It's the ones managing to flourish on a small, apparently inhospitable, plateau on the side of a mountain.

We are all impressed when we see life struggling to be, to succeed, against all the odds. Charles Darwin, the famous naturalist and biologist, would say that we have only evolved as a species by being physically tested by our environment. From adapting. By realising our potentials through the challenges we face.

Alone, ego could be represented by the tree which wants to be the tallest in the forest. The one that wants to outgrow the others in terms of size and stature. Left unfettered, it would draw all the nutrients it could through its roots from the ground on which it stands, showing little concern for the other trees. Although it knows they also need a share of the same nutrients. It would judge its own needs as being the most important and view the soil, the sun and the rain as something purely to be used and consumed.

Using the same analogy, our deeper self wants us to flourish through a sense of complementary connection and cooperation, rather than of pure consumption. It calls upon us to appreciate all the other elements that have come together that allow us to grow externally - physically - for us to be free to decide how we wish to grow internally. To work *with* the planet, knowing that we grow in partnership with it. Not just upon it.

There is scientific evidence now to suggest that trees communicate with each other. Nurturing younger trees via their root networks and warning each other about potential pests and threats. Further proof that everything in nature is part of a larger system that is always communicating with itself. One that is designed to be in a state of relational, and reciprocal, balance with the other.

An important question we all have to ask ourselves at some point in our lives is how do we want to manifest our unique opportunity for growth?

What sort of metaphorical fruit do you want to bear on your tree?

Perhaps you choose to harvest it for yourself. Keeping it hidden from others and stored away for a rainy day. Or do you choose to share it in a way which adds to the beauty of life? To the service and betterment of others. To the 'relationship' of which we are all a part.

Think about the work that you do. It may be paid, voluntary, running the family home or looking after children. When you take away the immediate, tangible benefit of this work, such as money or acknowledgement, notice how what you do plays some small part in the development of the whole. In the service and betterment of the lives of others.

Are the most satisfying jobs all about gaining the highest tangible reward?

Or are they about making the lives of others just a little easier or better?

"Work is love made visible."

Kahlil Gibran (Lebanese writer, poet, philosopher and artist)

The realisation that we are ultimately free to give something back to the flow of life is one way to begin to challenge the dominance of ego. It fears inner resources are finite. By embracing our deeper self's motivation to want to share and give of ourselves, we can soothe this fear-based ego cry.

EGO HUNGER AND SPIRITUAL HUNGER

Hunger is a natural human state for us all. In fact, for every living thing. It is what drives us both physically and mentally. Symbolically, and spiritually, it reveals the source of our questing. A need for satisfaction. To be nourished. A yearning to fulfil and to be fulfilled.

Channelled purely through an ego perspective, this evolutionary drive manifests in a more selfish and self-sustaining way. Left unchecked, ego monopolises this universal energy and transmutes it into a hunger purely to satisfy its own needs: 'This is what *I* want and what *I* need and that's all that matters!'

Ego creates specific desires within us. Then it uses pain blocking emotions such as anger, jealousy and hate, if the achievement of those rigidly held desires is thwarted. Often blaming the actions of others. Or it gloats on the sense of pride when the object of our specific desire is achieved. As if our very life depended upon it.

How often have you set your sights on achieving something, or getting somewhere, and, on finally reaching that place, find that the 'victory' feels empty or hollow?

Remember as a child waiting so long to get the birthday present you really wanted. Then the big day arrived and you were up really early tearing open the parcel. After a few hours playing with your new toy, the painful reality started to hit that it may not actually be making you as happy as you had dreamed of during the weeks beforehand.

This is how ego's anticipatory mechanism works, keeping us hooked into the perpetual drama of desire. It tells us that we'll only be truly happy when we get this or when we achieve that. The anticipation of this illusory state of endless bliss keeps us hungry. Living in some fantastical future moment. Any moment other than the present one.

All the while we are caught up in this ego drama our deeper self remains unnourished. It craves a more emotional experiential nourishment from life. Ego misinterprets the spiritual yearnings of the deeper self and morphs it into a constant material need. This is why we so frequently want to *consume* rather than to *relate*. Missing the opportunity to simply bear witness to what a particular life experience may be trying to show us.

Next time that you become aware that you desire someone or something, take a moment to contemplate the inner void that you are seeking to fill. Is there any hidden pain or fear in that space?

By delaying the immediate gratification of an ego-based desire we give ourselves the opportunity to see that what is merely material does not define, or add to, who we really are.

Literally, there is a 'quest' in question. Contemplating the bigger existential questions of life opens up a fertile inner space for our deeper purpose to bubble up. And it is our very willingness to ask them that allows the clarifying light to enter:

❑ *Is there a point to my life?*

❑ *Does what happens to me make a difference to who I really am?*

❑ *Do I want to make this world a slightly better place to be through my presence within it?*

What happened to your sense of being a separate ego self when you read the questions above?

Selma's Story

Selma came into therapy after receiving very upsetting news. She had been unexpectedly diagnosed with a cancer condition following a routine check-up. This naturally came as a real shock. Selma was only in her early forties and had never faced any serious medical issues before.

Initially, our time together focussed on the relationship Selma had with her body. Up to that point in her life, she had largely defined herself through her physical self. Her looks and her body image. Yet now she had been told that there was something wrong with the mechanics of this physical self, she was lost. Confused. How could there be anything wrong when she didn't feel any pain?

This added to Selma's sense of disbelief about her diagnosis. She danced between conflicting feelings of denial, anger and fear. If, in her head she was fine, but her body was not, then who was she really?

As our sessions continued together we navigated the raft of difficult emotions that came up. Selma tried hard to make sense of everything. Then, in one particular session, she shared a new found sense of inner peace. It was a kind of peace that she had never experienced before.

Through her tears Selma described talking to herself in the mirror a few days before. Really staring at her reflection, but not in the way she was so used to in the past. She saw past her physical form and described a sense of overwhelming peaceful connectedness. A place without any fear, just as she was concentrating on the bottomless centre point of her eyes. Although it was for the briefest moment of time, this sensation gave her a sense of expansion. Of limitlessness.

By being able to see beyond her old sense of self, Selma gained a new perspective. Her feelings changed from resentment to ones of surrender. She began to be at peace with her diagnosis. As she did so she also sensed a deeper message within it.

Selma described her cancer as shattering the old image she had always had of herself. Whilst the news rocked her externally, she realised it had also broken through a layer of illusion that she had carried for many years. The illusion that her limited, fragile physical body was the totality of who she was. The only source of her personal value.

Selma decided to make changes in her life. She gave up her old job as a beauty consultant and retrained as a nursery school teacher. She had always wanted children of her own, so teaching seemed a natural vocation for her to pursue. A way for her to share her, up to now, thwarted maternal instincts. Following ongoing treatment, Selma is currently in remission from her illness.

By being brave enough to see through the veil of ego-based fear and anger her diagnosis had triggered, Selma revealed a message. One which was to prove meaningful in how she now chose to live her life. And one which she may never have fully understood, had it not been for her diagnosis.

Just as Selma did, we all hit plateaus in life of confusion and bewilderment. Where nothing initially makes sense. When we just don't know where to put our next step. When it appears that the old self we once knew, that once defined us, cannot now happily stand upon the new plateau that life presents to us.

It is at just these stuck points that we need to be even more open to the subtle signs trying to reveal themselves. These frequently occur through meaningful coincidences. Synchronicities in our lives. They are the kinds of serendipitous events where we may hear ourselves saying: 'Someone else mentioned that exact same thing to me yesterday' or, 'how strange I was just thinking of you earlier' to, 'I keep meeting people like you who are doing exactly the same thing'.

When you wake up and notice these kind of 'coincidences' ask yourself:

What is life trying to tell me, show me or encourage me to try here?

It is in these moments we know our deeper self is speaking to us. Acting like a compass to guide our next step.

Sadly, given its sense of separateness from the world, ego will often dismiss synchronistic occurrences as mere coincidence. It offers up little meaning or significance to a sign that may be encouraging us to see ourselves in a new light. To try something outside of our comfort zone:

> "Synchronistic events offer us perceptions that may be useful in our psychological and spiritual growth and may reveal to us, through intuitive knowledge, that our lives have meaning."

> Jean Shinoda Bolen (Swiss psychiatrist, Jungian analyst and author)

Through the journey of counselling therapy, clients bring what they initially think is a raft of challenging, seemingly unconnected, life experiences. Given enough therapeutic space and holding, there is often a theme which reveals itself. A common thread running through the client's life in terms of repeating relationships, inauthenticities or stuck emotions.

Counselling works by effectively pulling on this common thread. Bringing together seemingly unrelated experiences in a way which offers up a connective meaning. By being able to make sense of what the client's ego will merely dismiss as insignificant or painful, successful therapy can help to reveal what our deeper self is trying to show us.

Take a moment to think of the last time you dismissed something as mere coincidence. Maybe you were thinking of an old friend you hadn't seen in ages and then bumped into them unexpectedly and they admitted that they had just been thinking of you too.

Or you met a new work colleague who had faced the same health issue as yourself, and they shared a helpful complementary therapy that had helped them.

If you allow yourself to see meaning in these types of events, what happens to your sense of trust in life? And in the greater wisdom of the universe?

◆ ◆ ◆

We all need nourishment to grow and develop. Our deeper self is no different. If we cook too much food for one meal, we wouldn't likely throw the excess away. We might keep it until we are hungry again later.

The deeper self sees life experience in the same way. If we have not extracted all the spiritual nutrients in terms of personal growth, it will seek out further similar life experiences containing the same lessons.

This gives rise to the familiar cry of: 'Why does this keep happening to me?' Or 'what have I done to deserve this?' Cries which we have all, no doubt, heard ourselves uttering at various points in our lives.

When you hear yourself repeating these words, know that there is an unexplored or repressed part of yourself that your deeper self wants to wake you up to. To learn to love and accept. Trust, wherever and whenever you can, that there is a 'higher' reason for it.

What similar life situations do you keep finding yourself in? It may be similar partners in relationships who take you for granted. Or work colleagues who do not give you enough credit for what you contribute.

Through these experiences, what might your deeper self be trying to wake you up to, regarding how much you personally value who you are and what you do?

Left to ego, we give the power we need to sustain our self-worth and respect over to the hands of others. We lose the ability to self-value. To recognise for ourselves who we are and what we do. Our deeper self knows, if we want others to reflect value back to us, we must first recognise and value ourselves. And acknowledge the real work we have done on our own spiritual muscle.

SURRENDER

Surrender has all sorts of negative connotations for the human condition: giving in, defeat, weakness, powerlessness.

But is it not also true that to be spiritually powerful is to realise, and to accept, the limits of our personal power? Of our ability to control what is?

Perhaps, spiritually, surrender is about having the courage of humility. To accept how things and people are right now, just as they are in the present moment. The energy that rejects how something is refuses to accept the world as it is. We then live in a state of perpetual, exhausting resistance:

> "God, grant me the serenity to accept the things I cannot change, the courage to change the things I can, and the wisdom to know the difference."

> Reinhold Niebuhr (American theologian professor, ethicist and commentator)

We spend a great deal of time and energy trying to change things or wishing people were different. Much of this desire comes from our conditioning. Persuading us that everything has to be a certain way - a way which we specifically define - for us to be happy. Ego too convinces us that unless we are busy controlling or manipulating something, there must be little positive benefit to be had from it.

The trouble is that all this effort takes energy. Energy that is sadly wasted. We tell ourselves we will be happy when I have this, or when my partner is like that, or when I arrive at this place in my life. All of these require us to feel in control. We can so easily become 'control freaks'.

Ann's Story

Many clients come for therapy because of issues in their personal relationships. They often want to solely focus on understanding why their partners act, or treat them, as they do. Ann was one such client. She had been with her partner, Bob, for 8 years. Whilst she loved him dearly, as he did her, Ann had felt insecure for much of that time. Bob did not show her the kind of demonstrative love that she felt she showed to him.

Ann's feelings were a mix of frustration, anger, sadness and loneliness. To add to this she also carried a burden of guilt. She felt that she had no right to feel these insecure feelings in the first place. Yet her mind kept obsessing with them. Did Bob really love her?

Ann spent a lot of time in counselling wondering why Bob could not be different. He was an all round 'nice guy' she said. But why couldn't he just be more affectionate and tactile with her? Her father had been a very loving man. She was the apple of his eye, particularly as she was the only daughter with three older brothers. Now her father had passed away, Ann was missing his love more than ever.

Ann recounted what it was like for her to be constantly at the centre of her father's attention. At first she described nothing but positives. She could do nothing wrong. Even when she was naughty, and her mum would tell her off, it was her father who first forgave her. Together we explored how much pressure Ann was putting on Bob to be like her father. Was it fair to require Bob to be so?

The deeper we dug around Ann's relationship with her father, the more she realised that it was actually quite suffocating too. Her father had fairly rigid expectations of how he wanted Ann to be. Nonetheless, all the while she won his love and devotion, she felt that adapting herself to his expectations was worth the reward.

As Bob showed his love in such a different way it was not surprising that it left Ann confused. His love was more 'laid back'. Less demonstrative. Yet more freeing and liberating, Ann decided. With Bob she was free to live a life she wanted which, in theory, was a good thing. Why did this leave her feeling insecure? Was there really no conditionality to Bob's love? No expectation?

I asked Ann, if she were to know all the historic and genetic reasons that made Bob who he was, would she then be able to accept him more? Could she then be happier with the love that he offered her in his way?

Ann admitted that, even with a full understanding of how Bob interpreted his world, she could not be certain that she would feel secure. This internal honesty allowed the therapy to move onto what it was that Ann really needed. To be able to offer greater security both to, and from, herself. To accept that having freedom does not mean that someone doesn't love you. It might even mean exactly the opposite.

With the recent passing of her father, and the loss of his physical presence and love, Ann's insecurities were heightened. Yet she also realised that she was now completely free to be who she wanted. Even as an adult she saw that she still did her best to please him. Now there was no longer any need for that. And turning to Bob to replicate her father's love was ultimately not helpful. Or psychologically healthy.

Retreating into the mindset of seeking to change how others are, we convince ourselves that all our problematic feelings will magically disappear, if they were to just behave differently. This was true for Ann. Until she realised that accepting how Bob is was more of a gift than a concession. His style of liberated love was the key to her own spiritual growth. And her existential freedom.

If we decide that we are truly not happy with how loved or secure we might feel, it is up to us to communicate that. And then to either change ourselves or our personal circumstances. To have the courage to 'change the things we can'.

Surrender, in terms of our deeper self, does not actually involve any sense of defeat or powerlessness. It is, instead, like an opening and acceptance of what is. Of loving what is. If we immediately reject the current state of a situation, how can we ever allow it, or us, to be in a different state? We have to accept where something or someone is now, before it/they can ever have the opportunity to move to a different state or way of being.

This calls for a brave trust in this form of surrender. A trust which accepts that, wherever someone else is emotionally or psychologically in relation to ourselves, is exactly where they need to be. Both for their own spiritual growth *and* ours.

Given our own current awareness and sense of personal resource, we too are doing and being what we need to be. Others are on their pathway and we are on ours. Who said that they should be the same? Or that one is 'better' than the other?

> "Your whole life is a rehearsal for the moment that you are in now."

> The Chassidim (Jewish mystic movement)

Try to sit back for a moment and imagine (or accept if you can), that everything is perfect as it is. Everything is as it should be right at this moment in time. Really try to breathe into that idea. Become aware of the peace and stillness that lies within that thought form.

There is always perfection and order underlying superficial chaos. Just as perfection and wholeness only appear chaotic, when perceived solely through the fragmenting eye of the fearful ego.

By loving and accepting what ego only sees as chaotic, we at least give ourselves the chance to sense the underlying perfection. The perfection waiting to show itself through our meaning revealing, spiritual 'in-sights'.

If we are always trying to change something we interfere with an underlying order that has yet to fully reveal itself. Within an all-encompassing mindset of acceptance, we even learn to love and accept those insecure tendencies within us that seek to control and manipulate.

By putting down our ego tools of control, and lowering our defensive shield, we see the reality of our horizon more clearly. We benefit from seeing the beauty of the whole horizon before us because we stop focusing on only part of it. Usually the part that we think needs to change. We never wish that the rainbow could be a bit more to the left or that the sun would set in a different colour.

Imagine being presented with a jigsaw puzzle which is virtually complete, apart from one missing piece. Ego will tend to fixate on that one missing piece. Less so on the appreciation of the rest of the picture already pieced together. Our deeper self remains centred and calm, even when presented with the reality of a missing piece. It knows that true completeness lies within us:

Ego says: 'Once everything falls into place, I will find peace.'

The deeper self says: 'Find peace and everything will fall into place.'

Embracing spiritual surrender means we let go of the traditional idea of the white flag being waved from behind defensive lines in everyday ego battles. We relinquish primal fears that our imagined enemies will somehow overpower us. Ego favours movement and doing. When we appear to be doing nothing in terms of wanting to change or manipulate, it feels impotent and powerless.

As an example of how this ego characteristic manifests, think about how you tend to be within social situations where others have a differing political or religious view from yourself. We are frequently quite opinionated around these subjects as they represent fundamental views as to how best we feel our world should be ordered.

How accepting, or resistant, are you when you find yourself among differing viewpoints? Contrary opinions?

Are you able to surrender to the idea that others may see things differently, given their own unique personality filters, life experiences and aspirations?

How much space can you hold, or access, within yourself to allow others to be different?

Ego needs to know where it stands and also to take a stand. The antithesis to surrender. Through this stance it knows whether something else is a threat to its superiority of needing to know first. And to know better. It adopts a tailored defensive reaction rather than an open deeper response. (See Defences.)

We all develop particular coping mechanisms when confronted with emotional stressors in life. Maybe you always deny being upset, when you actually feel very sad, because you don't want to appear vulnerable. Or you reach for a drink rather than discuss a painful family issue.

What personal historic coping mechanisms do you tend to over rely on?

Do they continue to be appropriate for how you want to respond to challenging times now?

The surrender sourced from our deeper self encourages us to drop the weapons of protection that ego seeks to retain. It means giving up the urge to control events. To become more open to seeing, listening to and witnessing what is happening, without immediately interpreting or judging. It means having the courage to trust and to step into the unknown:

> "The heart surrenders everything to the moment. The mind judges and holds back."
>
> Ram Dass (American spiritual teacher, author and clinical psychologist)

The spiritual truth is that the 'enemy', which ego fears will overpower us in any act of surrender, does not lie somewhere outside of us. It lies somewhere within. The amygdala-driven ego can become obsessed with searching for danger outside of itself, as a way of avoiding our own internal fear. It will even seek out situations and people which it judges as 'bad' and use them as a screen on which to project our unreconciled fears. (See Fear.)

This type of projection not only happens on a personal level but also on a group, cultural or race level. The attitude of the Nazis blaming all their internal woes on the Jewish people. Or the current Trump administration holding immigrants responsible for much of the country's economic difficulties.

Perhaps the act of giving in to something, within the traditional meaning of surrender, could be spiritually redefined as an opportunity for 'going within'. To have the courage to get in touch with all the inner parts of our own selves that we are conditioned to believe are unsavoury, unattractive or worthless. The parts that ego fears acknowledging and wants to keep locked away. Hidden in the shadowy vaults of our psyches.

OUR SHADOW SELF AND
THE ROLES WE PLAY

As children on a bright day, we no doubt played the game of chasing and hiding in each other's shadows cast by the sun. We felt safe when we could conceal all of ourselves in the shadows. Or 'exposed' if we could not move quickly enough to remain there.

The difficulty was, as we ran and played, the shadows kept changing size and direction according to which way we twisted and turned. At the times the shadow cast was longer, it was easier to hide in someone else's shadow. We were winning the game. But when the shadow was much smaller, it became impossible to stay out of the light. If only you could make yourself a little smaller, you could stay 'safe' in the shadows.

As we grow psychologically we develop a self which we believe works well in the world. When we expose this self into the light of public scrutiny, it is affirmed. Accepted. We have little need to hide away these proven 'acceptable' manifestations of ourself within our shadow parts.

Recalling our original definition of ego, this trusted public self is made up of how we want to think and feel about ourselves, combined with how we prefer others to think and feel about us. This is the self we feel most comfortable to inhabit. Its core personality traits form the basis for all the roles we have to play in life. So, if we like to be seen as a caring person, this will manifest to varying degrees in all the different contexts of our lives.

There are a myriad of life roles we are called to play. They differ according to the group context we find ourselves in: gender, personal, family, sexuality, work, social, religious, cultural, race. We adapt ourselves depending on how we personally perceive the demands and expectations of our role in each life scenario.

Consider how differently you might act when you are with your immediate family, as compared with a group of work colleagues. How much more real and safe can you be and feel with your loved ones, compared with people you need to impress in a certain way?

When meeting people for the first time, we tend to be more formal. On our best behaviour. Once commonality is found and rapport built, we can risk showing and disclosing more of ourselves. Providing this is reciprocated by the people around us.

Being a fly on the wall in these situations is like watching a game of poker unfold. Each person taking it in turns to put one of their cards down until, eventually, everyone is happy to 'show their hand'. Authenticity and a certain vulnerability builds as people's humanity appears from behind their social facade. But, if one person refuses to play their card, this inhibits the others from doing so. Disclosure leads to disclosure. Inhibition to suspicion.

I love the beautiful gesture behind the Zulu African tribe's word for hello, 'Sawubona'. It literally means: 'I see you. By seeing you I bring you into existence.'

We often act in our various life roles based on the expectations we perceived as being placed upon us from our original family group. If we were the eldest sibling, we will probably have felt a need to help our parents with the care of any younger brothers and sisters.

This may have been in the form of literal help, direct caring, or indirectly helping by curtailing our needs and so placing less demands on our busy parents' time. Either way, we will have carved out and established a family role in response to what we perceived as being required of us. In this case, one which is built upon seeing the needs of others as preferential to our own.

If we had health issues as a child we would have naturally needed more attention and extra care. Here we establish a default role of continuing to seek care from others into adulthood as a principal way of feeling affirmed and loved. Given our childhood experience, we would have little idea of how else to do it.

For us all, our principal role will centre around one of the following fundamental personality types: rescuer, carer, protector, peacemaker, questioner, reformer, performer, observer, challenger or victim.

Which of these personality role types best described you growing up? Is it still your natural or default role today?

What benefits do you gain from sticking with your default role?

Would these benefits still be there if you were to adopt a different type of role?

Imagine, or recall, being born into a culture where you are expected to marry a partner of your parents' choosing. Where you feel obliged to be with someone without necessarily feeling any love or attraction.

If we come to believe, and accept, that other's approval is more important than our own, we will likely develop a low opinion of our own needs. We become adaptive to the wants and needs of others. We might lose a sense of what *we* really want at all:

"No man, for any considerable period, can wear one

face to himself and another to the multitude, without finally getting bewildered as to which may be true."

Nathaniel Hawthorne (American novelist)

Or, envisage being born into a family of farmers who had worked the same land for generations. There would typically be an expectation, maybe a huge pressure, that you would continue to work in the family business once you had left school. You might find it almost impossible to leave to go off to pursue a career of your choosing.

Were you able to follow a love life and/or decide upon a career of your choosing or were you influenced by others?

Does your current partnership, or job reflect, allow you to repeat a default role from childhood?

As far as ego is concerned there is always a perceived pay back, a benefit, to maintaining our various roles. They include both tangible and felt things: approval from parents and family, a paycheck from an employer, popularity amongst friends, love from a partner, acceptance into a social group.

The perceived benefit for maintaining these roles is very persuasive. So much so that they become automatic. Second nature. We can lose touch with our deeper, more authentic, self and its role or purpose. This part of us frequently cries out, asking us to show a different side of ourselves, to rebel against family patterns or to take us off on a different path in life.

Ego deals with these rebellious parts and yearnings by compartmentalising our various behaviours into acceptable and non-acceptable categories. Any characteristics it deems unsavoury it pushes down into our 'shadow self'.

As this name would suggest, the shadow part of ourself is like a dark cellar under a house. It is here that we hide those qualities which, for one historic reason or another, ego has decided are not worthy of being in the light of our everyday awareness.

Similarly, many traits we feel may be outside of our desired personality are also pushed down. Perhaps anger, greed, selfishness, timidity, assertiveness, creativity, self belief. Any of the traits that our particular perception of the world has taught us are not palatable, healthy or attractive to others.

Which traits or emotions were you told as a child were not desirable?

Were you scalded for showing frustration and anger or scorned for crying when you were upset?

To keep them suppressed, ego shrouds shadow traits behind a cloak of shame, fear or guilt. Here they remain well hidden, making it difficult to access, or even feel, them.

Imagine your psyche - the conscious and unconscious parts of our mind - as being like a house made up of many rooms. Each room representing a different characteristic or quality of yourself. So there are potentially hundreds of rooms to explore.

When we are young, and less restricted by the developed ego, we have a greater unfettered access to all of our rooms. This makes it possible to interact with the world completely freely and uninhibitedly.

These accessible rooms include the less desirable traits. Hate and greed, for example. We all remember our parents telling us to be 'nice' to our friends and how it is not appropriate to be 'greedy'. All long before we had come to understand that these were socially undesirable qualities.

The rooms representing the opposite, or compensatory, traits of hate and greed are love and generosity. Unless we are able to reconcile and accept our natural human potential to be greedy, the repressed greed will express itself by tainting our sense of generosity. In other words, when we give, we will do so with an agenda of secretly wanting something in return. Our unacknowledged human capacity for greed will still continue to express itself, only from our shadow.

Free of ego's need to judge things as good or bad, we allow ourselves to see, and reconcile, both the dark and light of every one of our traits. We give ourselves access to their whole spectrum. We do not deny their complementary, and natural, opposites.

When we combine our capacity for love and hate we strike a healthier balance of love. One which is more objective, discerning and realistic. A love which is not blind but is not purely cynical either.

Through complete access to this healthy internal discernment, we free ourselves to both choose and accept that there are some people we have more in common with and others less so. We find peace in the fact that we will not like, or be liked by, everyone we meet.

Insecure ego insists that we should be liked by everyone. Yet, when we step away from its dominance, and the shadow it creates, we no longer feel compelled to either blindly love or vengefully hate.

This gives us the permission to accept people as they are. To surrender to the reality of what is. Here we will naturally feel less compelled to want to change others through a manipulating type of love or hate. Instead we maintain a non-attaching, accepting, objective, witnessing stance. A liberated live-and-let-live self attitude that brings light to the shadow of our psyche. And to others.

Through a reconciliation of our internal capacity for both hate and love, we do not constantly expend energy on hating or disliking anything. We instead balance the resulting loving energy between appropriate love for others *and* love for self. Here there is no selflessness. Only a recognition and acceptance of both how we, and how someone else, happen to be.

With an acceptance that we all have the capacity for love and hate, generosity and greed, does this help you to accept yourself more completely?

Psychological theory suggests that every one of our behaviours is motivated by some sort of perceived payback. Even the ones that we convince ourselves are completely altruistic. When we bring this basic, self-serving, need out of our shadow and into the light of consciousness, we regain the power over how it functions. We understand how we are *really* motivated to behave as we do.

Only in wholeness, and without shadow, we recognise that as we help others through our generosity of spirit, we also help ourselves. We realise our spiritual power by witnessing its beneficial effects on others. And that is ok. Part of the role of our deeper self is to find where we can serve and make a difference to the lives of others. It feels nourished and animated. We evolve.

This is part of the payback. Yet when considered in this light it does not seem selfish. Despite the fact that it is self-serving. It also reinforces the notion that we exist as part of a connected system. As we help others we cannot help but help ourselves.

From humility to confidence, rejection to acceptance, fear to bravery, doubt to trust and success to failure. All traits have their light and dark aspects. Depending on whether they operate through us consciously or from our egoic shadows. When we are less conscious of our shadow traits, they will continue to play out in our behaviours in ways which restrict us:

❑ If we have no sense of humility our confidence will

appear merely as conceit

❑ Our strive for acceptance driven only by a fear of rejection

❑ Our outward bravery constantly tainted by internal worry

❑ Our success sought only as an escape from the spectre of failure

❑ Our need to be loved rooted only in a fear of abandonment

Unless we allow ourselves to feel the light and the dark of each of our traits we cannot unconditionally express any point along its spectrum. We will always have a hidden agenda. As ego creates shadow, qualities and traits we keep there will be reflected back to us through others. Often in an unwelcome way. What we repress internally eventually manifests externally. Just as a mirror cannot help but reflect back a true, and complete, image of the subject standing in front of it:

> "We meet ourselves time and again in a thousand disguises on the pathway of life."
>
> Carl Jung (Swiss founder of analytical psychology, psychoanalyst and psychiatrist)

As we grow, and become more susceptible to the power and control of the developing ego, we close doors on certain rooms in our house. This pressures us into only fulfilling those roles that our interpretation of our early environmental experience has seemingly carved out for us.

Rooms which contain traits which we are told, or believe, are not desirable, we remove ourselves from. We lock the doors behind us. Then our house appears more 'attractive' to passers by. When we cast these parts into our shadow, there is less of ourself to share in the light. We become less than who we truly are. Or could potentially be....

PART TWO

ANGER

Let's begin part two of this book by looking at anger. A powerful emotion that many of us tend to push down into our shadow. Is that because we judge it poorly? Possibly fearing its energetic consequences?

It is true that anger is used by some as an attribute. It has the potential to bring a lot of personal attention when unleashed. For the rest, the recourse to anger is normally avoided. Ego regards it as not fitting with how it wants us to be viewed, and potentially judged, by the world. Socially it's a 'no go'.

Much of how we feel about anger depends on our childhood experience of it. Whether it was expressed appropriately by our parents or whether it was used as a tool to dominate or intimidate.

As we do with many emotions, we will either repeat or rebel against anger. If we choose to repeat we will have interpreted it, from the example of our caregivers, as having been an effective way of being acknowledged in the world. Indeed, perhaps as a method of getting what we want. Here, we appropriately keep the door to our anger room open, entering it as and when we choose.

However, where early experiences of anger are less positive, or maybe we witnessed its destructive potential, we will likely rebel against it. We may remember, and still feel, the pain of its inappropriate use and so decide that it is not an emotion that serves any particularly constructive purpose.

When this personal rebellion becomes too great, all the powerful energy behind this potent emotion is pushed down into our shadow. We will continue to deny ourselves any access to even an appropriate expression of it as adults.

Ego is happy to repeat or rebel in this way. But our deeper self will view any formative experiences that result in the forming of a shadow as being incomplete. Unprocessed. As far as it is concerned, there is still some growthful value inherent in the repressed emotion. And in the original life experience which led to its repression in the first place.

Deborah's Story

Deborah first came into therapy because of a worsening eating disorder. She was very driven and career focussed. In her job as a journalist she had faced many highs and lows, striving towards her goal of working for a national newspaper.

Now she had got the break that she had always wanted and been offered a position in a busy central London office. On one level she felt extremely proud and yet, on another, a gnawing unease that she did not really feel good enough to warrant the prestigious opportunity.

To anyone looking in on Deborah it seemed as if the wheels of her life were turning in a way that she wanted. It was clear that outside validation was very important to her, but inside she felt that things were just moving too fast. So, in order to get back some semblance of control, she began to over-control her relationship with food.

Over our sessions together Deborah started to get in touch with a well of raw internal anger. She recalled that, in her childhood, expressing how she really felt was often belittled by her parents. Their attention had largely been devoted to her chronically sick sister. Now she was with a partner who, whilst being rationally supportive, offered Deborah little empathy in how she was actually feeling. Particularly when it came to her unhealthy relationship with food.

The anger that Deborah connected with had been suppressed for a long time. In many ways understandably so. How could she possibly be angry with her parents when they were having to care for her more physically vulnerable sister? She really had little choice but to be the 'good child'. The one always helping. Taking on more responsibility than was normal for someone of her tender age.

As an adult, and with the appropriate therapeutic support, Deborah began to objectively understand that what she had had to deal with as a child was not really fair. And she realised that she had a right to be angry about it. Not angry with any-one in particular, just frustrated that there was little room for her own emotional needs.

Now she was also with a partner who, whilst acknowledging her rationally, did not really do so on a deeper emotional level. This added to Deborah's sense that there was never any place in her world where she could freely express her re-pressed anger. It was little wonder that her ego had judged it so harshly. It seemed it was not welcome anywhere.

Any sensitive witness to this could see why Deborah had de-nied herself a healthy access to her anger. There was simply nowhere 'safe' for her to go with it. Without an outlet for the energy behind it, Deborah was unable to access any level of self-compassion either. It seemed the door to her self-com-passion room required that she first navigate the 'hallway' of her anger. This may have explained why she sought to com-pensate for this by valuing herself solely through her career achievements.

It was difficult, indeed often frightening, for Deborah to get in touch with her primal anger. She would dance around it and share feelings of nausea and butterflies in her stomach. It was not surprising this affected her healthy relationship with food. It seemed she held a lot of this raw emotional energy in her stomach. If she were to fully feel it, she might lose touch with the person she knew herself to be. The 'nice' person her ego wanted her to continue to be.

Over time, as Deborah started to tap into her trapped anger energy, she understood it did not actually want to cause destruction and chaos. It simply wanted her to be seen. To be acknowledged emotionally. To be valued for who she was, rather than how 'successful' she could be:

> "The inner voice has both gentleness and clarity. So to get to authenticity, you really keep going down to the bone, to the honesty and the inevitability of something."
>
> Meredith Monk (American composer)

Through its innate tendency to seek wholeness and to heal the internal psychological split caused by the shadow, our deeper self leads us into life experiences where repressed feelings are provoked. For Deborah, this took the form of a partner who effectively recreated her childhood experiences of offering little empathic space for her emotional expression. Once she found this through therapy, and developed a sense of control over the energy behind her repressed emotions, her relationship with food improved.

We may find if we repress some of the deeper messages contained in the energy behind raw anger, we will tend to meet people who frequently express anger at us. This can be particularly unnerving when we fear our own.

Alternatively, we may react to life's frustrations with an irrational and disproportionate degree of anger. As we are part of a connected emotional network, what we suppress will inevitably rise up somewhere else.

Imagine for a moment two people on either end of a metaphorical anger see-saw. As one person suppresses their anger and is going down on one end, the person on the opposite end will have little choice but to go up with theirs.

Ego does not want to take responsibility for managing a shadow emotion. It will only see the anger in the other person at the opposite end of the see-saw. It doesn't readily admit, or accept, that we may be carrying unresolved anger within us. It has already judged it as serving no useful purpose at all.

When we bring anger into the light of its natural opposite - a context of calmness and gentle acceptance - we allow the primal energy behind it to feel safer. Here it has the space and holding to feel more understandable. It has the chance to be more clearly articulated.

Next time you feel it, try to listen to your feelings of anger within this more balanced context. What new awareness do you think it's trying to convey?

Maybe you hear words describing a fear of not feeling understood. Of needs not being met or acknowledged. Of feeling undervalued or taken for granted by others?

We often get angry when we think someone is not wanting to see the world as we see it. Or refuses to at least try to understand our point of view. The child within us that experienced the destructive, or frightening, power of anger when we were young, may be locked away in our anger room crying out: 'I feel unseen, frightened, ignored, rejected, disrespected ....'

Recall the last time you were really angry or lost your temper. Was there part of you that was feeling ignored, abused, helpless or frightened?

When we consider the other feelings that are lying just beyond our level of anger, we usually uncover a quality of sadness. Maybe even of compassion, for the part of us that is being overlooked. When we feel really angry our tears are frequently somewhere close behind.

When we push our anger down we are literally ignoring, or rejecting, part of ourselves. A frightened and ashamed 'inner child' part. If we do this often enough, and for long enough, we can become very adaptive. The sort of person that is always changing to suit others' expectations.

As we do this we continue to deny ourselves the positive qualities of what much of our anger emotion is trying to achieve. These may be a healthier degree of assertiveness, of self-respect and acknowledgement of our own needs.

The deeper self wants us to feel our shadow emotions more openly. Only then can we start to see what's contained within the subliminal message of their repressed energetic power. It is interesting that we only tend to 'lose' our temper when we are desperately battling to keep it inside!

If we can allow ourselves to feel the underlying contributors to this emotion, rather than entering into an internal conflict with it, we will probably find that we don't need to lose our temper at all. Through self-respect and self-compassion, we realise we don't have to fear, or fight, the energy behind it. Instead we can express it in a more articulate and constructive way.

As Deborah experienced in her therapy, when we allow ourselves to feel the component messages of our anger, it tends to take us back to a past memory where we did not feel seen or valued for who we were. This is where we may need to go back and do some healing work around our own inner child. (See Our Life Scripts.)

Our English word for healing originates from the ancient Greek word 'holos', literally meaning to 'make whole'. When we repress parts of our natural emotional self within our shadow, we feel fragmented. The antithesis to wholeness, balance and health:

❏ *If you find that you keep meeting angry people, how are you suppressing your own anger?*

❏ *If you cannot bear people who are conceited, what part of you does not feel free to celebrate yourself and your own achievements?*

❏ *If you are jealous of another's success, where are you sabotaging your own greatest potential?*

❏ *If you feel intimidated by another's confidence, where and how are you inhibiting your own?*

It is the quest of the deeper self to make us whole, to complete us. To have our whole presence in each present moment. Through this practise we come to realise that it is the people who we would normally avoid that manifest the qualities we hold within our shadows. Ironically, it is these very people that have the capacity, and ability, to teach us the most about what we are hiding from ourselves. This is doubtless where the origins of the phrase 'our enemies are our greatest teachers' comes from.

Take a moment to bring to mind some of the people that you admire the most, and some of the people that you dislike, or find the most challenging.

Both sets of people will, no doubt, actually have qualities that you want to develop for yourself. For people we admire, these qualities will likely be utilised by them in a constructive way, creating a positive atmosphere for those around them. This is probably why we enjoy being in their company.

For the second set of people, who we instantly dislike or avoid, think about what it is they actually do which you find abhorrent or challenging? Maybe it's the kind of people who have an unquestioning self-belief. Or those that can hold court when they walk into a room? Whilst their method of getting attention may disgruntle us, we move into a state of annoyance when we see them getting the recognition we secretly admire, and crave, for ourselves.

It seems that both categories of people have the potential to inspire us. Albeit through very different methods. By seeing them as signposts, showing us what we repress in ourselves, we have the opportunity to bring the disowned parts of ourselves back into the light of our everyday awareness:

> "Everything that's brought into the light eventually becomes the light."

> St Paul (Turkish Christian apostle and Jewish Prophet)

SADNESS

Whenever we lose touch with a part of ourselves, shut it away, or banish it from our awareness, we are bound to feel a sense of sadness. Sadness because we know, or just sense, that part of us is 'missing'.

But what do we mean by sadness? It is a very commonly used, generic word which we use to describe a multitude of our underlying states. Taking time to truly reflect on it, we find that it is also made up of other feelings:

- ❏ regret
- ❏ hurt
- ❏ frustration
- ❏ guilt
- ❏ rejection
- ❏ grief
- ❏ shame

Remember the last time you felt sad. How many of the above feelings were also wrapped up in it?

All of these states represent different nuances and textures of sadness and they all derive from a perception of some degree of psychological pain. From an ego perspective, this pain arises because something, or someone, as we observe it in our environment, has changed. It is no longer in a position that we judge as good or conducive to ours, or another's, state of well-being.

Consider for a moment what it means to be in physical pain. Normally it signifies that something is happening to our tangible bodies that hinders us from doing what we want to do in life. It makes it more difficult to focus our thoughts on more positive things.

Emotional pain has a similar effect. It prevents us from feeling 'good'. It inhibits our natural thought processes by taking our attention from a positive thought or aspiration and requires us to reflect on what has changed to cause us the pain in the first place. Ego doesn't like to acknowledge change. It threatens its comfortable status quo. In any way it can it will avoid fully acknowledging the sadness arising from some shift in external circumstances. It denies the grief.

There is a great societal pressure and expectation for us to remain superficially happy through the avoidance of pain. So the state of sadness generally gets a poor reception. We instinctively feel compelled to belittle, deny or even to fear it.

If sadness is ultimately about change, then the avoidance of it means we are also avoiding an acceptance that something has changed about, or around, us. It is ironic that life is, virtually by its definition, in a constant flow of change. Science has now proven that our Universe is continually expanding. Being an intrinsic part of it, our lives and our consciousness naturally expand and grow too. If we allow them.

*Consider this acronym that reflects the concept of L I F E as being a state of perpetual motion and expansion: **Living In Flowing Existence.***

Take a moment to imagine life, its events and experiences, as a never-ending movement of water. Picture a stream where the water is gently, but constantly, flowing. Notice how mesmerising and engaging this is. Now imagine yourself standing in this stream. Sense the cool and refreshing water lapping around your feet. See the ripples that your physical presence creates as the water passes by on its journey downstream.

Now picture that same water as being still. Not flowing. Stagnant and staid. Feel how lifeless it is. How stuck you may feel as your feet sink down into the mud. It is not easy for any life to exist in this stagnating water at all.

How much better does a life 'flow' feel, when compared with a state of stagnation?

Being able to be with sadness, in a relational sense, suggests being able to be with the constant flow of change. We cannot have growth without change. After all, growth *is* change. Internal growth represents a change in perception of how we see and understand ourselves. By avoiding change, we close ourself off from the possibility of being wholly present to new experiences. We remain trapped in old ones:

> "Be not afraid of growing slowly; be afraid only of standing still."
>
> Chinese Proverb

Sadness becomes suffering when we avoid or deny change. It takes more psychic effort in the long term trying to maintain a self concept of the world which is not in alignment with a new reality. It is this continued fruitless effort, akin to fighting with reality, which causes us to suffer. Because ego is so programmed to avoid pain at any cost, it would have us suffer in the long term, rather than face the shorter term pain of change.

When we resist a reality or a feeling, that state persists. It stagnates rather than flows. Until we face and acknowledge it. Latent, or repressed, sadness pushed into our shadow will continue to have an influence over our potential for happiness. It will be the one cloud which, annoyingly, keeps passing back and forth over our sun.

How do you relate to sadness?

If that feels too difficult to contemplate, ask yourself instead, would you really always want everything to stay exactly the same?

I have so far described our tendency to avoid pain and sadness. Yet, at the same time, there is often a fundamental spiritual pull towards this emotion. It's frequently said that it's helpful to have a good cry. Or to go and watch a 'weepy movie'. Our tears contain stress hormones which are released through our tears. We feel calmer and more peaceful after releasing the energy within this emotion.

There is a strange allure about sadness. It gives us a sense of mutual belonging. If we witness someone else's sadness or pain, something within us is stirred too.

Perhaps there is something about us which enjoys being moved to tears and touched in this way?

Could this be as a result of the mutual stirring of the waters of our connected deeper selves? Of the momentary transcending of our ego's sense of separateness?

If we can be honest enough with ourselves, it is possible to sense a kind of spiritual satisfaction in both our capacity, and ability, to be able to connect profoundly with the world around us. And through a shared pain connection we can more closely sense what someone is going through. We can feel it. Almost directly. Imagining, through this medium of emotional connectivity, how we would feel if it were happening to us.

Without sadness we would lose touch with our ability to commune in this way. This potential for connection allows us to build a profound sense of community. To share our common humanity. In its absence, true joy and happiness would have less meaning. It would be a sterile type of happiness that exists only in isolation. Without an awareness of the human experience beyond ourselves as individuals.

This, in itself, would be a kind of living hell. Imagine no appreciation of the warmth of human connection. Of empathy. Understanding. A comforting embrace. All the gestures we value most and which are, ironically, the most healing when we are feeling sad.

But what of the state of acute sadness, of raw pain? Imagine fearing being totally overwhelmed. Of drowning. As if you are lying on a beach with the waves coming in. Sometimes submerging you. With the constant worry that the next sadness wave may totally overpower you. Ego compels us to want to run out of the water. It dreads drowning in the high tide of emotional intensity.

By momentarily ignoring its 'rational' advice, we may feel secure enough to be able to stay in the water. Trusting that it does not have the capability of actually drowning us. When we surrender, and trust, we allow the water to let us float on its surface.

Without the heavier density of ego we are much more buoyant. We realise that we have the ability, somewhere within, to let the emotional waters support us. Not simply to overwhelm us:

> "When you swim you don't grab hold of the water because, if you do, you will sink and drown. Instead you relax, and float."
>
> Alan Watts (English philosopher and Zen theologist)

In our dreams water, in whatever form, represents how we are expressing our feelings. It can also highlight what emotions we are repressing. If you feel you are drowning within your dreams, this is probably an indication of some sort of sadness that you do not want to face, or are frightened of facing, during your waking life.

Can you recall a dream where you dreamt of water in any form? Was it flowing, leaking, stagnating or dripping? Causing stress or creating beauty?

See if you can remember how you were feeling in the dream. This will give some clue as to how you were relating to the emotional situations in your life at that time.

Water is an essential element to our existence. It gives life and sustains us in it. We are, ourselves, made up of around 60% water. When we accept that it is essential, both physically and metaphysically, our relationship with the sadness of our emotions evolves spiritually.

When we allow, and trust, the water to support us, we float rather than drown. Just like when we are lying back and floating in the sea. We begin to see the world from a whole new perspective. We can look up at the beauty of the stars. And not down towards the ground.

GRIEF

So what of the ultimate sadness. The rawest of pain. The grief of losing someone we love. What does grief actually mean to us?

Our relationship with the reality of constant change is brought into the sharpest focus through grief. For grief is about facing death and loss. The ultimate ending. The ultimate change.

The relationship we have with this given of human existence has a direct bearing on the attitude with which we live our very lives. Death, and ending, is a fact of life. We cannot have life without death. We cannot have death without life.

Through a reconciliation with the reality of grief we accept that everything we know in its present form will, at some point, transition from the one which we are currently experiencing.

Grieving is a personal process. There is no one formula for explaining how it expresses itself through each of us. However, there are various psychological stages. The Swiss psychiatrist, Elisabeth Kubler-Ross, in her book 'On Death and Dying' (1969) identified six common phases of grief:

- ❑ denial
- ❑ anger
- ❑ bargaining
- ❑ depression
- ❑ acceptance
- ❑ hope

We all work through these stages in our own way, at our own pace and sometimes even in our own order. No one really tells us, or should tell us, how to grieve. The process is unique for all of us. But if we can work through the various stages and arrive at 'hope', this is a sign that the experience has brought us into a more conscious relationship with our deeper self. (More on these stages a little later.)

Perhaps that is why, when we lose someone, we are forever changed. Because the way we relate to ourselves has to change too. We no longer have access to the traditional external dialogue with the deceased loved one that we used to have. Instead, the dialogue becomes an internal one. We 'talk' to them inside our own hearts and minds.

Working through grief calls for a redrawing of the road map of life. We have to re-orientate ourselves upon new, unexplored territory, whilst grieving the old, familiar landscape. It can be helpful to remember that the way we are able to view that very landscape is forever changed *because* of the impact left by our loved one. They leave their 'footprints' on our pathway. That is part of the beauty of their, ultimately timeless, legacy.

So following loss we are left with the impressions of someone we love only without their physical presence. Alone, ego has difficulty in conceiving this holistically. It tends to want to attach either to the pain of the physical loss or to the gratitude for the footprint impressions that are left.

The deeper self does not need to fragment. Rather than seeing the separate pieces, it sees only wholeness. Spiritually, gratitude and pain can coexist together when we honour both the person we knew, and the loss we feel, following their physical departure.

From this perspective there is a beauty hidden within the pain that gives birth to gratitude. And a timelessness within the gratitude that began only as pain. As I touched on in 'Sadness', it is our universal experience of pain that acts as a conduit. A channel through which we can connect most profoundly, not only with each other but, with the deepest parts of ourselves too.

If we can embrace the idea that we are capable of feeling loss holistically, we become more able to nurture our own internal relationship. That between the pain of loss and the joy of knowing.

This inner relationship parallels, and epitomises, the outer relationship between life and death. Between opportunity and threat. Between our deeper self and ego. It is here we come to realise that we can both smile and cry at the same time. Be both in pain and yet thankful. And know that that is ok.

Ego, resisting change and seeking permanence, constantly anticipates the pain of loss. The fear of the 'ending'. It taints the joy inherent in each present moment. As ego fears death and loss, it cannot help but project it into the actual living of life.

How often do you try to freeze and totally immerse yourself in a moment of time?

The scene of a family member enjoying the garden. Holding the hand of a loved one. Your pet staring lovingly into your eyes. The setting sun just at the point it disappears on the horizon.

Try to remain mindful of taking mental snapshots of these important moments in life. Commit them to memory. For these *exact same* moments will only ever occur once.

As you mentally and emotionally absorb each moment, it effectively becomes timeless. As you live it and feel it to its absolute fullest, from the deepest part of you. With sufficient practise, when the passage of outer time presents painful loss, we can soothe it with our developing sense of inner timelessness:

"Death is not an event in life: we do not live to experience death. If we take eternity to mean not infinite temporal duration, but timelessness, then eternal life belongs to those who live in the present."

Ludwig Wittgenstein (Austrian philosopher)

It's not until we lose someone that we can begin to understand the full impact that they have had on us. How often is the true value of a life not fully realised, until we are left to contemplate the space that's left?

We use the word 'loss' a lot around grief. It is the opposite of 'gain'. But a gain is what the person has literally brought into our lives. It is the loss of the gain for which ego mourns. Our ego wants the person back.

However, from the wisdom of our deeper self's intelligence, we can start to contemplate a new way of relating to our deceased loved one. One that is freer from the fixed, prescriptive ideas that ego normally insists we follow.

Let's have a closer look at Elisabeth Kubler-Ross's grief cycle to see where, when left unchecked, ego dominates. And at what stages our deeper self's wisdom shines through:

Denial

Given the inherent pain involved in the grieving process, ego tries to soothe us by persuading us to shelter within the initial stages of the grief process. Denial, anger and bargaining. Denial is the first, and most common, stage in which we can remain caught.

Denial is ego's 'anaesthetic'. It initially numbs our senses to pain. We feel like we are safely cocooned against the harsh reality of the outside world. Just as we squint when we walk out of a dark room into the light, we need time to adjust to the new exterior. A healthy initial reaction to protect our vulnerable eyes.

We may need to reach for our metaphoric sunglasses to shade our eyes from the reality of this new light for a while. Sometimes we continue to wear these sunglasses of denial, eventually forgetting that we have them on at all. Then we effectively miss the rich colours of our future emotional landscapes.

A common weapon in the denial armoury is ego's incentive to keep us busy and 'doing'. While we are doing, we have less time to think and just be. Painful feelings of grief have little room left to be felt. The Chinese symbol for 'busy' contains two meanings. The first meaning 'heart' and the second 'death'.

The busier we keep ourselves, the more energy flows into our head and away from our heart. The busier we are, the more distance we maintain from others and from our heartfelt emotions. This tendency to a 'doing' type obsession prevents us from asking the painful, but important, 'why' question: *Why did they have to leave us?*

Yet is it not through the true and honest contemplation of this question that we can start to uncover a greater purpose and meaning to their life?

Is it not by facing, and working through, the pain that we can come to really see and appreciate the 'gain' that the person has left us with?

So often we hear that when someone dies a part of the surviving loved one has 'died' too. Any positive legacy the deceased person may have left is lost to denial. The grieving person is all consumed by the fear and avoidance of their own pain.

At some point, usually due to sheer exhaustion, the busy doingness has to come to an end. The 'being' catches up. This is the process of, what is described as, a delayed emotional reaction to loss.

Anger

Anger, in this case, is ego's reaction to not feeling in control of the situation. Death, in the main, is outside of our control. When confronted with these incompatible realities, ego will often project our raw hurt anger onto people around at the time of a loved one's passing. Doctors, nurses, paramedics, other relatives, police, ourselves or possibly even our loved ones.

In this stage we hear ourselves saying things like: 'How dare you leave me so soon!' 'I told you to stop smoking sooner!' 'How can the world carry on normally when this has happened to me?'

All of these mechanisms are designed to try to regain a sense of control that has been taken away by death. It is a natural and healthy initial reaction. It gives us a sense of power that we convince ourselves will help to defeat the raw pain that we are feeling.

However, holding onto this superficial power for too long can become toxic for our system. Sometimes consuming and defining us for much of the rest of our lives. Particularly if we cannot understand how, or why, ego uses it. Eventually, any positive impact of the deceased person's life is lost, hidden away behind the potency of this blocking emotion.

If you find yourself in this anger stage for what seems like a long time following loss, try to contemplate what the energy behind your anger is trying to achieve.

From the perspective of ego, this energy will frequently seek justice, revenge or to regain some control, as it seeks to resist the reality of physical death.

When you feel ready, notice what happens when you begin to use some of this energy to focus on gratitude and appreciation for your loved one's life.

Having the courage to channel this anger energy in a more constructive way honours the positivity of someone's legacy. We might undertake some sort of charity work, form a support group or raise health awareness which benefits others in the wider community. From this higher perspective we start to be able to process the painful 'why' question. To give greater meaning to someone's life. To be grateful for the 'gain' from their earthly presence.

Bargaining

This is another ego-based coping mechanism which tries to get us to contemplate the 'what if' and 'if only' question around loss:

'What if I had managed to get to the hospital earlier?' 'If only I had encouraged her to see the Doctor sooner!' 'Why didn't I spend more time with him?'

In many respects this bargaining stage represents a form of self-blame. Ego looks toward our *own* actions to try to comprehend the, rationally inexplicable, nature of death. We replay these types of questions over and over in our minds in some vain hope that, if we could just arrive at a different answer, we might be able to create enough power to somehow bring our loved one back again.

It is really only from our deeper perspective that we are able to see the whole picture. To finally forgive ourselves for whatever self-created misdemeanour with which ego tries to hold us to ransom, continually berating ourselves. (See Forgiveness.)

A strong faith and trust in the wisdom and power of our deeper self helps us to navigate through these initial, but necessary, ego dominated stages of grief.

Depression

This stage indicates a processing of the real spiritual sadness initiated by the loss. It is a sign that we are beginning to acknowledge the grief of the loss at a deeper level. Because of this it is important to seek any outside support, if we feel that the effect of the pain becomes too much to bear at any point. (See Depression.)

Summoning the courage to enter this more profound point of the journey through grief allows us to authentically connect with the heartbreak. To admit that our heart is both broken and cracked open. That the raw pain of the loss has crushed us on one level, yet somehow expanded us on another. We slowly become aware of our greater capacity to be able to 'let something in' again.

Once more, by facing and acknowledging the depth of the pain, we eventually see through its veil to the love and gratitude that lies in the spiritual space that is created. Just beyond.

Acceptance And Hope

Within the early whispers of gentle acceptance also comes a sense of peace. As we allow peace in we find that hope follows closely behind it. We contemplate the future once more with a renewed sense of spiritual awareness, and gratitude, for all that our grief work has shown us.

In these latter stages we appreciate more of the joy, happiness and love that our loved one has brought into our lives. We accept that, once this has been given and experienced, it cannot be taken away. Once loved, no one ever actually 'dies':

> "Goodbyes are only for those who love with their eyes. Because for those who love with their heart and soul there is no such thing as separation."
>
> Rumi (Persian poet, Islamic scholar and Sufi mystic)

Taking time to focus on what we want to do with this love, as we move forward, pays the greatest honour and testament to our beloved. We offer up a greater meaning to their life. For we come to realise, accept and celebrate how they have given value, and meaning, to our own.

WHO AM I REALLY?

After we lose someone close, a natural part of grief calls for a re-assessment of ourselves. Of who we are now that they have gone. Logically speaking, once our parental figures have passed on, we can no longer readily define ourselves as someone's son or daughter anymore.

Ideally, during our early formative years, our caregivers will have acted as affirming 'mirrors' for us. They will have supported and nurtured our optimal development by reflecting back to us the positive attributes of our characters. This motivates us to continue to behave in socially constructive ways, maintaining a healthy degree of self-esteem.

In reality, this cannot always be the case. No parenting is, or can be, perfect. All parents and caregivers will have their own complexities and emotional wounds. They can never be clear and complete mirrors for all that we are.

Consequently, there will always be parts of ourselves about which we feel insecure. This is, of course, an innate part of our universal human condition. The parts of us which were not affirmed, or adequately mirrored, leaves us with the healing opportunity to do this personal work as we grow.

Optimal parenting ideally requires the mirroring of the traditional qualities of both the 'yin' (female) and 'yang' (male) archetypes. So, no matter what the specific genders of the parental figures, the child of such a partnership will ideally have degrees of both nurturing (yin) and potency (yang) qualities reflected back to them. This helps to develop an appropriate balance of both self-confidence, through potency, and of self-care, through nurturing.

Once our parental figures have passed on, we no longer have the same physical access to their affirming mirror. A psychologically healthy, and honouring, response to this change is to internalise the qualities that they showed us. Then we can continue to appropriately nurture and motivate ourselves from within.

How much are you like your own parents or caregivers?

What characteristics did you inherit from each of them?

How do you utilise them in a way which works constructively for you?

Perhaps you inherited your father's shyness, yet you have managed to grow in social confidence more than he did. Or you saw how your mother figure always had unrealistic expectations of herself, and seemed constantly stressed, so you learnt that being 'good enough is good enough'. Maybe you combined the influences of an overbearing mother and a more cool, detached father and developed a healthier balance of emotional attachment?

Just as we bear witness to the continual external flow of life, and do our best to internalise as many positive influences from it, our physical bodies too are constantly changing. Every single cell in our body renews itself over a seven year period. Many much more frequently. Our whole physical self is literally changing all of the time.

Given this reality, it is interesting to consider how we instantly respond to the question, 'who am I?' Instinctively we define and identify ourselves primarily through our ever changing physical body. We use our name, gender, age, physical well-being, race, job, place of birth, in order to define our apparent 'permanent' physical existence in the world. Even when that very permanence is in a constant state of flux. Both internally and externally.

We attempt to define ourselves in so many ways. Can any one of them singularly sum up who we really are in any given moment?

Give yourself some time now to sit back and think about who you are, and I mean really think.

Consider how you describe yourself to others when you meet someone for the first time. Now contrast this with how you describe yourself to someone who you know well.

The differences usually centre around a more surface description of who or what you are with new acquaintances, through to a more honest assessment about what you are currently thinking and feeling with people you know better.

The subtle differences in response parallel the developing relationship we have with ourselves as we grow. Where we take time to know ourselves better, we see beyond our physical exterior. We come to understand ourselves as being something 'more'. Through our very ability to reflect and feel, we become a mirror to ourselves too. Mirroring different aspects of ourselves via the very thoughts we choose to focus on.

What parts of yourself do you tend to fixate on?

Physically, is it attributes or perceived inadequacies?

Emotionally, is it strengths or insecurities?

What sorts of things would you be saying if you were to be a kinder mirror to yourself?

How we wish to tangibly appear to others is a product of ego. Much of how others initially see, or perceive, us is a product of theirs. If we move away from this rather one-dimensional, limiting approach, we free ourselves up to contemplate the question, 'who am I?' from a more timeless, spiritual perspective.

From this more aware place the question, 'who am I' evolves to, 'how am I in relationship to myself?' We become able to provide ourselves with this gentler self-enquiry once we have undertaken some of the healing opportunities that our imperfect childhoods offer up to us. When we have bravely faced our inner pain, worked through our grief and reconciled with the trauma in our lives, whilst staying connected to our deeper wisdom. And our spiritual muscle.

If you look inside now, how do you *find* yourself? I intend that to be literal as well as metaphorical. An easy question to pose, yet one which is much more challenging to answer. Particularly when we remove recourse to everyday ego status or the 'physical body' type responses.

Consider how often you stop and actually take the time to have a good look at yourself. Not just at your reflection in a shop window as you're passing, but a real deep look. What do you see? Do you ever take the time to look?

Usually, the only occasion we stop is when fate steps in and forces us too. Sometimes this takes the form of an illness, an accident, the loss of a job, the breakdown of a relationship or some other life crisis that conspires to knock us off our regular pathway.

When these types of life events happen, try to acknowledge the signs and opportunities of what deeper message may be within them. What are they encouraging you to stop and think about?

How well can you nurture yourself when outside support systems change or give way?

Do you have to wait for the next unsettling life event to undertake this sort of internal enquiry?

Sarah's Story

A man had collapsed in the street near Sarah's home. Being a trained first aider, she ran over to try to help him. Sadly he passed away. Sarah had done her best to save him. Despite her efforts and quick thinking, she had difficulty in forgiving herself. For not preventing his death.

Sarah battled in the bargaining stage of the grief cycle, asking herself the typical 'what if' and 'if only' type questions. 'If only I had got to him sooner' to 'what if the ambulance hadn't been so delayed!' She continued to berate herself. The constant internal questioning prevented Sarah from moving on from the unsettling experience.

In our second session together I felt moved to ask Sarah if she had found out the name of the man who had sadly died. She said she had. His name was David. From that point on in our time together, we referred to David by his name.

At first this seemed difficult, and more painful, for Sarah. It made the man's life, and his humanity, seem all the more real to her. But David came to represent a significant figure in Sarah's life. Someone with whom she could poignantly relate. Particularly as she had shared with him the very intimate, final moments of his physical life.

Through the closer contemplation of her grief, Sarah began to recognise a theme running through her life. A role she had, up to now, unconsciously played out in her family. Being the only daughter with three older brothers and divorced parents, she had always taken on the responsibility of sorting out her family when disputes and arguments occurred. As far back as she could remember, she had been the archetypal peacemaker.

I shared my sense of the amount of pressure that Sarah 'willingly' took on. She saw how her family had disregarded her own emotional needs for many years. Particularly since their mother had left. They even appeared to blame her for their own problems. Whilst Sarah struggled to fulfill her default role of peacemaker, her brothers and father conveniently cast her as the family 'scapegoat'.

Since the death of David in the street Sarah battled with her own confused emotions. She became a lot less able to continue to manage those of the men in her family. Her emotional capacity bucket was overflowing. This was compounded by the burden of guilt she carried for not being able to save David's life.

Through the additional pain of this loss, Sarah started to acknowledge her own frustration and sheer exhaustion. Constantly trying to 'save' the men in her own family too wasn't fair. Either on herself or them. It not only hindered her own growth and emotional freedom, but that of her brothers and father too. They would never be able to offer themselves the self nurturing that they were capable of, if Sarah continued to bear the responsibility of both peacemaker and scapegoat.

With her new-found insight, and by refusing to blindly follow her default roles, Sarah noticed her father and brothers begin to change. As she honoured herself more they were less willing, and less able, to readily blame her for their own problems.

Finally, Sarah found the closure that she had been seeking in relation to David's death. Just not in the form that she had originally anticipated. By personalising an unexpected relationship with a dying man, Sarah began to see her own self as a person too. Not merely a selfless dumping ground for other's shadow emotions.

Sudden and dramatic external change, such as Sarah experienced, often forces us to redraw the map of our lives. And of our place within it. The Chinese symbol for crisis can be interpreted as opportunity. That is why these points in life offer up both challenge and opportunity.

Within the 'crisis' there is a chance to question, examine and deepen the relationship we have with ourselves. To start to view it from a renewed perspective. We come to appreciate our inner being as the only force that truly endures and sustains. Despite all outer physical cellular reproduction and change.

Rather than wait for fate to require, or force you to, try this simple exercise for yourself now. Sit comfortably where you won't be disturbed and look at yourself in a mirror. Look deep into your own eyes. Concentrate intently on the pupils within your eyes.

How does it feel? Easy or difficult? Do you see yourself more physically or can you begin to go past that and sense your deeper self? Notice how challenging it can be to stay really focussed on your own reflection. Try and stay looking into your own eyes. What are your pupils trying to 'teach' you?

When you can concentrate for long enough, you may feel flashes of a sense of expansiveness. Of connectedness. When you can get past any feelings of self-consciousness, the inner chat of ego quietens and a more peaceful, calming sensation can often be felt. These are the echoes of your deeper, timeless self.

Few people take the time to do this simple, yet powerful, exercise. Try and do it regularly, or even fleetingly, when you are cleaning your teeth or brushing your hair. Use it as an opportunity to get to know yourself better. If you encounter negative self-talk, be aware that this is simply the voice of ego trying to prevent you from seeing beyond itself.

This exercise can be a great introduction to practise stilling the mind by reducing the constant monkey chatter that frustrates us all. Use it as a focus to step into contemplative meditation too.

Taking a little time to invest in these kinds of mind-stilling moments gives us a chance to get to know ourselves better. We spend so much of our time concentrating on how we are when relating to others, we leave little time to consider the important question of how we are when actually relating to ourselves.

How do you nurture yourself?

What do you do to take care of yourself which involves no one else?

Moments that we spend self-nurturing are frequently few and far between. Activities such as taking a long bath, reading, meditating, exercising, yoga, dance, being in nature, painting, listening to music are important to our mental health. And our spiritual well-being.

When you do spend time alone do you tend to have the television or radio on or do you use social media a lot?

If, and when, you are on your own do you always find it necessary to have some sort of external stimulation in your environment?

Who are you when alone in silence?

What self nurturing activity can you plan to do that just involves you, without any sort of external distraction?

As a natural progression, think about how you tend to motivate yourself. Call to mind an aspiration or life goal. What motivates you to achieve it?

Often we imagine only the feelings of what it would be like once we have reached a personal goal. We become obsessed with *what* we have created or achieved, rather than on drawing satisfaction from the actual creative process towards it. We fixate entirely on the destination. Less so on the journey.

Next time you are completing an everyday activity such as preparing a meal, a household chore or walking to the shops, try and focus less on just finishing and more on each present moment whilst undertaking it.

Experiment with placing the focus of your attention on the knife as it cuts the vegetables, the cloth cleaning the plate or your feet as they make contact with the ground.

Focus with positive attention on the activity in hand. Be aware of the temptation of ego mind to keep jumping ahead to having everything 'done'.

Use this mindfulness technique when eating too. Take time to notice the texture of the food in your mouth. The sensation of the flavours as you chew each mouthful.

The quality of the present moment improves, when we allow ourselves to be totally in contact with it:

> "Nothing ever happened in the past; it happened in the now. Nothing will ever happen in the future; it will happen in the now."

> Eckhart Tolle (German author and spiritual teacher)

Ego fears us having a deeper relationship with ourself. It knows that when we are away from the stimulation and chatter of people and things, we have more opportunity to hear our own inner voice. This inner voice contains truths and insights that threaten the dominance of ego. It will continue to do its level best to keep us occupied in completing the doing of life, in an attempt to drown out the dialogue of our own internal relationship.

This is why we are conditioned to think that being alone is nearly always unhealthy or sad. Ego tends to interpret aloneness as if we are literally 'worth-less'. Just because there is no other immediate person to validate our worth. In times of solitariness we are left to do that for ourselves. If we take the first 'l' from loneliness, we get 'one-liness'. Spending more time with our 'one', literally *by* our own self, we build a better relationship with ourselves. One which is authentic and profound:

> "Loneliness doesn't come from missing someone, it comes from being disconnected with yourself."
>
> Ranae A Sauter (American mind/body/spirit therapist and psychologist)

Our inner dialogue reflects how we treat ourselves. Take time to listen to it and we 'hear' whether we treat ourselves well or harshly. The quality of the company that we keep within ourselves will be mirrored back to us via the quality of the relationships that we have with others.

Frequently, when we spend time both beside, and by, our self, we see more of what it is we want to change. And less of what we can peacefully accept and be still with. By accepting right where we are, right who we are, and right how we feel, we save a lot of energy typically wasted in wishing we were somehow different.

To put this sentiment into practise use this spiritual mantra as and when you might need:

'Even though I currently feel (insert difficult feeling e.g. guilty, angry, jealous, fearful, depressed, resentful etc), I still completely love and accept myself ....'

Until we can make peace with our 'difficult' feelings, and accept our inner foibles and natural idiosyncrasies, we use them as an excuse as to why we cannot thrive. Why we are not lovable. We self-sabotage our plans and lose confidence in our abilities:

'What is it about myself that I am currently using as an excuse not to be all that I can be?'

Ego is the source of our annoying inner voice of self-critique. This may seem difficult to understand. Traditionally, to be egotistical is all about convincing the world of our strengths and importance. Less so about succumbing to self-doubt and perceived weaknesses. It is surprising how punitive and self-deprecating ego can also be.

Yet the overall effect remains the same. Ego inner critique makes us feel small and less spiritually powerful. We focus entirely on how we should be changing through doing instead of accepting where, and who, we are as a being. Ego maintains its power over us through control rooted in a perceived sense of lack. Of not feeling good enough.

We are conditioned to think that constantly berating ourselves in some way is the right thing to do to motivate ourselves. It is responding to the typical messages inherent in our conditioning: 'You have to conform to be accepted.' 'You must please others to be happy.'

When we feel that we are not conforming, or adhering to external norms, the internal ego critique is the first to let us know. We *individually* interpret these messages from our generic external conditioning. Ego then stores them like a set of rules which act as our guide for living a happy and successful life. The book of these rules could be entitled the 'shoulds and oughts' of our life.

'SHOULDS AND OUGHTS'

When did you last hear yourself saying: 'I should be more like that person.' 'I ought to be less sensitive.' 'I hope I impressed that person.'

Whether we are able to admit it or not, we are all subject to these kinds of 'shoulds and oughts' in our lives. They represent our own set of rules for living. The personal sense and assumptions we made of our childhood. The unique conventions we *individually* interpreted from the group programming of our youth.

This explains why siblings can be so unlike each other. Given they were brought up by the same parents, attended the same school, lived in the same town and so on. Because we were all born with unique characters and unique aspirations, we all interpret our environments differently. A singular clay spinning on the same wheel of life yet making an unparalleled pot!

Underlying all of our individual interpretations of early experience is a common striving to be accepted. And to feel good enough to be accepted. This is when we start to write the first lines in our shoulds and oughts rulebook.

As I covered in 'Conditioning', we are all biologically and psychologically designed to want to please our parents or caregivers. A vital mechanism when we are young, since we depend on them for our physical survival. Once ego starts to develop - triggering our sense of feeling separate - from the age of 6 months or so, we come to understand what pleases and what displeases them.

Basic endeavours from impressing them when we begin to struggle to walk, to upsetting them if we scream too loudly.

All give us an early indication of what is good and bad in their eyes. We swallow whole our parental expectations of us. Internalising them without question.

If we do not question something we tend to accept it as a given without consciously understanding, or personally approving, it. The result is that our foundational shoulds and oughts take root. They unconsciously pervade much of our thinking, attitudes and actions as we grow.

However, at this point, I would like to draw some distinction between how ego reacts to these general contexts of conditioning - giving rise to our individual interpretation of personalised shoulds and oughts - as compared to the part our deeper self plays in their formation.

Ego's shoulds and oughts will nearly always be created with some sort of personal pay back or benefit attached to them. We might adopt the same career path as one of our parents or follow a course of study which *they* believe is worthwhile. Here the message of our parents, as filtered through ego might be: 'I should do what my mother and father expect of me.'

But, when a should or ought emanates from our deeper self, it has a different feel. It is not purely driven by an obvious benefit, or observable reassurance, such as parental approval. Instead it feels more like a yearning. A pull or attraction *towards* something that fulfills us. It contains no fear of disapproval if we happen not to surrender to its calling. It is an inner calling for completion. A motivation for personal expansion.

Maybe you had a yearning to become an artist, rather than an accountant like your father was. 'I want to follow my heart', might be the compelling voice of the deeper self. Even though it may, at first, appear to make little economic sense!

Claire's Story

Claire felt disillusioned and bored with her life. She was approaching middle age, did not have a partner or children, and excelled in her career as a management consultant. She referred to herself as being 'married to her job'.

During our time together, Claire often talked about her younger brother Dee. He, by all accounts, led a very different life to hers. He had tried several different jobs and travelled around the world. He was always the rebellious one, according to Claire.

Sadly, Claire and her brother had never really seen eye to eye. She had always been the 'good child'. Doing what was expected of her to keep the family peace and harmony. Dee, on the other hand, was the free spirit. He chased his dreams and followed his passions. Claire didn't think that was reasonable at all. He was 'irresponsible and immature'.

I frequently referred back to Dee during our sessions together. I felt he represented something to Claire that was the key to her feelings of boredom and pointlessness. But Claire was very resistant to talking about him. I sensed, at some deeper level, that she knew she was envious of him, yet couldn't bring herself to admit it. He was living the life that would give hers more fulfillment and meaning.

This was why Claire's ego viewed her brother as a threat. He represented a risk to her established, but now shaky, work-defined sense of importance and status. Her ego despised her brother. Her deeper self was fascinated and admiring of him.

Over time, Claire started to question whether her historic shoulds and oughts were still relevant to the person she now wanted to be. She became aware that she had always sought the approval of her emotionally detached mother. This continued to drive her to prove herself through her working life.

Within the holding, non-judging environment of the counselling relationship, Claire slowly began to esteem herself more. Recognising and celebrating all that she had achieved in her life. Instead of seeking the absent permission of her mother to be able to love herself, she focussed on where that was present. From her father and, indeed, her brother. She came to realise that her repressed envy of Dee had blocked her from feeling his love for her.

Claire worked on 'reparenting' herself. She learnt to hold up her own affirming mirror that her mother could not. She stopped giving her own power of self-validation over to her. Allowing herself to grieve for the love that she so wanted, but which was not available in the way that her ego sought, enabled Claire to be more tender in how she treated herself. To develop greater self-compassion.

As her therapy came to an end, Claire reduced her working hours. She planned trips and joined an amateur dramatics group. She began to internalise the ego-feared 'rebel' archetype her brother had represented to her for much of her life. She used this rebel energy to bend some of the rules of her dictatorial shoulds and oughts rulebook. She reclaimed the person she had always, secretly, wanted to be.

Have you ever wanted to do something that seemed completely out of your 'normal' character?

If you define yourself as shy, do you ever look at a stage and wonder what it might be like to stand upon it, acting in front of an audience?

Or do you ever stare out of your office window and fantasise about getting a job working in nature?

It is strange that what we fear, or shy away from, is also what we secretly fantasise about moving towards the most. This highlights the, often contradictory, nature versus nurture struggle present within all of us. Are we merely a product of our conditioning and perceptions of our experiences? Or are we indeed born with an innate blueprint - an agenda - to move towards a specific potential or flourishing?

As I discussed in 'Our Quest to be our Best', our ego-based shoulds and oughts frequently persuade us into following a specific life path. Yet, if we are prepared to open our sails and trust the guiding winds of our deeper self, we can end up somewhere totally different and unexpected. The round-about explorations of Christopher Columbus again remind us that there is no such thing as being blown off course!

The familiar anecdotes 'man plans and God laughs' and 'life is what happens when you're busy making other plans' really resonate here. An injection of humour into an unchecked egoic agenda helps to gain a more light-hearted, yet spiritually insightful, perspective on our unquestioned shoulds and oughts rulebook:

> "Life is too important to be taken seriously!"
>
> Oscar Wilde (Irish poet and playwright)

What balance do you strike in your life between rigid planning and spontaneous diversion?

When your initial best-laid plans seem to go awry, how much energy do you expend in frustration and anger, rather than philosophically accepting that your deeper self may have other plans for you?

Can you trust to go where fate appears to be directing you?

When can you next risk to take a step into that flow?

Whilst our internal shoulds and oughts form a basic foundation on which to live our lives, unless we are prepared to question them, they can become like a straitjacket. They restrict our ability to grow. As we tend to swallow them whole, we have little sense of their true flavour. This makes it difficult to fully understand how they are covertly running our lives. What we cannot see or understand, we shroud in suspicion and fear.

It is said that fear and desire are close bedfellows. When we follow our innate 'nature' tendency, we feel a movement toward something which we initially fear. Facing our fears means facing ego's conditioned warning system. Reminding us that we may not 'survive' if we ignore its alarm bell. This is what produces the tension between our primal nature versus nurture drives.

These ideas reflect Sigmund Freud's (Austrian neurologist and founder of psychoanalysis) structural model of the psyche. In his 1923 'theory of personality' study, he identified three distinct, but interacting parts: the id, ego and the superego.

Freud's 'id' can be represented by the pure and unbridled deeper self's instinctual drives to follow dreams and desires. His 'superego' more closely identifies with our overall generic conditioning. And his definition of 'ego' is that which grows out of, and attempts to negotiate between, these two other influences.

It is in the very tension between these points that we write the personal shoulds and oughts rules of our life. The word tension in that last sentence is important. It indicates that our life rules are written primarily from a place of fear, rather than one of joy and freedom.

Have a think about how your ego mediates between your superego (societal conditioning), and your true id (deeper self). What every-

day personal shoulds and oughts are you consequently subject to?

Do they permit you to live the life that you really want to be living?

As a useful tool to explore the source of your own shoulds and oughts try the following exercise:

Begin to list your shoulds and oughts under various headings as they are required from the differing roles in your life.

Examples of some of these roles may include partner, son/daughter, father/mother, friend, employee, work colleague, neighbour and so on. Importantly include a heading for 'self'.

Without overthinking it, write down what comes to your mind in terms of personal expectations that you feel are important for you to fulfill under each role heading. For example, you might find that you are expected to be subservient to your parents but always have to take the lead with your partner.

When you have got some ideas down on paper, see how they may differ from one heading to the next. Reflect also on which role traits appear most frequently.

Under the heading of 'self', what does it feel like when you read back what you have written? See if what you expect of yourself is similar to what you assume others, appear to, expect of you?

If you can, have an open conversation with those others. Ask them what it is they expect of you within the role that you find yourself with them. See if it concurs with what you have written about what you expect of yourself. You may be surprised how much higher an expectation you place on yourself, compared with what others *actually* want from you.

You will probably find those role expectations closer to the top of your lists are the unquestioned assumptions making up your shoulds and oughts. 'I should be strong for my partner' or 'I ought to always look after my mother's emotions'. Examples of common attitudes which are formed at an early stage in our lives. This is why they surface quickly and feature higher up on our lists.

Within these higher placed expectations, it is helpful to review them within the natural and balancing context of your deeper self. This adds a greater degree of perspective and mutual inclusivity to your unquestioned shoulds and oughts: 'I can be there for my partner but I don't have to *be* their strength.' 'I want to look after my mother, but I need to balance that with looking after myself too.'

When you reframe your shoulds and oughts in this way, you find that they seem to transform into a sense of mutuality that includes your deeper self's aspirations too. They feel a lot less dictatorial and punitive. They become more encouraging and nurturing.

The listed expectations which occur further down your lists are, most probably, ones which are more inspirational and motivational in their tone. The further down the list they are, the deeper from within your authentic self they come. If none of them seem naturally encouraging, go back again to the mirror exercise for a period. (See Who Am I Really?) Spend some quiet reflective time relating just with yourself for a while. Then come back and try this exercise once more.

See if you can get in touch with the part of you that wants to encourage, rather than chastise. How different does that feel?

In order to be a functioning inclusive member of society, there have to be some shoulds we need to follow and oughts we have to heed. A healthy balance is struck when we interpret the outer ones in such a way that they become more aligned with, and so more closely serve, our inner ones. This allows us to motivate and nurture ourselves. To express our unique potential in a way we choose. One which best reflects who we *really* are:

"What matters is how quickly you do what your soul directs."

Rumi (Persian poet, Islamic scholar and Sufi mystic)

HOW ARE YOU FEELING?

The simple, very commonly asked, question from one person to another. But what happens if we ask ourselves the same question? After the last chapter, you may find that your feelings are different, having questioned your real motivations for meeting the varying role expectations in your life.

Think for a moment, not what you are feeling, but HOW you are feeling what you are feeling?

What relationship do you have with your capacity to feel?

Can you create a better internal space to honour and acknowledge your feelings?

Sometimes it is really difficult to know how we are feeling from our deeper self's perspective because it is blocked by the overpowering judgement of ego. And its innate fears of the very expression of those feelings.

Let's briefly focus on anger again. When we become angry it is usually because we feel, at a deeper level, that we are not being seen, acknowledged or valued. To vocalise this openly and honestly feels threatening to ego. It would mean naming a source of potential personal vulnerability. Of 'weakness'. Where ego senses vulnerability it will attempt to defend us vehemently. Frequently to such a degree that we become aggressive or enraged. (See Vulnerability and Shame.)

What can start out as a deeper sense of not being seen culminates in an explosion of defensive anger. This is merely ego's attempt to regain some control in an environment it fears loss of control. Sadly, much energy is expended, but often to little growthful effect.

When we more *honestly* contemplate the above question, 'how are you feeling' again, we have the opportunity to answer more comprehensively. This is because our feeling states will depend on which 'level' of ourselves we answer from. From what level we allow ourselves to have access to.

So, the next time someone else asks you, 'how are you feeling' think more of the *how* you access your feelings and less of the *what* you are feeling. Contemplating how we access our feelings indicates to what internal depth we go to, to access the what!

Given the example of anger, depending on the level of awareness of how we answer, we might react simply with, 'I feel mad', through to a more authentic response such as, 'I'm feeling scared, vulnerable or out of control'. By taking an extra second before answering this 'how are you' everyday question, it helps us to become more emotionally aware of the deeper messages our emotions may really be trying to convey.

The challenge is to get past our restrictive shoulds and oughts of what we think we *should* feel. And to give ourselves the chance to have a clearer idea of what we *actually* feel, beneath the top layer of emotion.

When you ask someone how they are and they abruptly and defensively reply 'fine!', we instinctively know that this description does not match their true inner state. So we may ask again and get the same, ego-based, defensive answer.

Frustratingly, both sides then become entrenched. They feel stuck. Each knows that there is something not being communicated, but neither feels equipped to know how best to open the door to it.

If the person being asked the question took a moment to think of the *how* am I choosing to access my real feelings, they may give themselves the opportunity to respond differently. Perhaps more authentically. The questioner could also recognise the initial ego-defensive response of 'fine', and just allow the necessary extra processing time. Saying something like: 'Okay, well when you're ready to say more, I'm ready to listen.' This less defensive, more balanced, approach leaves the door open for a greater possibility of genuine contact to be established over time.

There are times when we all find it hard to access our deeper emotional states. This may be because our deeper feelings may not align with how we superficially want to appear to the world. Or simply because we have buried them away for so long.

One useful method to try to get back in touch with them is to consider how other people react in our company. We project outwards into the world the type of internal atmosphere we hold inside. If you harbour an inner struggle, or unreconciled pain, then you may find that you unwittingly create conflict or disharmony in the people around you.

When was the last time you felt angry with yourself, yet only expressed it by being angry at others?

If we do not feel particularly positively towards ourselves then we may, out of our awareness, try to create an environment where other people do not feel good about themselves either. This may be obvious, such as deliberately patronising people or putting them down. Or it may be more subtle, whereby we create socialised traps into which we wish others to fall. Both with a covert intention that these others also feel less good about themselves.

Through this kind of social manipulation we attempt to normalise our own uncomfortable inner state by getting other people to match it. All in a fruitless effort to relieve our own suffering of it.

Do you ever catch yourself patronising, criticising or shaming someone to feel better about yourself?

We often don't do this with any deliberate or conscious intent of malice. Usually we simply cannot help ourselves. Our own internal state of insecurity, self loathing or pain is just seemingly intolerable.

In psychological language this type of social interaction is called projection. A method ego uses to protect us against difficult feelings. Feelings that it is fearful of acknowledging.

We have all been in situations where we have had a strange feeling that somebody is actively looking for us to make a mistake or to show our apparent ignorance. Just so that they may appear smarter than us. The psychological reality is that the other person wishes to transfer their sense of inadequacy onto us. Only in such a way that we feel as if it is actually coming from *within* us. This ego tendency to project is a major reason for much of the strife and confusion within personal relationships.

Ego normally projects out difficult emotional states we hold within our shadow. Anger, low self-esteem, guilt, shame and jealousy are amongst the common ones. It passes, projects onto or attempts to blame others for difficult, unpalatable feelings hidden inside:

> "The most dangerous psychological mistake is the projection of the shadow onto others; this is the root of almost all conflicts."

> Carl Jung (Swiss founder of analytical psychology, psychoanalyst and psychiatrist)

Within counselling therapy the relationship that forms between therapist and client will directly reflect the kinds of relationships that the client creates outside in the world. If a client has a tendency to blame others for everything that's wrong about their life, at some level and at some point, the therapist will also feel the weight of this blame. By maintaining an open and non-judgemental stance, the therapist can share their sense of this projected blame, in a non-shaming way. Bringing it into the light of the client's awareness.

In essence, the therapist can effectively offer themselves as a metaphorical blank screen, giving the client the opportunity to safely project their shadow qualities onto it. Hence, they get an unbiased view of the 'movie' of their complete, whole self. By seeing and making this kind of shadow emotional material conscious, the client becomes more aware of how this may be affecting their personal relationships.

If we have low self-esteem we may project this outwards in one of two ways. The first may be to demean, patronise or psychologically dominate others by putting them down. This has the effect of elevating our own position. Then we can feel relatively more 'powerful'.

Alternatively, our low self-esteem may attempt to heal itself by looking to others to praise or affirm us. We might say how much we admire or love someone, but with a covert agenda of wanting them to say the same back to us.

Through this kind of projection ego attempts to manipulate others into offering back to us the very qualities we feel we are unable to offer ourselves. Its vain hope is that once the other person has done this for us, we may be able to love and accept ourselves more. All without having to do the real work of looking at what it is about ourselves we actually have difficulty in loving.

Both of these manifestations of projection point to a deeper self-desire to want to communicate difficult feelings of inadequacy. Frustratingly, this innocent healing quest frequently gets hijacked by the control and coping mechanisms of ego.

When was the last time you paid someone a compliment, or attempted to make them feel better about themselves, with a vague awareness that you would have liked them to say something similar back to you?

What stops you complimenting and validating yourself?

If our unexpressed painful emotion is more challenging, such as internalised trauma or irrational fear, naturally we do not want others to directly reflect this back to us. After all, we are doing our best to avoid it. The dynamic of projection in this case is often more covert and insidious.

Here the pain or fear contained within us may be so repressed that it tries to show itself by manifesting in other people. When we are in great psychological pain that we just don't know how to deal with, we will attempt to recreate it in another person close to us. Usually a partner or family member.

As this projection is less conscious, the types of behaviours used to achieve this transfer of pain are even more covert. They include subtle mind games and controlling power struggles. They usually start off slowly, building below the surface, so are not easy to recognise. Nevertheless, they are felt at a deeper level within the person being subjected to them. Eventually they start to feel confused and less able to healthily esteem themselves too.

All too frequent self-doubt and inner questioning arise when we find ourselves in these situations: 'I feel so insecure in this relationship, but I just cannot rationally understand why. On the surface everything appears to be okay.'

We cannot understand how we have lost, or have apparently given, our personal power to the person who is projecting their pain onto us. This building level of frustration and confusion leads to a felt sense of internal unease. The egoic aim of a transfer of unreconciled pain from the projector to the other is therefore successfully achieved. (See Power within Relationships.)

Have you ever felt drained of your personal power and self-esteem in a relationship and not really understood why?

Did it give you the opportunity to esteem yourself in a whole new way once the relationship was over?

As I touched on earlier, a less insidious type of projection is when we want others to feel how we would like to feel within ourselves. Perhaps we always go out of our way to make others welcome and comfortable, but with a covert agenda that we want them to offer the same qualities back to us. Here, the deeper healing self-enquiry is: 'Do we feel we genuinely deserve someone to offer us these same qualities?'

If you have a strong urge to constantly help or rescue others from their problems, are you still able to take care of your own?

If you find you can always make time for others, are you also as good at making time for yourself?

We cannot really give to others without also giving to ourselves. Just as we cannot truly love others without first loving ourselves.

When we get embroiled in this kind of psychological entanglement we imprison ourselves and hand the power of our release over to somebody else. We mistakenly come to believe, if we can just get others to behave in a certain way toward us, we will finally be free. Unfortunately, we will always be a victim to this futile endeavour. Surrendering our personal power to others, simply because we no longer know how to access our own:

"The most common way people give up their power is by thinking they don't have any."

Alice Walker (American novelist, poet and activist)

Whether difficult emotional states are projected outwards from ego or from our deeper self, they share a common goal of needing to express inner pain or fear. Whether they are shot like arrows out into the world causing chaos where they land, or are doorways opened from the deeper self wanting to experience the very thing we offer, they represent insecurities which require healing and self-love.

PERSONAL POWER

Strength, energy, capability, dominance. When we traditionally think of the word power these are the first words that generally come to mind. The ability to achieve. To conquer. To be
powerful requires an unquestioning trust. A faith that it will
not let us down. A deep knowing that we 'have what it takes'.

To have a trust in our own power we have to be able to 'objectively' look at ourselves. To know ourselves well enough to
understand what *our* power is and how it works. The ability to
consider the implications of how both our actions (doing) and
our presence (being) has on others in the world.

When we are in touch with our power centres we are most
effective and potent. We appear to achieve more, win more
and generally have more success. Both in terms of what we
do and who we are. Some people describe this as being 'in the
zone'. Everything we say and do appears to be helping us to
shine. To prosper and win. This happens most obviously with
sports people when they appear to be unbeatable. Or speakers
who have the audience in the palm of their hand.

On a more superficial level, what is it that makes us feel more
powerful? Money, status, physical strength, attractiveness,
possessing a particular skill or talent, coming first in a race,
being the best, winning the argument?

Traditionally, and materialistically, the way we acquire, use
and hold onto power helps ego to define who we are. 'I am rich,
I am strong, I am clever, I am beautiful, I am fastest, I am witti-
est.' All ways of proving egoic power in our modern world.

But notice that, in all of these examples, to acquire this type of power - and to therefore *feel* powerful - there is an implicit necessity that others relinquish theirs. And subsequently feel more powerless.

In order to feel rich there must be a relative reference to someone who is poor. In order to feel strong we must feel that we are able to overcome someone who is considered weak. In order to be fastest there must be those that appear slower.

This all holds true for a sense of ego-based power sourced outside of us. It always centres around adulation, money, materialism or public position. This is because it is about a measurement of relative status and the necessity of comparing ourselves with others to assess our own relative position. On this basis, how we perceive someone else as having power, or being powerful, will have a direct affect on how we measure our own.

When we compare ourselves via ego, we will always find someone who appears more powerful than us and always someone who is less so. This perpetuates a growing fear that tells us this external power source is limited. We must compete with one another to get enough. Before it 'runs out'.

This fear leads to much of the manipulation, abuse and control of power that we see manifesting in society today. Particularly within government, industry, even religion. The classic, seemingly eternal, power struggle.

Becoming aware of our inner, or deeper, power feels quite different. I also like to think of it as our silent power. It is not loud or domineering. It has no requirement to feed off, or compare itself with, anybody else. It has nothing to prove. It has no need to manipulate or control.

Personal power coming from within, by its very definition, is self-resourced and therefore self-sustaining. As its strength does not depend on comparison it has no need to compete. It naturally knows when to express itself and for what greater effect. And always with the inclusive aspiration of a blossoming of self and benefit to others.

Have you ever stopped to ponder your own silent power? Do you focus on empowering yourself or on empowering others?

When we act from our authentic, deepest centre we bear witness to the real source of our personal, infinite power. Others may not even perceive it as such. It is not always immediately recognised on an ego level. But they are nevertheless subtly moved, or touched, by a sense of its presence. Of our essence. Of our spirit.

You can recognise when you are around someone who is acting from this inner silent power. You get a sense that they stir something within you. They seem somehow inspiring. Without having to prove, dictate or do anything specific. After being in the presence of someone who connects with their silent power base you come away with a stronger sense of, and connection with, your own.

It feels like a gentle breeze. A refreshing, renewing breeze people sense, often very subtly. One which is welcome, constructive and keeps life moving in a gentle, evolving motion.

Ego-based power can be likened to a biting wind, demanding to be noticed. It has a need. An agenda. People are knocked over, numbed, by its presence. It tends to throw things around causing chaos and confusion. A biting wind frequently runs out of energy in its haste to make an impression. A gentle breeze lasts a lot longer using the same amount of energy. Enduring yet profound.

Who can you call to mind that, in their rush to make an impact, makes you feel diminished or 'squeezed out?'

And who do you know that leaves you with a feeling of being seen and fully acknowledged for who you are?

But how do you go about trying to get a greater sense of, and become more connected with, your own silent power?

A good indication is when you notice you don't have an agenda to want to change anything or anybody around you. Your silent power has a wonderful quality of groundedness. Of peace and calm. Still, even when everything else is in chaos:

> "To interfere with the life of things means to harm both them and oneself - he who imposes himself has the smallest manifest might, he who does not impose himself has the greatest, secret might."

Martin Buber (Austrian Jewish philosopher)

What Buber describes here as 'secret might' is an intelligence which is able to bear witness to life without being compelled to change or fix. To maintain a spiritual presence which shines a powerful clarifying light on the folly of the insecure ego power trying to compete with it.

People operating from ego power are at first confused when coming up against inner silent power. The familiar power struggle game is not played out. There is no need for it. For this psychological game to be played there has to be at least two willing, and competing, ego participants.

When one side decides not to play the resulting confusion can have a lasting effect on the ego-dominated person. Imagine if we were to challenge someone to a genuine game, and they apologise saying they've got more important things to attend to. We're likely to be intrigued as to what could be more important than the game that *we* want to play!

The resulting intrigue leaves a positive legacy. An important questioning of how someone chooses to use their ego-based power in the future. When we come up against someone utilising their deeper self-empowerment the effects are subtle, but far-reaching. Ego is intrigued and moved in ways beyond its normal comprehension.

Any of you who have ever been in any form of counselling therapy will hopefully have experienced the non ego-based power of the therapist. The ultimate goal of therapy is to encourage the client to feel empowered from within. To begin to recognise and trust their own deeper self-power. By offering the 'core conditions' of empathy, unconditional positive regard, genuineness and acceptance, the therapist creates an atmosphere of silent power presence. (The core conditions form the basis of the humanistic psychological approach as founded by Carl Rogers in 1957.)

This therapeutic ability is not obvious, overbearing or always directly vocalised, but subtle and intangible. These core conditions need to be intrinsically *felt* by the client in counselling. It is the feeling, and receiving, of the presence of the therapist's silent power that provides the fertile ground for the client to grow and heal.

When a client begins to feel more spiritually empowered they take more responsibility for how they perceive their life experience. For what they want to do with what life is showing them:

> In a word, each man is questioned by life; and he can only answer to life by answering for his own life; to life he can only respond by being responsible."
>
> Victor E Frankl (Austrian neurologist, psychiatrist and holocaust survivor)

To develop a sense of your own silent power try to spend some time without external distractions. Ideally in silence. Meditate. Still your mind by focussing on a candle flame or listening to your breath.

During early meditative practise, ego-based power sends our thoughts darting off in all directions about what else we should be doing. We normally try to *actively* defeat this 'monkey chatter' through even more internal chatter: 'I really have to concentrate harder!'

The problem lies with the word actively. This is merely an indication that ego power is trying to suppress *itself* through more mental activity. We cannot achieve a greater sense of stillness simply by further doing. When you meditate, and your mind wanders off, which it inevitably will, simply notice this and come back to your breath and stillness. Accept the wandering mind as a part of your meditation practice. Don't chastise it. Or yourself.

Allow your deeper self presence to gently accept and understand this ego-mind endeavour. Imagine it to be a vast flat lake with an ego 'boat' floating upon it. By calming the waters on which the ego boat floats, we can honour and hold it. We do not feel so troubled when it tries to make waves.

If you like, use this imagery to frame your meditation session. Identify with the waters of the lake representing your vast, calm and infinite deeper self. Notice how it supports and allows the ego boat to float only because of its very existence.

Perhaps ego's oars occasionally break the tranquility of the waters, appearing as insignificant ripples, when compared to the vastness of the lake.

Feel how, without the lake, the boat would have no purpose to exist. At the same time, the lake is only aware of its real buoyancy power by supporting the boat which floats upon it:

> "While meditating we are simply seeing what the mind has been doing all along."

Amit Ray (Indian author and spiritual teacher)

At some point, through the practice of mindful awareness, or perhaps a life crisis where we are shaken to the core of our being, the presence of our inner silent power will make itself known to us.

Sometimes it is only through a process of betrayal, of sacrifice and pain, where we feel broken, that we can begin to see who we really are through the cracked mask of ego. Once ego facade is dismantled, we have the opportunity to rebuild again. But this time from a felt, known, limitless power centre.

Our own silent power illuminates us, calms us, grounds us, helps us to trust. Its source reveals the reason we are all here. It acts over and beyond personal advancement of external status or standing. It wants to have a positive impact on others. To help others too in the expression of their own silent power.

How do you tell if you are expressing the power from your deeper self? Ask yourself whether it is facilitating others to do the same....

POWER WITHIN RELATIONSHIPS

Team spirit. Group energy. Marriage 'made in heaven?' The place where we are most immediately aware of our own power, and how we choose to use it, is within our personal relationships. When that relationship is loving and equal, the deeper power each partner possesses complements the other. Working harmoniously together the whole creates something larger than the sum of the two 'parts'.

An obvious symbolic example of this is the birth of a child. Through the combination of the archetypal male and female energy, the biological power sharing, the yin and the yang, something greater is created.

It takes time, effort, patience and, above all, good communication to reach a point in a relationship when both partners use their power appropriately. Where it is both acknowledged and respected by the other.

For a relationship to endure, after the initial 'honeymoon' period is over, respective roles ideally evolve which both honour and encourage each partner's power contribution. This is not always an easy process. Particularly when ego-based 'traditional' roles are fixed or taken for granted. Where one partner goes out to work while the other looks after the children, for example.

How often do you verbally express gratitude to your partner for bringing unique qualities into your relationship?

Do you, at times, take these qualities for granted?

How could you let your partner know that you appreciate what they bring to the relationship?

To experience our wholeness, we need to feel free to experiment with being protector, nurturer, peacemaker, initiator, enthusiast, romantic, and the myriad of other role traits on offer within couplings. Rigidity, and a lack of freedom, inhibit deeper power expression. If we feel entrenched within a default role, our ability to use it creatively is stifled. We can feel frustrated, suffocated, unappreciated.

For example, a father may have deep nurturing qualities, and so choose to spend more time at home looking after the children. While the mother pursues a career which allows her to express her corporate abilities. Or one partner, who normally assumes responsibility for being the 'peacemaker' following a disagreement, offers some space for the other to do so. Will, or can, they take the opportunity to grow into that space?

This complementary sharing of deeper power potential facilitates the best opportunity for spiritual growth in a relationship. Rigid external conditioning, with all its limitations and inherent disempowering qualities, is distilled away to leave a freer, more fluid environment. An environment in which natural power can blossom and contribute to the overall positive expression of a partnership.

Many of us will have been in relationships where there are ego-power struggles leading to conflict and frustrations. A seemingly never ending battle of wills. These can even show up in simple everyday scenarios. Who decides how best to discipline the children. Who gets to choose the new colour for the lounge walls. Who always has to have the last word in the argument.

If we become obsessed with getting our own way, we miss out on the *inclusive* nature of our deeper power. It is this that appreciates there is always another way. If a relationship is to be successful, we must be prepared to try this. To understand the alternative perspective.

How open are you to trying something in a different way or being able to view it from your partner's perspective?

Can you remember a time when you tenaciously attempted to achieve something, thinking that your way was the only way, only to finally realise that your partner's idea worked better?

Did you feel spiritually expanded or contracted as a result of a more power sharing approach?

The fraught journey of reaching a healthy power sharing in relationships is summed up by Bruce Tuckman (1965), in his well known model. Although he applied his four stage model primarily to teams of people working together towards a common goal, it also describes the rocky road of personal relationships too. The four stages are:

- ❏ Forming
- ❏ Storming
- ❏ Norming
- ❏ Performing

See if you can recognise yourself in the following typical relationship journey:

Forming

During the initial forming phase of a new coupling, partners come together sharing their hopes and dreams for their 'perfect' union. Children, travel, pets, projects, property, wealth creation, passions and pastimes are often among the typical aspirations discussed and compared. How much do we have in common? Do we laugh at similar things? Are we on the same trajectory?

Storming

When it transpires that any concerns and aspirations are not totally in harmony, the differences and disagreements will start to come to light during this second storming stage of the relationship journey. Here each partner tests out how strong their ego willpower is. Will I be able to achieve my *individual* aspirations and emotional needs from this burgeoning partnership?

What cements initial romantic ideals into enduring love and respect is how we go about managing these inevitable differences as they arise.

So the storming stage, although tricky, is vital. It allows for repressed emotional needs to be acknowledged. These needs are rooted in our inescapable insecurities arising from the formative relationships we had with our own parents or caregivers.

Within healthy adult partnerships we get to explore all of the different parts of us which may have otherwise been left dormant. Languishing in the shadows of our psyches. This is particularly true of our unmet childhood needs. Being loved is wonderful. It gives us the chance to enter more safely into our vulnerability. Particularly the vulnerability of our wounded 'inner child'. (See Our Life Scripts.)

How often have we heard ourselves, or our partner, shout out in an argument, 'don't be so childish!'

Can you express your early unmet emotional needs in a relationship without 'throwing tantrums' or regressing to a more infantile state?

When you notice your partner acting immaturely, or particularly unreasonably, it is likely that unfulfilled childhood needs are resurfacing. Inevitably, they are trying to meet and heal these needs via the container of the adult relationship.

This is why the storming stage can be particularly difficult to negotiate. The material that arises is historic, fragile and painful. This is not dissimilar to the effects of a literal weather storm. Neither party quite knows how long it is going to last or how many umbrellas they are going to need!

There is both opportunity and threat at this point. Souls become bared and childhood psychological wounds surface. Does my partner love me enough to hold, and heal, my childhood insecurities too? The raw, primal emotion triggered can ultimately cement and strengthen the partnership, *if* the energy behind it is sensitively nurtured and effectively communicated. This calls for both parties to act from their deeper power 'inclusive' centres. And to be willing to seek outside therapeutic support, should the evoked material feel too overwhelming.

If egos are allowed to run riot at this stage then, given the fragility of the emotions exposed, inevitable superficial power struggles and psychological game playing ensue.

Norming

If the relationship survives the storming stage we move into norming. Here each partner has come to accept, and respect, the expression and nurturing of the other's needs. There is joint acknowledgment and clear communication of how each other's deeper power adds to the value of the relationship overall.

A more profound love blossoms. A realisation that every part of the relationship, and of the people within it, is important. Where real love is present normal ego boundaries dissolve. Both partners feel, and act, as one. The combined 'one' seemingly taking on a separate energy identity all of its own.

Buddhist philosophy describes a partnership as having three 'people' within it, for this very reason. The two individuals, plus the third entity which is created as a result of the other two coming together. They say that each of the three need identity, love, understanding, respect and recognition.

Take a moment to think about personal relationships you are currently in or have been in. How much is/was this third entity acknowledged and nurtured?

To try and visualise this part's presence, think about what was created out of your joining of forces. Out of the 'team spirit' that ensued.

Performing

A cause for celebration is the universal force for greater good arising from healthy power sharing, cooperation and joint aspiration of personal unions. The positive *product* of the relationship is what needs to be fought for, honoured and nurtured. This is what the optimal performing stage is all about.

Here the potent third entity created via the team spirit is both maintained and sustained. An inherent relational strength that endures the future trials and tribulations of unavoidable life challenges. Even when external circumstances change, as invariably they will, the partnership is robust enough to go back to the storming stage again. Strong unions perceive this revisiting as an opportunity to assess what further spiritual growth needs to occur.

We are all here to learn about the true potency and creative potential of our deeper silent power. As we do so, we will need to pass through the tricky, but seductive, ego stage of its expression. Relationships - and not just couple relationships - act as both a container and a testing ground. They give us an opportunity to witness the effects of the expression of our personal power, via the feedback and mirroring of those closest to us.

If we can listen to this feedback, we will know whether our power expresses itself solely to feed ego or whether it contributes something to the greater good. Relationships of all sorts are the perfect, and at the same time the most challenging, place to discover, test and explore this. There is no place to hide!

A healthy, appropriate power sharing unit emits positive energetic ripples out into the world. These relationships may not just be personal, but within larger social, work and other contexts too: orchestras, choirs, sports teams, dance groups, unions, theatre companies.

An effective, power complementing entity has the potential to create something bigger than itself. To move and to stir others. Proving that the whole can be infinitely larger than the sum of the individual parts:

> "The day the power of love overrules the love of power, the world will know peace."

> Mahatma Gandhi (Indian activist and leader)

THE POWER IN OUR EMOTIONAL WOUNDS

We all go through pain and suffering in our lives. From the death of a loved one, the break-up of a relationship, the betrayal of a friend, the trauma of an accident to the challenge of an illness. We cannot avoid becoming emotionally wounded by life. Emotional wounds are an intrinsic part of our physical existence. Perhaps, even, a spiritually valuable part.

For an emotional wound to impact us, it may not need to be anything particularly dramatic or traumatic. It could be defined as any event or experience where we have difficulty reconciling, or accepting, what has happened to us. Something as apparently 'insignificant' as the realisation, as children, that adults are not actually as perfect as we had once hoped. That they cannot provide all the security we feel we need. We all had to face the reality of this particular growing pain wound. An acceptance that the world may not be as stable, predictable and controllable as we first hoped that it was.

Wounds become acute when we cannot make sense of our resulting feelings. When they remain confused and fragmented. Wounds come to represent the gap between how we had planned, or expected life to be and feel, versus how it actually turned out and felt.

For this reason our wounds are highly personal to us. Only we know what expectations we have of life. How we interpret the meaning of what happens to us. By their very nature these types of experiences are painful and consequently fear-inducing. We have to accept that things are not going to be as 'perfect' as we might once have hoped.

Ego uses this fear emotion to try to avoid, or deny, post wound reality. It attempts to push away the inherent pain. Our deeper self knows our wounds may actually hold the key to a greater meaning. Helping us to see life, and ourselves, in a particular and unique way. As gifts, but not always wrapped in the nicest of paper.

Lost within these competing agendas, our wounds can be pushed down for years until our deeper self conspires to bring them back to our attention. Often through repetitive life experiences. Again we hear ourselves crying: 'Why does this keep happening to me?' We find ourselves facing all too familiar personal challenges.

Our most common wound experiences are centred around three primal themes. They are a fear of:

- ❑ Failure
- ❑ Rejection
- ❑ Abandonment

I use the word 'primal' here because it is these same foundational fears that we must all face as we grow up in a less than perfect world. And it is the perpetuation of them that leads us to continually feel disempowered. To be frightened of fully being ourselves.

We seek out relationships as adults hoping to be protected from having to face old historic wound fears again. We hope that prospective partners will provide us with the power and security ego tells us we need to feel safe, often placing a great deal of unconscious pressure on our relationships. (See Our Emotional Wounds and Our Relationships.)

When similar life challenges re-occur, it provides us with an opportunity to recognise the theme of our wounds. And to begin to heal them.

If you feel able, recall a time in your life when you remember feeling rejected, abandoned or a failure.

As the memory becomes clearer, did your face the full pain of the feeling at that time? Or did you protect yourself from it?

However you dealt with it, try not to judge yourself harshly. These themes represent some of the biggest threats to the security of the ego.

As an adult, are there people around you now who you could share your emotional wound stories with?

Fear Of Failure:

Michael's Story

Michael came into therapy traumatised. A close friend of his had tragically committed suicide. They had known each other since school days and had grown to be like 'brothers', as Michael described it.

During our sessions together, Michael began to acknowledge difficult feelings beyond his surface shock and grief. Huge regret and guilt that he was not able to prevent his friend from taking his own life.

Yet these feelings still did not seem to adequately describe the extent of Michael's unease. There was also a repressed sense of failure hidden beyond the surface shock. A failure of not being able to help his friend in his time of greatest need. A failure because he should have been able to 'read the signs'.

These words were really difficult for Michael to hear himself saying. Yet they represented the start of a process of untangling historic, painful feelings.

To admit we feel we may have failed at something is difficult for many of us to face. Let alone accept. This was particularly true for Michael. It took a lot of bravery for him to be able to bring some healing light to this shamed part of himself.

To protect him from shame, Michael's ego had kept him numb and in denial. By summoning up the courage to fully face his existential fear of not feeling good enough - the bedrock of failure - Michael recognised that he had carried this for much of his life.

He first remembered feeling this when his beloved grandmother, who had been like a mother to him, had died. Michael was in his early teens. He recalled feeling totally inadequate that he could do nothing to prevent it. A 'failure'. This deep, historic, inadequacy wound had been re-triggered by the tragic loss of his friend.

Once Michael was brave enough to step into the shadowy unknown, just beyond his surface feelings of guilt, he was able to take back the domineering power from his fear of failure. He understood that he would be failing *himself* if he were to continue to deny that he was, in fact, a good enough support to his friend.

By working through the entrenched layers of his sense of inadequacy, Michael was able to navigate through his primal wound. From the raw, yet solid, ground state of his childhood 'failure', he saw just how actually loving and supportive he had been as a friend. And as a grandson. He was, and is, enough.

An emotional wound is painful, just as a physical one can be. A physical wound is more outwardly obvious. Simpler to deal with in a conventional sense. We instinctively know how to tend and bandage it, until it heals and we can return to some sense of normality.

Emotional wounds are quite different. Alongside the pain, we have to contemplate what has happened to us and what that means to us. How we go about trying to treat them is as varied and unique as we are individual.

There is no prescriptive ointment or bandage to apply, protocol to follow or medicine to take. The external world can never completely understand, or appreciate, what has happened to us. There are often no external scars to see. Only internal ones.

There is a powerful parallel we can draw with a physical flesh wound, however. An emotional wound allows us to 'see within'. To glimpse and appreciate what lies below our surface. As a flesh injury heals, the scar tissue transitions through many differing colours before disappearing away. With the right treatment, an emotional wound similarly enables us to see our 'true colours'. Perhaps revealing, spiritually, who we are underneath.

Ego sees emotional wounds as enemies. They represent diversions away from the specific plan it has in place for us. To how our lives 'should' be. The events that lead us to feel wounded are only threats. Inconveniences. Ones which should be quickly defeated and avoided. Now and in the future.

Ego attempts to deal with our wounds in several ways. It may:

- ❏ Resist or deny the pain. Perhaps by building a wall around ourselves to keep it either in or out.
- ❏ Run away from the hurt by keeping us busy or occupied.
- ❏ Fear feeling the pain to such an extent that we create it in others (projection).

❑ Use drink, drugs, food or other addictive habits to try to numb us from its effects. (See Addiction to Things.)

The myriad of ways ego will attempt to counteract the pain are as many and varied as the deeper self will attempt to heal it. Yet, there is one endeavour that unites all egos in their attitudes to our emotional insecurities. To create life strategies and develop personality traits designed to stop us from feeling again the painful emotions arising from the original wound.

Fear Of Rejection

Constantly being told to be more like our 'clever' brother or sister growing up, we would likely feel rejected by our parents for who we were. As a consequence of not feeling like the favourite we might develop a low self-worth. An insecurity in what we felt we were capable of doing.

To try to avoid feeling these sorts of painful emotions again, ego constructs strategies attempting to disprove these childhood messages. Perhaps a stronger compulsion to study hard and get good grades. Becoming the best hockey player in the school. Most probably achieving more than we would have otherwise done, had we not been trying so hard to disprove the indoctrinating message of our youth.

Later, we may find ourselves in careers where everything *appears* successful and satisfactory, but where we still harbour childhood fears of inadequacy. While having some superficial benefits, such as well paid employment, if this rejection wound continually drives us unconsciously, it will manifest in less constructive ways. Perhaps an insecure state of never quite achieving, or being, enough to feel 'acceptable'.

If you think you may carry a fear of rejection wound ask yourself:

Have you ever prematurely rejected a budding partner at the first sign of a problem?

Do you sometimes sabotage otherwise healthy relationships?

Does this enable you to feel more in control by rejecting, before risking being rejected yourself?

When a wound continues to unconsciously act through us, it can control much of our automatics behaviours. And we can feel completely disempowered to know how to change it. In this example, we could be seen as having 'commitment issues'.

The healing of this kind of wound lies in contemplating the parts of ourselves we have difficulty in accepting. To bravely face what we reject within. Rather than trying to heal solely through affirmation from others, to do the work for ourselves:

> "Healing emotional wounds will yield more true happiness than any type of external validation ever will."
>
> Renae A Sauter (American mind/body/spirit therapist and psychologist)

Being bullied as a child can often be the source of a rejection based wound. Feeling ostracized by the crowd. Our response at the time might have been to speak up straight away to seek help. Or perhaps we kept quiet and suffered, maybe for many years, obeying a paternally conditioned belief that we should 'fight our own battles'.

Through the understanding of this type of bullying victim pain, we may have developed a heightened sensitivity, enabling us to empathise with others who are also being treated unjustly. Carrying a childhood sense of not feeling protected, we may later be attracted into careers which involve protecting others: police officer, firefighter, social worker, lawyer. Or we might be drawn to vocations that support those that have been abused. Working with victims of domestic abuse or refugees, for example. We are driven to offer others what we didn't get for ourselves *because* we carry the original pain of not having it.

Imagine emotional wounds to be the engine that powers our 'vehicle of self' to reach its intended destination. With enough self-awareness, we can utilise their power to both propel us forward *and* maintain a sense of our own self-care.

With sufficient insight, the consequential exhaust fumes created from our 'wound engine' cannot choke us. We drive our vehicle with an understanding of the source of the fuel that powers it. We can happily sit in the front seat with a plan of where we are going and a clear sight of where we have come from, via the rear view mirror.

However, with less awareness of the potential gifts in our wounds we effectively leave our vehicles locked in the garage. We cannot get to where we *really* want to go, even though the engine is left constantly running. The trapped exhaust fumes only end up suffocating us....

Take a moment to reflect on the following:

Boiling water hardens an egg but softens a potato.

The contemplation and understanding of what our wounds may be trying to show us provides us with, not just the route to inner acceptance and healing, but also to outer benevolence. It is the benefits we derive from our *interpretation and treatment* of what happens to us that describes our readiness for spiritual evolution.

The confusion within the psychology of wounds for ego is that it cannot simultaneously reconcile the pain with the inherent opportunity. It defines opportunity only as a chance for outer material achievement. Not so much for deeper inner connection and awakening. Given the pain of a wound ego can simply feel overwhelmed.

The subliminal question ego asks us is: 'How can there be any opportunity, or gift, when I am faced with only hardship and threat to my currently known self and my intended plan for living?'

What effect could an enlightened awareness of your wounds have on how ego operates through you?

Part of the challenge in how we heal our wounds is that ego is very effective in keeping them hidden. Just below the surface of our everyday knowing. The question therefore is, how do we even know we have any?

Contemplate those areas of your life where you feel most vulnerable, defended, angry or insecure. I call them our 'red button' triggers. The more vulnerable we feel in the face of particular issues or experiences, the higher ego builds walls around them. Rationally this makes sense. It not only protects us from further harm, it also prevents others from knowing we are fallible. Or just human.

When someone comes along and appears to be pressing our red button, our internal alarm system will go off. We will overreact or attack, often to an extent that's completely out of character. A sure indication that someone, or something, is approaching our ego-defended wound. (See Defences.)

Fear Of Abandonment

That childhood dread of being left alone. Of losing sight of our parents in the supermarket or the park. This core fear is programmed into us by Mother Nature.

Nonetheless, at some point we had to feel 'abandoned' by our parents as we grew up. Our first day saying goodbye at the school gates. Perhaps a night alone in hospital. The appropriate retreat of close parental influence allowed us to be free to mature. To discover the opportunities of being a separate individual. Without the psychological rupture and pain of facing abandonment, we would never really learn to fend for ourselves. Or learn to take responsibility for our own lives.

But if this infantile fear becomes reinforced as we grow up, maybe through the premature death of a father or prolonged absence of a mother, the abandonment theme may develop into a highly sensitive personal wound. A red button trigger.

We may not consciously be aware - or want to be aware - of this heightened degree of sensitivity we carry. Inevitably, though, it will play out within adult relationships. We may remain so fearful of not being abandoned again that we work extremely hard on trying to appear interesting and appealing to our potential friends and partners. We might go out of our way to be constantly helpful, adaptable or attractive. Anything to avoid someone retriggering our red button.

The potential gift in this strategy is a more friendly and socially pleasing disposition. We may actively nurture a potential of helping people to feel safe and secure in our company. Qualities that lend themselves well to many professions working with the general public. Particularly those where it is important to win the confidence and trust of others.

Despite the outer benefits of the power of our wounds, at some point we need to channel that same power into healing and deepening the relationship we have with ourself. With abandonment, this may require spending time alone, in our own company, getting to know and to relate to ourselves without having people around us all the time. By withdrawing ourselves from others through the power of our *own* choosing. Until we fully face ego fears of abandonment, we will never create the opportunity to 'make it' on our own.

If we do not, or feel we cannot, do this inner work, we will continue to project an inauthentic image of ourselves out into the world. One which we hope will be more worthy or attractive than our genuinely frightened, and still wounded, self within. The irony is potential partners and friends, whether consciously or not, will eventually sense the lack of authenticity of our presented 'false' self. Relationships built on inauthenticity are unlikely to endure in the longer term.

Sadly, our original fears around abandonment then become a self-fulfilling prophecy. Despite our best efforts to the contrary, when inauthentic relationships break down our red button is pressed, old fears reignited and our original wound re-triggered. All this without us possibly even being aware that we are still carrying unhealed pain from our past.

How do you feel this common abandonment wound operates through you?

If you have a latent fear of being abandoned by others, offer yourself this deeper self-enquiry:

In what ways do I abandon myself?

If you find yourself in repeating patterns, such as people leaving or letting you down, this is a sign your deeper self wants to draw your attention to an unacknowledged wound. It is opening up an opportunity to heal it.

The Point Of Pain

If we are to fully reconcile with, and heal from, a painful experience, we have to be able to see through the window 'pain' of our wounds. To trust the process enough to grasp the gifts of spiritual muscle waiting for us, just on the other side:

"Where a man's wound is, that is where his genius

will be...."

Robert Bly (American poet, essayist and activist)

How we manage to negotiate a path to this place can be one of the greatest struggles we will ever face. Often necessitating a tricky navigation through a fog of confusion, isolation and fear. It is easy to drown in the pain of our wounds. Become a victim to them. And most of us will be a victim for a time, at least. We feel sorry for ourselves for the suffering we face and seem to have to endure. But we suffer until we don't have to, because suffering finally burns away all that doesn't truly serve us. All that ego thinks that we are.

Once we can complete this journey, turn and face our deep existential pain and transmute it into spiritual gold, we set ourselves free to connect more profoundly with others through theirs. A peaceful acceptance and awareness of where we have suffered helps us to understand, and to alleviate, the suffering of others.

Consider this initially challenging, but ultimately spiritually true, acronym for PAIN:

Perhaps All Is Nurturing.

How many stories do we hear of someone who is touched by cancer being committed to raising funds for the very wound which has blighted their physical life? Or how Princess Diana used her own sense of personal solitude to reach out to patients in the 80's, who were dying in isolation from AIDS?

Remember Simon Weston, the veteran who was facially disfigured through fire in his line of military duty. He used his obvious physical wounds to bring light and compassion to others living with similar disfigurements. He even found the strength and courage to forgive, and befriend, the pilot of the aircraft that dropped the device on his ship which led to his horrific injuries.

With enough spiritual muscle we can begin to see that our wounds don't happen to us, they happen for us. When we summon the courage to turn and surrender to them, we cannot help but liberate their wise, silent power. Power that operates, not from us but, through us:

"What is to give light must endure burning."

Victor E Frankl (Austrian neurologist, psychiatrist and holocaust survivor)

EMOTIONAL WOUNDS AND OUR RELATIONSHIPS

Ever felt that instant connection with someone you meet for the first time? The sense that you've known them for ages? Our wounds can act like magnets, pulling us toward potential partners with similar, or compatible, ones to our own. Each inherently senses in the other an historic pain which needs tending and healing. One that each is unable, or unwilling, to heal for themselves.

What better way for ego to deny our own wounds than by focussing exclusively on healing others? We often circumnavigate our own pain by seeking *only* to take care of the other.

Ego's covert, bargaining voice says: 'I can sense where this person is vulnerable and needs taking care of. If I can care for them in the way that *I* need to, I will be able to feel better about myself. When I feel better about myself I won't have to face my own unreconciled pain.'

If our potential partner has a compatible wound centred around needing to be cared for, we can essentially become hooked into the other. The perfect double bind.

The outcome is a confusing codependency. Each partner becoming dependent on the other, albeit for different reasons. Nevertheless, it is a mutually beneficial arrangement on an ego level. Surface needs are fulfilled.

Have you been in relationships where your more superficial needs were met, but you still felt trapped and unnourished?

Looking back, was there a compatibility of your respective wounds? A similar history of personal challenges?

In psychological language ego states of carer and cared-for are frequently referred to as 'rescuer' and 'victim'. They are two of the most common to play out in social interactions, particularly personal relationships. Ego states can more simply be described as unquestioned states of mind. (See Our Inner Victim and Our Inner Rescuer.)

Different egos can develop different coping mechanisms to suppress the pain of, what is, a similar wound. For example, in this case, it might be joint childhood experiences of emotionally absent parents. However, this doesn't mean that there is no opportunity to heal it. We do not have to remain entrenched in codependency simply because of mutual, unexpressed pain.

If the nature of the codependency can be communicated openly, we have more of a sense of knowing what we're dealing with. We then have a choice as to how to support each other through enlightened healing opportunities, rather than outdated egoic diversions. It takes a good degree of brave soul-bearing and determination though, and possibly the intervention of outside therapeutic support. (See Defences.)

But, if handled appropriately, and brought into the light of awareness, the shared pain of similar historical wounds can ultimately strengthen a relationship. Particularly when each partner supports, rather than competes with, the other. The need for codependency falls away when the fear of vulnerability, lying just behind protective ego-coping, is faced together:

> "Relationships are laboratories of the spirit. They are hospitals of the soul. They are the places where the wounds that we hold can be brought up because that's the only way we can be healed."

> Marianne Williamson (American spiritual teacher)

Where wounds continue to be suppressed a psychological phenomena known as a 'game' gets played out. Games is a term coined by Dr Eric Berne as part of his Transactional Analysis theory first formulated in 1958. His 1964 book entitled 'Games People Play' was the best selling non-fiction book of the 1960's.

When two parties are seduced into playing a game there is always a mutual benefit. As I said, superficial needs are met. These needs generally centre around a sense of getting attention. Of feeling valued and worthy. All the time this benefit is felt, we are more able to feel good about ourselves. When we are lost in a game, or don't realise we are playing one, we never question *why* we need the affirmation of others to feel good.

Such is the seductive power of ego-based games, we unconsciously seek out people prepared to play them with us. As in the carer/cared-for game. We look for our 'match'.

Do you tend to find yourself in either the carer or cared-for role?

When you are in either of these two ego states, what personal benefits do they bring you that you are aware of?

Are you still loveable when you don't play out this game?

Frequently too, we project the wounds we don't want to feel onto our partners. How many times have you heard yourself saying:

'Look what you made me do!' 'You always make me feel bad when you say that.' 'Can't you see that I'm fed up?!'

Here we are simply trying to blame our partners for how we are feeling. We don't want to take responsibility for our own suppressed, difficult inner states. In any 'blame the other' type game our deeper self remains frustrated. Its job is to work with, and to heal, the original wound through ownership. To transform it into something more spiritually valuable.

Similarly, if one partner feels that they don't get enough attention or love, part of their game may be to deliberately provoke the other in some way. Possibly by criticising or nagging them. This at least evokes a reaction, albeit likely a negative one.

A defensive reaction from a partner often feels better than getting none at all. Of feeling ignored. This could be called the 'I will get you to pay me attention at any cost' type game.

What psychological games are you aware of that you play within relationships?

What personal needs are you trying to meet by initiating, or perpetuating, a game?

Sometimes, we find ourselves attracted to somebody who has a similar type of wound *and* a similar type of coping strategy to protect it. Mutual abuse of alcohol or food to provide escapism and comfort, for example. A partner mirroring our own unconstructive habits helps to normalise our own coping behaviours. It reduces the pressure on us to 'wake up'.

Consider another example where both sets of parents were not particularly tactile or emotionally supportive. Instead of showing their love through sharing quality time, they showered their children with gifts and money. The subliminal message passed down being that self-worth is directly related to money and status.

The adults of such childhoods may be drawn together through having similar aspirations of financial success. Of assessing their lovability based solely on relative material value.

Have you ever been involved in a relationship where you felt you have competed with your partner?

Was the object of trying to 'win' the competition to prove your worth to them ....or to yourself?

This kind of relationship dynamic acts as both a hook and challenge for ego. It sees a willing and available competitor to play out its fantastical 'I will prove my power to you' game.

It might be that these types of relationship games endure for many years, outwardly quite happily. In many cases they do. Nonetheless, the likelihood remains that any depth of communication between partners may well stay at a superficially 'safe' level. There will, no doubt, be many no go areas that risk going to the source of respective wounds. Sadly, playing and sustaining the game then becomes the primary raison d'etre of the relationship.

Are there many no go areas within your personal relationships?

Do they source from mutual fears of being vulnerable? (See Vulnerability and Shame.)

Who would you be able to be within the relationship without these no go areas?

Animosity abounds when relationships break down because of unacknowledged tension within wounds. We conveniently hold our ex-partner responsible for not helping us to heal our deep emotional pain.

Ego rightly feels frustrated. It has put a lot of work into maintaining psychological defences, probably over a long period of time. All the while our deeper self remains disappointed that the chance to grow through our mutual wounds has been squandered.

The original wound is likely to become even more sensitive in the period following a break-up. And easily re-evoked. Further emotional pain, triggered by the actual ending of the relationship, is piled on top of it. As this can feel overwhelming, we

readily pass it onto our ex-partners. We hold them solely responsible for its cause:

'All of the reasons we split up were to do with him/her!'

Even in the post-mortem period in the aftermath we can fail
to see any lessons learnt, or self-awareness gained, due to ego
tendency to blame the other. We continue to project all our
unreconciled personal woe at the feet of our ex-partner.

For the deeper self though, no experience is wasted. Everything is an opportunity for greater awareness and growth. Because personal relationships are one of the best conduits to
take us into the deepest recesses of ourselves, tensions with
ego are inevitable.

This may explain why many new couplings break down after
an initial degree of growth. Compatible ego coping mechanisms may have initially attracted partners together, yet neither is quite ready to peer behind them to face the primal pain
underneath. Some progress may have been made, but it is not
possible to go the whole distance. And that is ok.

At this natural end point of a relationship any bitterness
can be soothed *if* partners can share how they have grown,
and what they have learnt, through their relating to one another. Bringing this into awareness avoids the tendency to unwittingly becoming entrenched within similar relationship
dynamics in the future.

It might be that, even in the very painful and most challenging
moments, our deeper self has actually learnt the most. Despite our fragile ego trying to convince us otherwise:

> "Grief after a relationship ends gives you the win-
> dow to heal your wounds and to begin anew."
>
> Louise Hay and David Kessler (American authors)

Do you give yourself time to grieve after the ending of a relationship? Perhaps to reflect on what you have learnt about yourself both from, and through, it?

If the very source of our challenge and pain can be so spiritually rich and revealing, why do we fear our wounds? Why do we attempt to hide them away behind a cloak of shame, guilt and blame?

DEFENCES

Our skin is our physical body's protection against the harsh elements of the environment. A defence against microbes that could harm us. Without it we would die. The same is true of our emotional self. It requires a container, a metaphorical vehicle, to enable it to survive within the unpredictable drama of the human experience.

We rely on our psychological defences when faced with life situations we perceive to be emotionally threatening. By this, I mean any life event which we fear may be painful or difficult. Where there is a risk of us being 'exposed'.

The way we choose to defend ourselves depends on the degree of inner confidence we hold, in relation to the experience we face. In some challenging situations we will feel more comfortable and relaxed. In others less so. If your boss continues to criticize you when you know you have done a good job, how defensive would you be? This would, no doubt, depend on how much you personally believe in your own capabilities. How much you trust yourself to be self-affirming when external validation is lacking or absent.

As this is very much work in progress for the majority of us, we are naturally more inclined to be defensive around those parts of ourselves we are insecure about. Ironically, it is these very parts that we feel compelled to build our highest walls of protection around.

Returning momentarily to the example of a primal wound around abandonment, (see The Power in our Emotional Wounds). When life events occur which ego fears may stir it again, we will likely react with a primal level defence mechanism: panic or anxiety.

Once we have undertaken some inner healing work, our heightened self-awareness allows us to see growth opportunities in potentially triggering experiences. Our defences will then likely be less reactive and more responsive, evolved and constructive.

Here we give ourselves more space to *respond* to wound triggers with less primal panic or anxiety. Perhaps accessing a degree of inner trust that knows that we do not just survive, but spiritually thrive, by risking being less defensive.

Let's look more closely at some of the range of defences we adopt to try to understand when they serve or hinder our journey of self-knowledge. I've divided them into three categories:

❑ Primal
❑ Reactionary
❑ Responsive

Primal

Our primal defences are those which are the most reflexive. They are instinctive and unquestioned. Ego triggers this level of defence when it senses the greatest fear for our psychological safety.

Imagine for a moment that you are being physically threatened or that someone is encroaching on your personal space. Automatically your primitive defences take over. Very quickly, in fact instinctively, you work out how to protect yourself via our universal 'fight or flight' mechanism.

Fight Or Flight

This primordial reaction, managed by the limbic part of our brain, was originally hard wired into our psyches by Mother Nature. It was designed to be our personal survival alarm system. Our limbic system's amygdala gland plays a central role in the processing of our emotions, particularly fear. It acts like our internal 'meerkat'. Standing tall and constantly scanning the horizon to give us as much possible warning about potential approaching dangers. In bygone days, these would have been tangible threats such as wild animals, enemy tribes or thunderstorms, as we roamed the plains hunting for food.

In these moments stress hormones - adrenaline, noradrenaline and cortisol - flood into our bodily systems. They prepare us for either standing up and fighting to defend ourselves or fleeing from danger. These hormones cause our breathing rate to increase and become shallow, our pupils to dilate, our situational awareness to sharpen and our perception of pain to diminish. Our blood supply is re-prioritised from our digestive system out to our muscles and limbs.

Whilst this primitive defence mechanism may have served us well many centuries ago, it is less useful today. Modern day threats do not usually involve such obvious, tangible and time-limited dangers, such as wild animals or enemy spears. Instead, they are composed of more covert, ongoing stresses: rush hour traffic, time deadlines, family difficulties, overcrowded cities, work pressures, less quality face-to-face communication and so on.

These low-level, but nevertheless consistent, stressors continue to fire up our primitive survival mechanism. The result? Our bodies are flooded with stress chemicals over a much longer period of time. However, these background stressors tend not to peak into actual tangible physical threats. This leaves us charged up with action orientated hormones which have nowhere to go and nothing 'constructive' to do.

All this results in us being constantly hypervigilant, potentially aggressive and persistently anxious for no purposeful reason. Our meerkat amygdala is continually prodded by modern life, scanning for dangers it thinks could harm us. Dangers which rarely materialise. (See Anxiety.)

Have you ever felt anxious or nervous and not really known why?

In moments of high hormonal stress, do you tend to send worry-laden thoughts toward things that wouldn't normally concern you?

Next time you feel inexplicably anxious, remember how your meerkat amygdala may unnecessarily be provoking itself, rather than being directly provoked by actual life events.

The stress chemicals which continue to prime us for a bodily response simply get pushed back into our nervous systems, causing havoc with our ability to remain calm and centred.

Physically we may be more prone to things like headaches, high blood pressure, irritable bowel syndrome, depression and generalised anxiety. Our immune systems become compromised too. Our bodies have less energy to repair and maintain themselves. A background feeling of ego-fear perpetuates. All the while our deeper self knows that there is nothing that can *really* hurt us.

This same primal defence is triggered when ego senses an emotional wound's pain is threatened . Part of ego's job is to ensure firstly our physical, and secondly our psychological, survival. But from its one-dimensional viewpoint it perceives these as one and the same.

Consequently, when one or the other is threatened the reflexive fight or flight mechanism is activated. That is why solely relying on our primal level defences is so unhelpful for us spiritually. We simply don't give the chance for our more evolved prefrontal cortex brain to have an 'opinion' on what may be happening.

Some of the other defences at this primal level I have already discussed. These include the capacity for denial (see Grief), and also the projection of our difficult or painful feelings onto others (see How Are You Feeling?).

Regression

Here, when we feel emotionally threatened, we revert back to more childlike behaviours in an effort to source more attention from others. Psychological game playing would be an example of this. (See Our Emotional Wounds and our Relationships.)

With a regressive defence we naturally move into a more helpless or incapable ego state. Our agenda will be to try to subtly manipulate others, often using emotional blackmail.

At some point we have all employed this infantile type defence. Do you recall ever refusing to talk to someone, throwing something across the room in a tantrum or grossly exaggerating how bad something is? All with a covert desire of creating a drama in order to get noticed?

This superficial attention acts as a poor substitute for the real self-care that our hidden vulnerability is crying out for. We employ this defence when we have difficulty putting into words what it is we *really* want or need. Just as when adequate verbal dexterity eluded us as children.

When was the last time you remember shouting 'it's not fair', stamping your feet or slamming a door? Likely you were reverting to your child ego state, wanting to be understood, but unsure as to how to clearly ask for it.

Perhaps you feared that you were not actually understandable any-way because, in that moment, you could not fully understand your own feelings?

Next time you use this defensive style, try offering yourself the soothing that you would ordinarily seek from others.

'Acting Out'

This represents an attempt to externalise the bottled up emotional energy around a wound by channelling it in a purely physical or behavioural way. Here our behaviours are generally destructive either to ourselves or others. It differs from infantile regression in that we use 'adult' mechanisms such as alcohol, drugs, food, gambling, promiscuity, self harming or criminality in an attempt to act out difficult feelings.

Often we fear that to express our feelings verbally would render us vulnerable and open to abuse or ridicule. Sometimes our original wound is so repressed in our shadow selves we are unsure as to the true source of our angst. (See Vulnerability and Shame.)

What we can sense however is that these feelings are intense, frightening and potentially overwhelming. We simply lack the emotional dexterity to go within in order to begin to untangle them. This is particularly the case with a wound caused by prolonged psychological or sexual abuse. Where we have been disempowered by someone who has abused their position over us in some way.

When we feel unable to express our raw emotional energy, sometimes it becomes so pushed down that we can resort to self harm as a form of release. Smoking or drinking too much is a subtle attempt at this. Sadly, this self harm may increase in severity to causing ourselves actual physical pain or developing suicidal tendencies.

Paula's Story

Paula came for counselling because of her destructive pattern of acting out. She had become so obsessed with her beauty and makeup routine, it was taking several hours a day to prepare herself to 'face' the world. A vital part of this ritual was the incessant plucking of her eyebrows and any tiny traces of facial hair.

After several sessions together, Paula felt safe enough to explore her compulsions more deeply. She began to understand that her ego was actually trying to protect her. She had been sexually abused by an uncle when she was young. The momentary physical pain caused by her incessant hair plucking provided a temporary diversion away from having to face the emotional angst of her past.

Once Paula saw through her protective ego's acting out, she discovered that the physical pain she inflicted on herself did not block the emotional underneath. It compounded it.

By forging a greater level of compassion for herself, Paula recognised that she was carrying the pain of her abuser too. The self-blame that she had created provided a convenient hook on which to hang this additional pain which did not belong to her. She no longer wanted to carry it. She wasn't responsible for it. Her layers of makeup had acted as a security defence against anyone seeing her true self underneath. A self that she had assumed was guilty, ugly and unworthy.

Paula accepted that her deeper healing would require a rewriting of the negative messages that she had carried for so long. By continuing to hold onto these, she made herself less emotionally available for potential partners. This had the 'benefit' of keeping her psychologically safe but, at the same time, prevented her from finding love.

When Paula was able to esteem herself for the powerful 'survivor' she was, she saw through the superficial benefit of her ego's attempt to keep her safe. She expressed gratitude to it for doing its best to take care of her. Now she was ready to do this on her 'own'.

Dissociation

We use this mental technique when ego doesn't want to admit to what part we have played in something. The only way it can deal with the shame of some assumed misdemeanour is to temporarily disassociate us from its reality.

A simple example might be where we may outwardly describe ourselves as completely honest, but don't own up to being undercharged in a restaurant. Or we brag that we are completely law-abiding when we frequently break the speed limit!

An uneasy truce is struck by ego as it attempts to unify seemingly conflicted aspects of who we are, by forming them into one incongruent 'false' self. But, if this false defensive self is relied on for too long, we can lose touch with the reality of who we really are underneath:

> "Every one of us is shadowed by an illusory person: a false self. We are not very good at recognising illusions, least of all the ones we cherish about ourselves."
>
> Thomas Merton (French monk, theologian, mystic, poet and activist)

How close is your authentic self with your public 'false' self?

Do they get along well?!

Sometimes our wound can be so disorientating we create a

completely different 'alter ego' state. This effectively allows us to believe that an experience happened to somebody else, rather than to us, or that something we did was carried out by somebody else.

When the originating event is particularly traumatic, people often report a sensation of having an out-of-body experience. A sense that they were not actually fully present when an unsettling event happened. This coping mechanism is particularly common when there has been a misuse of ego power from others: bullying, physical intimidation or sexual abuse.

Pretence

This is where we respond in a totally opposite manner to how we are really feeling inside. For example, you may feel very upset about how someone has treated you but never let them know that they have done something to hurt you. We paint a false picture of ourselves.

Here, ego fears that we will lose power if somebody sees our vulnerability. By relying on this defence for too long, we sometimes lose touch with how we authentically feel inside. When we don't allow ourselves to occasionally check in with our feelings, it makes it much harder to act in constructive, self caring ways. (See How Are You Feeling?).

How much do you value and honour how you really feel?

When you express your real feelings, do you also feel vulnerable?

Reactionary

This second category of defences represent a mix of both ego reaction and deeper self wisdom. Consequently these defences are more inward focussed. They tend to be concerned with the inner impression we want to maintain of *ourselves* for *ourselves*. They are therefore more contemplative and have greater potential for our spiritual growth.

Displacement

This is when we acknowledge that we harbour difficult feelings but sadly only discharge them onto others.

We might be frustrated with ourselves for not hitting a target at work and then vent our frustrations on our partner later. Or we may be angry at ourselves for leaving the house too late, but only blame the heavy traffic en route.

Where we over rely on this defence it may indicate that we didn't feel safe expressing our in-the-moment feelings as children. Maybe we were ridiculed or belittled when we did so. This wound is particularly common because, in order to appropriately discipline us, our caregivers had to let us know whether our behaviour - driven by our internal feelings - was socially acceptable.

Seen through the eyes of a child this necessary parental discipline often feels like a judgement of who we are as people, rather than simply based on our actions. We will therefore likely develop a defence mechanism based on the belief that it is not safe to express genuine emotional reactions to people we perceive as having power over us. Parents, teachers, bosses, bullies, abusers etc. We may become 'passive-aggressive' later in life. Storing up frustrations and resentments only to vent them later onto others we have 'secure' relationships with. With those we so often take for granted: partners, employees, siblings, children.

How easy do you find it to give honest feedback, or to express how you feel, to someone who is in a position of authority over you?

Perhaps it is a parental figure, a boss, or anyone else who seems to yield superficial power?

If you were to practice doing this, try to maintain a connection with your adult ego state, rather than your powerless childlike one.

The reason I place this displacement defense above the re-flexive primal level is because difficult feelings are at least given an outlet. The growth opportunity lies in working them through by, and for, ourselves.

Repression

Here we try to repress difficult memories around a painful wound whilst having a vague awareness that it is taking a good deal of mental effort to do so. It is this vague awareness that distinguishes it from primal denial.

By mental effort I mean the busy mind syndrome that fills our heads with superfluous activities, or thoughts, leaving lit-tle room for deeper contemplation. Adopting this type of de-fence over long periods can result in exhaustion and anxiety. We perpetually run from our historic demons.

The deeper self will attempt to bring these 'demons' back into the light of our consciousness, so that they have the chance to be healed. It will draw us into situations which act as associa-tive triggers to repressed feelings.

An example might be if one of our parents abused alcohol and we find that we keep attracting partners with similar addic-tions. Breaking this relationship pattern calls for an exercis-ing of our spiritual muscle. To forgive, and therefore release, caregivers who may have let us down in the past. Whilst, at the same time, understanding that it was not up to us to 'save' our parents, or partners, from their self destructive behaviour in the first place. So the forgiveness needs to focus on ourselves, to release ourselves, as well as on any parental figures who could not be the caregivers we so dearly wanted them to be. (See Forgiveness.)

How many times have you found yourself in unhealthy relationships with people who have very similar character traits?

On reflection, do they bear any similar traits to those of your original caregivers?

Rationalisation

At the reactionary level we may also use forms of rationalisation and intellectualisation to avoid the feeling part of a wound. Here we effectively compartmentalise experiences in our head.

The left side of our brain is where we employ our rational thought processes: reasoning, logic, language and analytical thinking. The right side of the brain is where our imagination, intuition, creativity, 3D recognition and holistic thinking take place. It is from this right hemisphere that we source our emotional literacy, connectivity and empathic qualities. Where we are able to tune into what others may be feeling.

Wherever we are entirely rational, or traditionally intellectual, we tend to operate more like a robotic computer. Experiential information goes in one end and we print out a fixed, predetermined clinical conclusion at the other. Hence there is normally only one possible outcome because of our prescriptive interpretation rooted in our historic conditioning.

An example might be when someone we initially trusted appears to later let us down and we immediately say: 'I knew all along they were not a nice person!' Or, 'that's what you get when you mix business and pleasure!' We subsequently miss using our right brained emotional literacy. Ego likes to defend us against the 'shame' of admitting that we are in some sort of pain because of someone else's actions.

The sad consequence of this purely intellectualising approach is that our minds remain closed to new ways of thinking. A closed mind has little capacity for play or creativity. We can become increasingly cynical and dogmatic.

By becoming aware of situations where you are normally particularly inflexible, try to contemplate how you are feeling as opposed to merely thinking.

Notice whether you tend to say 'I think' when referring to an emotional experience, as compared to 'I feel'.

Try using 'I feel' more as a response and see if different words come out!

Rebalancing

This is where we may do, or say, something that we realise is hurtful and then try to make amends later in an indirect way.

Where we know that we've been unreasonable, ego doesn't quite allow us to outwardly apologise. Instead we attempt to recompense by being overly nice.

An example might be buying a present, or doing a favour for someone, who we know we have hurt, but without ever verbally expressing the reason why we're doing it.

Responsive

Our responsive propensities allow some time to reflect before we respond. Here, we rise above our stressed reactive amygdala, allowing access to the contemplative wisdom of the prefrontal cortex part of our brain.

Sublimation

An example of this might be where we previously would have automatically reached for a cigarette, or a drink, to numb a level of stress we are facing and instead choose to talk it out. Or perhaps we choose to channel our pain energy into a constructive activity, such as exercise, artistic pursuits or helping others. Here, we effectively transmute a denser emotional energy and refine it into something less destructive. We feel it *enough* to make it into something more healing.

There is, however, a secondary type of sublimation which can be less constructive. We might use humour to dumb, or numb, our pain, feeling compelled to make light of it through joking or self ridicule.

Similarly, when we hear ourselves saying: 'There is always someone else worse off than me', or 'I've got nothing to complain about when you think of what happened to our neighbour'. This again represents a diversion away from working through the deeper messages of our own internal anguish.

These types of sublimations may appear helpful but, if over relied on, convince us that we don't deserve to show ourselves any compassion. Compassion for self is a vital component on any healing pathway.

Compensation

This is the most sophisticated and self-aware responsive level of defence. Here we are aware of, and fully reconciled with, a perceived weakness or vulnerability, and then turn it to our advantage.

For example, if we were born with dyslexia - word blindness - we might nurture an ability to play an instrument 'by ear', as we cannot easily read sheet music.

Or perhaps we suffered with a stammer when speaking, but found that when we sang the condition magically disappeared. We compensated by developing our singing voice in a choir.

At this level we accept that, in order to truly know our strengths, we must have made peace with our apparent weaknesses. When we are at peace with our own fallibility, we can accept that everyone excels at different things. That is reality and that is okay.

Where we can see that, outwardly, life doesn't always appear to be fair and yet this is part of what it means to be alive, we naturally become calmer and less defensive. From this reconciled place we offer more of ourselves because less of that very self is locked away behind a defensive wall.

Being less defended we are also less fearful. The lowering of our defences naturally reflects a greater self-acceptance of who we really are and of the spiritual wisdom that we have tapped within our wounds. Here we free ourselves to see that our 'weaknesses' do not have to be a source of fear. Only of spontaneity and creativity:

> "The walls we build around us to keep sadness out also keep out the joy."
>
> Jim Rohn (American author and motivational speaker)

We all need to employ a certain degree of defence to survive in this unpredictable world. The path moving from primal through reactionary to responsive defences reflects the healing journey of increasing awareness and self-trust.

However, the first steps along this path do not require that we immediately change our defensive positions. Just to simply become aware of how we currently react to various emotional threats.

Take a moment now to consider what your emotive triggers are. In what sorts of situations do you react rather than respond? When do you feel threatened rather than grounded?

What can you offer to yourself that would support you in these kinds of situations?

As a guide as to how you can better nurture yourself, what do you feel a good friend would be saying to you to show you support in such circumstances?

The very silent power we realise through our ability to *observe* our default defence mechanisms helps us to evolve them. To inspire us to move towards the more emotionally literate, responsive level.

Ego falsely believes that if we keep our inner wounds defended and hidden away long enough they will somehow magically heal or, at the very least, remain dormant. Our deeper self knows that the wound energy needs to be released and channelled creatively. Just as with a physical wound, it needs to be able to breathe through the defensive dressing which we use to protect it, in order to work for the greater good.

FORGIVENESS

We all experience hurt. Sometimes others betray, manipulate, take advantage and overwhelm us. Where we have been brave enough to lower our protective walls to let someone close and they hurt us, how can we ever hope to forgive them? Or ourselves?

In the height of the pain our ego defence clicks back in and shouts: 'You see, that's what happens when you open yourself up and make yourself vulnerable to someone. They hurt you and let you down. From now on you need to protect your own heart and defend yourself from further hurt.'

How many times have you told yourself this after your heart has been broken?

For ego, any recourse to any concept of forgiveness feels like defeat, a weakness. We lose control. Left to its own devices it will want to win back some sense of control by planning revenge. Replaying anger or passing the hurt we hold straight back to the perpetrator who betrayed us.

Where we appear to have lost control is where ego perceives it has also lost its only source of power. It convinces us that we cannot have power where we do not have control. To entertain forgiving someone in these circumstances is completely counter-intuitive. A form of surrender, a weakness of character, which can only lead to further potential hurt. From ego's perspective, the only give in 'for-give' feels like a giving up or a giving in.

Through the eyes of our deeper self, this same give evolves into a 'giving forth'. That is, a kind of giving through reaching out to the world, even though we're hurting, in order to give back to ourselves again.

This manifests a different kind of power. It nurtures a willingness to realise what potent energy we have inside of ourself. Energy that can only be unlocked *through* the pain of another's betrayal.

Here we can begin to understand that this gentle, inclusive spiritual power does not actually want to cause further hurt to others. Instead, the embracing of its energy lifts us. Freeing us from being pulled back into a repetitive karmic cycle of anger, revenge, pain and more suffering.

The deeper self sees through the surface anger and grief of being betrayed and is prepared to feel the resulting pain and sadness that reside underneath. In this place, we gift ourselves a fertile space to contemplate the resultant self enquiries: 'Why has this happened to me?' 'What is wrong with me that someone could treat me in such a way?'

These are truly soul-searching questions. They are likely rooted in our primal wounds and serve to evoke hidden negative self beliefs we have stored away. When we view this same questions through a more spiritual lens they evolve to:

- ❑ How do I really feel about myself?
- ❑ Do I blame some part of myself for being let down?
- ❑ Do I deserve love?

While they may be initially painful to contemplate, these questions trigger a form of genuine self-enquiry. How do you *really* see yourself?

From this deeper self perspective a different light can be cast on the often quoted spiritual philosophy that 'our enemies are our greatest teachers'. Naturally, if someone we trusted and loved then only causes us pain, we may readily redefine them as an 'enemy'.

But, when we take the time to step back and consider the deep, enlightening questions that their actions have triggered, their position as enemy shifts. Particularly when we see their role in helping us along our journey of self-love. If we allow ego to take over, we will merely feel compelled to rebuild our lost reserves of power solely to reap revenge. This energy requires a constant, toxic supply of anger, hate and jealousy.

These states may feel superficially satisfying in the short term. If we act upon them we appear to momentarily regain some control. But the stress hormones they produce have a negative effect on our psychological well-being over time. They prime us for bodily action or movement so we will tend to focus our efforts on seeking out, yet more, enemies. Perhaps to the point of even creating them where none actually exist.

Can you recall an occasion when you wanted to get revenge?

If you bring that thought or scene back to mind, are you aware of any stress energy rising up through your body?

Does this energy feel conducive to your well-being?

Where we appear to have gained a degree of control and power back by acting out a form of revenge, this will only serve to perpetuate an insecure relationship with that very power. Any energy that is expressed negatively, or destructively, is spiritually impotent. It does not represent who we truly are.

The natural power we can develop via the journey of inner questioning, self-honesty and increasing integrity, necessitates that we release the external cause of this enquiry. That is the person, or people, who betrayed us.

This releasing can only be achieved through a process of forgiveness. Without this outer release we will continue to focus the energy of our enquiry on the external trigger. We look for answers there, rather than within:

> "Forgiveness is the fragrance the violet gives under the foot that has crushed it."
>
> Mark Twain (American author, humourist, publisher and lecturer)

Forgiveness is not a one-off decision. It is best represented as a flow. A continual way of being. We may find that, until we have journeyed a good way along its path, our deeper self will pull us into further situations with similar challenging circumstances. These will serve to invite us to look at what forgiveness really means again. Perhaps, on each occasion, from a subtly different perspective. As if to repeatedly test our commitment to this highly evolved spiritual practice.

As we become masters of this flow, we will find that we save ourselves from our own tripwires. The traps which anchor us in our past. Indeed, it is often said that true forgiveness requires the giving up of all hope of a better past.

Take a few moments to really think again about this last, seemingly paradoxical, sentence: 'Forgiveness is the giving up of all hope of a better past.'

It may be simple to say, yet a lot more challenging to face and accept. We spend so much of our time wishing things had worked out differently. Feeling regretful that we perhaps didn't take another pathway. We beat ourselves up again and again for apparently making 'bad' choices.

When we cannot give the past up then, by definition, we attach ourselves to it. We hook ourselves into it, replaying and reviewing it. As if the more we do it, the more we will somehow magically be able to change it.

Have you detached from the pain causers of your past?

If not, what benefit do you gain from continuing to relive the pain? Possibly a sense of egoic anger-powered revenge? Or victim ego state attention?

As I discussed in 'Surrender', there is a great silent spiritual power in accepting what is. Once we can successfully begin to accept, and to live by, this concept we break ego's obsession which seeks to identify us solely by what has happened to us. And less by what we can *do* with what happens to us.

A forgiveness practice liberates us to live more fully in the present moment. That is where our deeper self knows that our true power can be most effectively and constructively invested. If we can conceive forgiveness as not just a static attitude, and more like an emotional state, it takes on the felt sense of an energetic forward motion. One which has the capacity to take us into new realms and higher perspectives.

From this higher perspective, the vantage point which sees meaning and purpose over everyday ego suffering, we start to see why others may have acted as they did. Our greater capacity for empathy allows us to understand how those that have hurt us see their world through a more egocentric, less conscious, lens.

Greater understanding helps to fuel the light of forgiveness. That is not to say that we have to condone someone for being, or acting in, a certain way. But at the very least, we begin to realise what fears, and insecurities, drove them to behave as they did.

Ego will not rest until it has *all* the answers as to why someone has let us down. It searches for the answers to pain outside of itself. The deeper self knows that we have the power to define every experience, and ultimately ourselves, in how we choose to respond to the resulting hurt.

Through this process we become less judgmental as to whether something is good or bad. The deeper self knows that it is only an experience which has the potential to lead us to a place of greater self-knowledge and enriching compassion. It knows the answers lie within.

Residual anger and resentment fragment us. They leave parts of us isolated, stuck in the past. Forgiveness unites us in the present. In wholeness and completion. It is the greatest unselfish 'selfish' act that we can ever hope to offer ourselves:

> "To forgive is to set a prisoner free and discover that the prisoner was you."
>
> Lewis B. Smedes (Dutch Christian author, ethicist and theologian)

OUR INNER VICTIM

What happens when we just can't forgive? What happens when we adopt the attitude that bad things always seem to come our way? How many times have we looked to the heavens and heard ourselves crying: 'Why is this happening to *me* again?'

We all occasionally dance with this tendency to act from the victim part of ourselves. After all, it feels good to feel sorry for ourselves occasionally. Doesn't it?

It's not all about self pity though. Our inner victim self also holds the key that can open the doorway into self-compassion and self-love.

Our victimhood is part of being human. A natural option from the repertoire of human responses as we face life's challenges. Apart from the opportunity for acknowledging to ourselves where it hurts, this ego state also sends out a signal to the world: 'I'm in pain, and I need you to help me because I just don't know where to start!'

As babies and small children, being perceived by adults as helpless is a necessary part of our survival. At this tender age we are physically unable to look after ourselves. So, in many respects, we need to be seen as vulnerable, susceptible 'victims' in our caregiver's eyes.

The instinctual response that Mother Nature has hard wired into our guardians is to respond to this neediness in a way that motivates them to nurture their offspring. To be responsible for them. A vital role for the healthy continuation of our species.

In this early primal energy exchange we learn that, as children, where we are perceived to be weak, powerless or incapable, is typically when we receive the most help and attention from others. How could we then not naturally conclude that, by behaving in this way, we evoke reactions from others that help us feel loved?

To compound this sense of dependency, as parents, we are conditioned to also feel responsible for the emotional states of our children. We learn that a 'good' parent should be seen to pacify their child if they feel upset, in an attempt to lift their mood. We instruct them to be grateful when they are given something and implore them to be brave if they are scared.

But the pressure to be a good parent has been stretched to a point where we can now feel overly responsible for the ongoing emotional states of our children. Take this to the 'perfect parent' extreme and we dictate to them what *we* want them to feel.

This aspirational child/parent relationship can restrict our offspring from freely feeling more challenging emotions such as greed, anger or jealousy. Nevertheless, these represent an important part of their natural growing expression. Ultimately, we can restrict a child's unfettered access to their full emotional repertoire. (See Our Shadow Self and the Roles We Play.)

Consequently, when we encounter difficulties as adults, we readily revert back to a more childlike victim ego state. And why shouldn't we? We have become accustomed to others taking responsibility for how we are *supposed* to be feeling at any given moment.

The lazy ego is happy to sit back and allow someone else to carry the burden of our emotional predicaments. This state also makes it much easier to blame others when things go wrong. Because of the emotional limitation we carry, we frequently convince ourselves that we are unable to respond in more self empowering ways. 'It's not my fault I'm in this place and feel this way', becomes the helpless, impotent voice of our victim ego state.

Where we give ourselves constant recourse to blame others, it disempowers us to the point that we bear little responsibility for our helplessness. Hence the decreasing circle into victimhood becomes ever more narrow and alluring. We inwardly remain content to continue to give our power away to others. All in a vain attempt to feel powerful enough to change how we feel. A sure road to nowhere! (See Blame.)

My use of the word 'content' in the last paragraph is not an incidental one. In our victim state, the benefits of the extra attention perceived and received does indeed bring superficial ego contentment. Despite the fact that it was garnered through a passive, powerless state.

It is said that 80% of the human race's population regularly use this ego state to win favour and attention. This serves as a potent reminder of how powerfully it remains ingrained in our group psyche. And of how disempowered the majority of people actually feel much of the time.

Ego also utilises our victim state as a protective cloak to shroud our deeper pain-based wounds. As these wounds are a source of shame and vulnerability, the cloak of victimhood acts as an appropriate, protective garment. It fulfills the requirement of attracting attention to a part of ourselves that is in pain, whilst at the same time denies the deeper self need to fully reconcile with it. Ego's ultimate aim is, as usual, rationally positive. It secretly wants that part of us to be loved too. (See Vulnerability and Shame.)

If ego were to act with more emotional dexterity it might say: 'Hear me I'm hurting. There is the part of me that I am ashamed of. A part of me that, if I were to reveal to the world, I fear I may die. It feels so fragile. It's my wounded part. I cannot love that part because it is hidden away and I don't know how to locate or heal it. I would like you to try and do it for me. But that can only happen if I can get you to feel sorry enough for me....'

Do any of these words feel familiar?

If so, can you find another way of asking for what you really need?

Our deeper self knows it is our inner wounds that need our *own* love in order to begin to understand their wisdom and our potential. Ego victim state doesn't easily trust the true power of the love that is sourced from within.

So how do you go about rescuing your victim? Is it even possible? The antidote to this natural ego tendency is initially to simply *notice*. Notice during which life experiences you tend to go into your 'poor me' role.

In what sorts of emotional situations do you feel you have few, or no, options?

Do you limit yourself because the power of your conditioning feels greater than the power of your own self-love?

"You owe yourself everything you expect from others!"

Nicky Verd (South African writer and speaker)

From our victim's limited panorama, we give ourselves little room to acknowledge new or alternative responses. Paradoxically, it is through the *endeavour* of the acknowledging that we realise our deeper silent power. The power that knows we no longer have to be a victim to our victim. The power that knows we are creators and that our job is to create.

Think about how you could help someone you love who is stuck in their victim state. What is it that they might really need, beyond their ego desire for surface attention and sympathy?

Where we can feel resourceful enough to drop our victim cloak, even for a short while, we free ourselves. We begin to face, and diffuse, the limiting shame power contained within our wounds.

We understand that our victim cloak of powerlessness, rather than protect us, has instead hidden away our greatest potentials. That it has acted as less of a comfort blanket and more like a straitjacket. Where we allow ourselves to see that we have something valuable to offer, we crack the facade of the victim mould. The victim ego state only survives through the need to be needy.

The allure of our internal victim is forever present. Yes, it can open a door into a healthy respite of self-compassion. But, unless we pass through it, we can become trapped in its doorway of spiritual impotence and powerlessness. Our only option then is to attempt to manipulate others through continuing displays of self pity.

The very pity shown by others merely serves to deepen the trenches of our victimhood. It feeds our ego whilst starving our deeper self of its innate calling to live a more creative life. A life only won through an independent mastery of the deeper implications of our own pain.

By witnessing the potential released by the healing energy of self-love we throw a lifeline down to our inner victim. A lifeline up which it can climb into a light of new awareness:

"No power in society, no hardship in your condition can depress you, keep you down, in knowledge, power, virtue, influence, but by your own consent."

William Ellery Channing (American speaker and theologian)

OUR INNER RESCUER

At first sight, our inner rescuer propensity appears to be the antithesis of the victim ego state.....or does it? When we are under its superhero spell, enjoying the highs of 'saving the world', we can strangely become victim to the self importance that this role readily bestows upon us. Once identified by this mindset, we derive great personal satisfaction, fulfillment and a sense of self-worth through helping others. Even when those others may not have specifically asked for it!

If we primarily value ourselves when coming to the rescue, we unconsciously seek out people who are happy for us to take care of them. These others then become the energetic source and supply of our ability to feel good.

Naturally, this ego state meshes perfectly with someone in their victim. Alongside them we can look like the helpful heroes we believe we need to be to feel worthy and whole. People who identify strongly with the rescuer role often get drawn into occupations that give the most opportunity for its expression. And usually for the greater benefit of society at large.

Jobs such as nurses, doctors, the armed forces, social workers, emergency service workers, flight attendants, coastguards and so on, all fall into this category. In fact, any role, work or vocation where there are opportunities for the potential to help, rescue or care for others.

To a lesser, or greater, degree we are all programmed with this tendency to want to help. This is even more heightened when we witness others in distress. How many times do we hear of complete strangers doing the bravest things to save people in immediate danger, frequently without regard for their own safety?

It is the free expression of this human quality which develops a stronger community spirit. When we nurture and honour this spirit within, we often gain more from helping others than we do from helping ourselves. Making things better for others makes us feel good afterwards. Even if we had to work through a little bit of personal resistance beforehand!

It is, however, if we *only* feel valuable and useful when doing something for others that suggests a strong conditionality to our motivations. If this sounds like you, ask yourself the following:

'If I reached out to, or rescued, everyone that I feel might benefit from my help or expertise, would I then be at peace?'

If you think the answer might be no, it is highly likely that you have a hidden agenda of needing to help to feel good. The word 'needing' here is important. Often the need in the rescuer ego state is greater than that in the victim. This then raises the question, 'who is the real victim here?'

The tragedy is that this rescuing need rarely gets the opportunity to be expressed clearly and constructively. It acts out of, and is disguised within, the lauded 'selfless' human quality of wanting to help and care for others. As this quality is judged by ego as being *only* good, all sorts of subtle control and manipulation are covertly played out in its name.

Consider restrictive religious practices and belief systems that purport to be able to 'save your soul', only if you follow their doctrine. 'If you want salvation you will have to do it our way.' The domineering voice of the archetypal saviour quality endemic in these kinds of ego-empowered institutions. It's easy to see that any practice dressed up in this cloak of saving others is rarely questioned for its underlying motive: control.

This begs the question, if you are compelled to rescue, is it because you like to feel in control?

Does the need for outer control soothe an unhealed wound that sometimes feels out of control?

Having to be seen, and esteemed, through continually being helpful may grow out of an earlier wound where our needs, or achievements, were not sufficiently recognised. We all remember wanting our caregivers to be proud of us for things we had done, made or said.

This primal need is universal across cultures and nationalities. It continues to influence us, often unconsciously, throughout our adult lives too. 'I wonder what my mum would say if she could see me now?' Or 'I want to prove to him that I can do it!'

These represent the timeless infantile voices of our inner child. Always seeking parental approval or authority figure affirmation, no matter what our physical age may be.

Does it still feel important to want to make your parental figures proud of you, even if they are no longer alive?

If you are/were not close to them, do you still secretly harbour the opportunity of proving your worth to them?

The rescuer ego state is most commonly seen in the eldest child in a family. Because of the greater demands of younger siblings, there is frequently less time and energy available from busy parents. The elder child's own wants are subsequently perceived by them as less important, as they witness an environment where other's needs are more pressing. Hence a more selfless always-wanting-to-help type persona is a convenient way of getting approval and reduces pressure on mum and dad.

This developed sense of selflessness is not without its consequential gifts. This child often grows up with a strong capacity for empathy and intuition. This empathy stems from the requirement to be able to read the needs of carers, so that the child knows how to adapt their behaviours accordingly. Continued approval is then assured and becomes the sole source of self-esteem and worthiness. The rescuer is born.

If you have a strong rescuing tendency, can you use your associated empathy to empathise with, and value, your own needs occasionally too?

In order to move toward wholeness, our deeper self desires the person who is not putting on an ego act to be revealed to the world. This feels threatening, since there is a hitherto untested fear that there is nothing of any real worth behind the rescuer facade anyway.

The deeper self sees little spiritual sense hiding ourselves away behind earthly roles. It wants to experience *real* seeing and knowing. Not acting and playing. To have a chance to break our moulds, we may well find it draws us into life experiences where our rescuer is just not able to help anymore. This may be due to rising work pressures, illness or simple exhaustion. Particularly when others increasingly monopolise on our need-to-give mentality.

As levels of stress become unsustainable for the rescuer, old ways of coping and being in the world inevitably start to fail. Our rescuer self shouts: 'I just can't do this anymore!' (See Challenge and Stress.)

During these moments, putting on an act and simply playing the game seem exhausting and pointless. As life conspires to force us to drop our rescuer ego state, a feeling of sadness, even depression, can set in. We begin to feel like a part of us is dying. Perhaps because it is.

These feelings parallel those of actual bereavement and loss.

We find ourselves going through the familiar stages of grief. This is a natural process as we shed an old skin which no longer describes who we are. And, more importantly, no longer serves who we need to become. (See Grief.)

As a way of assessing how your innate rescuer operates, when someone gives you a thank you gift, or compliments you for something you have done, what is your immediate reaction?

Can you receive it comfortably or do you feel obliged to return the compliment in some way?

Do you tend to instantly belittle yourself when someone gives you positive feedback or praise?

Practice unconditional receiving next time by simply saying 'thank you'.

Try to see how you may be actually compromising the value of the gesture, through your attempts to want to *reactively* always acknowledge another's giving. Give yourself the inner space to let it in. If you cannot unconditionally value the generous gestures of others, you will never be able to truly value your own.

There are a large number of clients who come for therapy who describe themselves as being selfless rescuer types. Frequently they seek psychological support because of increasing levels of inner resentment. They see themselves as working harder and harder to please others, only to find that they are increasingly taken for granted and undervalued.

Initially, these clients express a clear need for the outside world to appreciate them more. Only then would they be able to appreciate themselves more. Much of the subsequent therapy centres around working on becoming a more affirming mirror for *themselves*. To be able to see themselves more clearly and more lovingly. To accept that they are human beings. Not human 'doings':

"No one saves us but ourselves. No one can and no one may. We ourselves must walk the path."

Buddha (monk, sage, philosopher and teacher)

The self-aware rescuer can use their developed empathy and intuition both for the benefit of others *and* for themselves. What people remember is how we made them feel, less so for what we actually did. If we are merely playing a role, we are less likely to be remembered for so long.

SELF-ESTEEM

As egoic moulds break and masks fall away, what are we left with? Perhaps more choice? More options to choose how we now want to define ourselves? To esteem ourselves?

Traditionally, we esteem ourselves through what we do or what we look like. Less so by who we are fundamentally. Our society is built around, and driven by, comparison and competition. Different models of perfection and 'ideal' states of being are constantly paraded in front of us. It's no wonder we are left with a sense of lacking. Of feeling 'less than'.

We assume that we need to make up for this lack. It becomes the only way available to feel better about ourselves. Especially when societal conditioning continues to bombard us with the message that we should somehow be different from who we are.

If we fall victim to the obsession of comparing ourselves, we limit the degree to which we can genuinely esteem our deeper selves. Particularly when this constantly varies, depending on who we are comparing ourselves with.

Feelings of low self-worth imply that we have been focussing on people who we think are better than us. Contrarily, we tend to like ourselves more when we have just proved our worth to someone else.

Fearing limitation in how we source our own esteem, we naturally look to others. We live in fear of how they might treat us. Their treatment then becomes the key to our ability to feel good. Our social anxiety increases. We give others the power to determine our own worthiness.

Ego loves to berate us by telling us that we are not good enough or as good as somebody else. Our inner voice becomes our worst critic. Berating us for not trying harder, being better, more attractive, as efficient, cleverer and so on.

Can you remember comparing yourself with other children at school, wishing you could be more like them? Then you would be more popular and life would be more bearable.

As an adult do you still sometimes feel similarly?

If so, contemplate how your inner critic blocks an acceptance of your own uniqueness. The qualities that make you different and individual.

Our culture of constant fear-based comparison only creates more conformity, uniformity and duplication. What a dull world that is. An aspiration to become the same as someone we revere. Just so we can be as happy as we perceive them to be.

We are frequently taught from an early age, not so much of what to positively aspire to be and to do, but more of what not to do. What not to be. What not to think.

With so many nots it's hardly surprising that we are beaten down. By what we should *not* be like. Nots, like 'knots', quite literally, tie us up, restrict and inhibit us. They give us less freedom to consider what we want to be. To celebrate who we are.

Think about how you primarily motivate yourself. Is it by telling yourself what not to do or be, rather than what you aspire to do or be?

Is it more about running from fears of inadequacy?

Ego seems strangely motivated by negativity. This is probably because fear is magnified by negative thinking. And fear is one of the primary ways ego controls us. This negativity enables ego to dictate to us: 'Isn't it awful that I have to think this or act this way because I am expected to. Yet what other choice do I have?' (See Our Inner Victim.)

Ego interprets restriction and limitation as a kind of bitter-sweet comfort. These boundaries imply sameness, predictability and therefore a sense of safety. But whenever there is a part of us which is not free, which feels trapped, we will feel an inner sense of disquiet. Of potential 'dis-ease'.

Affirmation from others feels like the only way to appease this inner dis-ease. As if this alone can release us from the endless pointless cycle of feeling compelled to compare.

'If I can get enough love and attention by meeting others' expectations of me, this may just give me enough power to free myself from my compulsion to solely regard myself through the lens of another.' The bargaining plea of ego. The voice of our deeper self would, no doubt, be saying:

> "Why do we buy things we don't need with money we don't have to impress people we don't like?!"
>
> Dave Ramsey (American author, radio host and speaker)

As we become more consciously aware of the brainwashing negativity that has been programmed into us, then we can see it for what it is: a societal way of manipulating us through our own ego insecurities.

How susceptible are you to media advertising that implies that you will have a more satisfactory life if you drive this car, wear these clothes or eat this food?

Or perhaps, if you can just get enough likes, followers or friends on social media, then you may somehow be popular enough to be able to, at last, like yourself?

When we can see through the false allure of this negative pro-gramming, we are more able to see and value who we really are. Only this time from outside the prison walls that it at-tempts to build around us.

An important part of the counselling therapeutic process is to allow clients to feel that, despite their individual quirki-ness, they are still understandable. Clients come into therapy seeking a greater understanding, not just of themselves, but also of what is happening to them. Many get lost in this endeavour because they have attempted to gain this under-standing solely by comparing themselves with other's lives. Of how they deal with stuff. Of how they cope.

This cannot help but lead to frustration and personal misery. We can never hope to fully understand ourselves through a comparison with others. We can never truly understand the pain of others and how they manage theirs. Just as they can never *really* know what it's like for us to sit with ours.

The gift of good therapy is that each person is seen as unique. As being acceptable for however they feel and for however they react to their life experiences. It is this non-judging en-vironment which helps them to see that, despite confusion rooted in compulsive comparison, their actions are under-standable.

Once we can begin to accept that we are all finally understand-able, we esteem ourselves from within. To be grateful for the people that we are. Indeed, gratitude and self-love are ul-timately one and the same thing. Energetically, the feelings of gratitude and love vibrate at the same frequency. They both produce the same 'feel good' hormonal response within the body.

Do you try to maintain an attitude of gratitude?

It is also a spiritual truth that the emotional states of gratitude and fear cannot be felt at the same time. Gratitude vibrates at a higher frequency. Maintaining an attitude of gratitude naturally lifts us out of denser ego-based fear states.

How grateful are you for the good things in your life?

What happens to your sense of everyday anxiety or 'wanting more' feelings in this higher state?

With the advancement of materialism, our natural ability to affirm ourselves has morphed into a self-valuing based on what one has. Not who one is.

Our innate tendency to recognise the value in our uniqueness has become lost through comparison. It pervades our very psychology. We try to esteem ourselves with the wrong things. We desperately look for value, but in spiritually empty places.

When we esteem ourselves from within, we free ourselves up both to share what we value and to value what we share. This cycle naturally continues upwards until we become less concerned with what people think. Less inhibited by the negativity. Less imprisoned by the fear:

> "If you really put a small value upon yourself, rest assured that the world will not raise your price."
>
> Jean Sibelius (Finnish composer and violinist)

FEAR

What keeps us defining ourselves by our past? What anchors us in protective fight or flight mode? What prevents us from growing spiritually? The answer, in every case, is fear.

We all live with fear to varying degrees throughout our lives. It pervades, infects and controls us. Both seen and unseen. Conscious and unconscious. Often to such an extent that we simply grow used to it. In fact, life would probably feel quite strange without it. Can you imagine a world without worry, wanting or concern?

We may have little real awareness of when, and where, fear continues to dominate us. But we know we have reached this tipping point when the purpose of life feels more about simply surviving. And less about thriving.

The superficial benefit of a fear-based culture is that we establish a comfort zone within ourselves. And we continually design and define ourselves as existing only within that. The parameter of this comfort zone provides a welcome security of containment. A sense of safety. Yet, at the same time, it prevents us from even imagining what our life may be like beyond its limits. Of risking the ascent to the highest peaks of our potential.

Fear acts like our internal alarm system, primed to alert us to dangers. It served us well in the past when dangers were obvious and tangible - wild animals or enemy tribes. However, in our modern world, where the real dangers are much less physically threatening, our alarm systems continue to be set to high.

Fear is the fuel which adds the hypervigilance to our meerkat amygdala. It primes our fight or flight reactors, ensuring stress hormones continue to pump through our bodies. Whilst all this extra adrenaline can make us feel more alive, it is not a spiritual present aliveness. It is a chemical high which simultaneously suppresses our immune system. (See Defences.)

Let's consider how this endemic latent emotion plays out in an everyday scenario. Imagine yourself having to enter, alone, a room full of people, none of whom you have ever met before. I suggest there would be very few of us who would not feel a little anticipatory angst at this prospect.

The fear here stems from whether we will feel 'safe' as we enter into, what is, an unknown situation. This primal emotion bubbles up and verbalises itself through worrying-induced internal enquiries:

Will I be accepted? Will I fit in? How should I act?

We develop many ways to allay these kinds of concerns. They may be adaptations of our natural personalities: falsified outward confidence or a persona designed to prove that we are witty, clever, funny or powerful. All are, essentially, coping mechanisms aimed to hide our underlying anxieties. To ensure some form of acceptance from all of the other egos in the room.

Our ego is simply doing its job here. Trying to protect us by gaining approval from the crowd. Encouraging us to rely on our socially winning formula.

Take a moment to consider how you go about breaking the ice with people you don't know. Do you tend to talk to others initially about problems or frustrations in your life?

Or maybe you talk about health challenges that you are currently facing?

Do you use humour or wit to win favour?

Perhaps you share ideas, aspirations or passions that you are currently pursuing?

Whether we choose to share our woes or our dreams, our opening focus gives a clue as to how we relate to our internal fears.

If we talk about our immediate life difficulties first, we are probably feeling overwhelmed by them. Possibly to the point of being frightened.

If we tend to refer initially to our dreams, aspirations and goals, this suggests that we inhabit a freer, creative, less fearful inner world.

Where we tend to refer to the problems or failures in our lives, before our dreams or successes, this may point to a fear of being successful. Of becoming all that we were designed to be.

Ego fools us into thinking that we should be frightened of the darkness within our shadows. In truth, it is the power of the clarifying light, emanating from our deeper self, that most frightens it:

> "Our deepest fear is not that we are inadequate. Our deepest fear is that we are powerful beyond measure. It is our light, not our darkness that most frightens us."
>
> Marianne Williamson (American author, lecturer, activist and spiritual teacher)

Feeling nervous before going out onto a stage is a natural human response. It is merely ego firing up the mind and body to encourage us to perform at our best. It usefully employs a degree of fear to ensure that we care enough to get the affirming applause from the audience.

If everyone is motivated in this way to perform at their best, then wouldn't the world be a better place?

Perhaps this is true when we allow ego to dominate. Problems arise when it feeds on latent fear in order to eventually 'take over the show', as it were. We lose sight of a healthier way of performing at our peak. We unconsciously seek out fear as the only option that can keep us on track.

Fear can be likened to a form of fire. Properly harnessed it can heat our homes. But when unchecked and stoked, it burns those very same homes down. This is both its allure and threat. In one hand it can serve us. In the other, destroy us.

Fear and wanting are the principal drivers of ego. It sees them as the only ways to motivate us. To keep us safe from 'danger'. It is a perfect double bind. It fears when it doesn't get what it wants and its wants are driven by a dread of never having, or being, enough.

Just take a pause to really think about the deeper significance of that last sentence.

Is that how you want to be motivated to achieve in your life?

There are numerous methods by which this double bind of ego manifests in our everyday behaviours. All of these behaviours are designed to keep us continually striving for some illusory finishing line. They are commonly called our drivers. Or, more specifically, the fuel which drives our behaviours in life. They were first defined in Eric Berne's Transactional Analysis theory (1949). The five principal ones are:

- ❑ To be perfect
- ❑ To be strong
- ❑ To try harder
- ❑ To hurry up

❑ To please others

They operate within all of us to different degrees and in varying combinations. Ego uses them to ensure that we can survive in what it sees as *only* a competitive and threatening world. They are designed to ensure the ongoing acceptance and approval of others. When we feel weak or judge our vulnerability harshly, ego relies on the superficial power within these drivers to get us through. All in an attempt to keep us from 'failing' completely.

Take a moment to consider which of the above drivers apply to you.

You may be aware that you utilise them to varying degrees, depending on the nature of your life events.

Do they serve you? Or do you serve them?

What influences which drivers we *automatically* rely on? Primarily, it's our parental or authority figures. If we see that certain drivers worked for them, we assume they will do the same for us. So if dad was always rushing around and had little time for us, then 'hurry up' might seem a natural option for us to adopt. Or if our rich boss had unrealistically high expectations of herself, we might assume that 'be perfect' is a sure winner to financial success.

Consider how ego uses our actual *fear* of fear to justify these drivers:

❑ If I am not perfect then I will not be loved
❑ If I am not strong then I will fail
❑ If I don't try harder then someone else will win
❑ If I don't hurry up then I will be left behind
❑ If I don't please others then I cannot please myself

All of these messages that ego mind tells us to keep us 'alive', root and nourish themselves in fear. If we were not to bow down to them, we may 'die'. It is this instinctual fear of death that ego uses to maintain its power and dominance. To keep us in check and to keep us checking ourselves.

Contemplate this acronym of FEAR:
False **E**vidence **A**ppearing **R**eal.

This describes ego's limited interpretation of the world. It sees fear in many situations where there is, in fact, none. Walking into a room of new people, and not impressing anyone, does not lead to death. Walking onto a stage, and forgetting your lines, does not lead to death.

Any embarrassment or ridicule that results from this may *feel* like a kind of death. But it has nothing to do with the physical death from which ego draws its dread-based conclusions. It merely attempts to ally them with that. It uses this 'false evidence' as a way to restrict us from trying something different. From thinking outside the box. From being vulnerable and more authentic.

When we find the courage to risk more, to risk being all that we are, more often and to more people, ironically our fear of physical death diminishes. When we are prepared to live more fully, we become less fearful of many different aspects of life. Including the end of it. A life which is fully lived, is lived in the present moment. From the most authentic part of ourselves. Not at some unknowable point in the imagined, fretful future. In the timeless present there is no fear. No ending. No death.

If we were to personify ego as being like that of a child, how would we respond to a child who was frightened? We would hopefully soothe and comfort them, assuring them that there is nothing to be fearful of.

Perhaps this is what ego really needs in order to grow up. In order to serve us more constructively. Love, understanding and peaceful acceptance. To feel safe the infantile, frightened inner part of us, must first be acknowledged and reassured. (See Our Life Scripts.)

When you momentarily feel overwhelmed by fear, bring your attention to your breath.

Breathing slowly and deeply, listen to your breath. Feel the cool air passing into your lungs. Notice how this shifts the frantic ego mind's focus back into the sanctity of the body.

Rooted here, your attention stays present and grounded. An awareness of the very 'aliveness' of our body disrupts the ego's usual recourse to 'False Evidence Appearing Real'.

Let's propose that the opposite of love is not hate. Let's propose it is fear. Fear that we may be seen to be different. Fear of the unknown. Fear that we will not be accepted. Fear that we may die.

If there was one assurance given for the experience of human existence, it is that we are all going to physically die, one day. So what is the point, rationally or otherwise, of fearing it? All the fear energy in the world is not going to change this prescribed outcome. The perpetuation of it during our earthly lives only serves to limit and restrict those very lives. This fear, like most others, serves little constructive purpose.

What we fear we reject. What we reject we push away into our shadow. Here our fears continue to control us unconsciously, keeping some part of us hidden, closed off from the world. Scared and spiritually isolated. What is within our shadows we cannot see clearly. What we cannot see clearly frightens us. There, we create superstition and false evidence, to try to justify our uncomfortable feelings.

Faced with this unending dilemma, ego does what it can to resolve this quandary. It projects its own unwelcome consequences of fear outwards, and onto, others.

Sadly, we subsequently berate or attack the external screen onto which we project our own terror. We seek out, or even create, a common enemy or a differing belief system. Again, this universal psychological tendency of ego leads to many of the conflicts in our world today.

Consider the word prejudice. It is made up of two root words 'pre' and 'judge'.

By definition, we can only pre-judge when we do not know something well. What we are not familiar with we cannot adequately, or fairly, judge.

But we tend to fear what we do not yet know because it is unfamiliar to us.

Therefore prejudice is actually less about critical bias. It is more about ego's continued attempts to control us through the illusion of fear of the unknown. Fear of difference.

Catch yourself next time you are aware that you are judging quickly or feeling prejudicial. Is there a part of you that feels threatened in some way?

When we see someone facing their fears, stepping out of their comfort zone and risking their vulnerability, we are often filled with admiration and respect. Even if they appear to make a 'mistake' in this process, our common humanity connects ours to theirs. It is our deeper self which both admires, and empathises with, their courage.

Interestingly, the old French word for courage (corage), derives from the Latin 'cor'. It means 'coming from the heart'. When we witness others who are prepared to have the courage to face their fears our naturally judgemental ego tends to quieten. We are moved by their brave heartfelt endeavours.

A more profound spiritual connection naturally ensues. We recognise that it is the human wide task of the deeper self to help us to face our fears. To reclaim our power back from them. From this springs a second acronym:

Face **E**verything **A**nd **R**ise!

"Fear is a reaction. Courage is a decision."

Winston Churchill (English politician and writer)

Where there is more love and heart-sourced courage there will be less fear. It raises the question:

What is your kindest driver? Fear or love?

Next time you make a mistake, or don't 'get it right', see which you offer yourself.

If ego thrives and dominates on fear then, in order to live a world with less, we need to give it less power. Less control. Where ego remains unchecked, it both seeks and creates more, both within and outside of ourselves.

In its blissful, but infantile ignorance, this is the only way it knows how to motivate us. It is only through our willingness to work on our own self-awareness, by seeing through the false illusion of our fears, that we can find another way:

"Everything you've ever wanted is on the other side of fear."

George Addair (American speaker, author and philosopher)

DEPRESSION

The state of depression is often described as a mixture of fear and anxiety. Fear that says life has no meaning. Anxiety that says I have no meaning to offer life.

When we are fearful and anxious about *how* to live our life, or what to do with it, of course we are going to wonder, 'what is it all about?'

We have more luxury, convenience, leisure, technology and communication than ever before. Yet rates of depression continue to rise. The chasing of these goals alone cannot be the answer. Perhaps we are increasingly seeing through the allure of their false gold? The relative ease of modern life makes the awareness of our inner emptiness - often used as a metaphor for depression - ever more inescapable. Even more 'contactable'.

Unlike our ancestors, we no longer have to struggle so hard to stay alive physically. We now have the opportunity of more space to grow psychologically, to evolve emotionally. But with that opportunity comes challenge; a more intimate relationship with meaning. With purpose. With the point of life.

Societally, we are conditioned to value our 'doingness' through what we achieve, how much we earn, how well qualified we are. Yet, when we take all these things away, we have no yardstick to measure our intrinsic value. Our core humanity, our 'beingness'. Of the richness of our life experience that is ever trying to nudge us into loving who we are. Even when it appears to be trying to do so in some very round about ways!

Without a clear medium through which to measure how much we have grown, how much more aware we are this year compared to last, we flounder and struggle. When our ceaseless doing begins to feel pointless we look within. To our deep inner space.

Just as a tree grows we are here to grow too, both physically and emotionally. Maybe depression is a turning point when we start to fully face the inner space that we have to grow into. One which we, initially, have no idea how to fill.

That's probably why, when we first summon the courage to enter, it seems dark and daunting. A well of confusion and disorientation. A void of little meaning.

And yet within this inner space the questions of our very existence call out:

- ❑ Who am I?
- ❑ What do I really want?
- ❑ What is my purpose?

When we begin to contemplate these 'bigger' questions naturally we feel overwhelmed, confused, lost. Based on our day to day experience they are overwhelming.

Remember pestering your parents with your big life questions, 'what does this mean mum' and 'why does that happen dad?' No doubt they probably replied with their own familiar patter, 'because that's just the way it is!'

Since childhood we have grown accustomed to seeking answers outside of ourselves. That they lie, somewhere in the ether, waiting for us to devour them. Only then we will be given the prescriptive meaning of our lives that we so desperately seek.

It's hardly surprising that we begin to feel depressed when we realise that no amount of consuming can satisfy the pang of the deeper questions we harbour. That previous coping mechanisms, exhausting drivers, material promises, just don't seem to do it for us anymore. When all around falls away, where do we turn?

Depression leaves us with little option. We turn within. As we grapple with the big questions we find that we are left with very little energy for the small ones. Everyday mundane tasks such as regular eating, washing, cleaning and socialising take on less significance. They just don't seem as important as they did before. For a while, at least, finding answers to the bigger questions of existence matters more.

When there are no external soul-satisfying solutions available, ego goes into a kind of panic. Its regular, default coping mechanisms and diversionary techniques break down. The subsequent feelings of depression can overwhelm us. Everything we have done in our lives up to that juncture may seem meaningless and pointless. We quickly realise that, spiritually, we have only ever contemplated the mundane, small stuff of life.

Depression is often a sign that there is a potential for a new shift in our thinking. An evolution of our spiritual consciousness. We start to see life differently. We realise the painful truth that there are no easy, prescriptive answers. Whatever journey someone else may be on, searching for their own meaning, is never identical to our own. Ours is one we must tread alone. That's why the journey can seem so anxious and lonely.

In certain native American Indian tribes, many of the common manifestations of depression were seen as a natural part of a tribesman's deeper awakening. The lethargy, a need to withdraw within oneself, a disinterest in everyday tasks. All signs of the 'dark night of the soul', as it is sometimes called. A challenging initiation into a more enlightened state of being.

Here, 'depression' was seen as an opportunity, a portal into a new awareness. Not something that had to be feared, stigmatised, denied or medicated.

In these societies, the person entering into their 'dark night' would leave the security of the tribe, possibly for many days, in order to be with themselves. They gifted themselves the space to contemplate who they really were, free of the labels, expectations and conditioning that had defined them up to that point. It was a 'right of passage', a form of ego death. A time to shed old identities.

The stress inherent in depression in our modern western world rises from the conditioned compulsion to get back to who we once were. While our deeper self wants to uncover new priorities and potentials. No wonder we feel caught in the middle of this tussle. Pulled in different directions. Dismantled. Unsure where to put our next step.

The inner space this enquiry opens feels vast and overwhelming. There is nothing ego can come up with to fill this infinite chasm. The concept of infinity is always overwhelming. Our rational minds frazzle when we even try to imagine it.

Depression is something that we are taught to fight, to overcome. To never contemplate or enter into. To ego the black cloak of depression is simply that. Blackness.

Try to envisage an infinite space, perhaps in terms of outer space. In this vast expanse, the traditional sense of ourself is lost. We feel tiny and insignificant.

Now try to imagine your limitless, deeper self within this boundless space. Does it feel any different, less foreboding, less threatening?

Do you feel you can relate to it rather than simply trying to fill it?

> "We too should make ourselves empty, that the great soul of the universe may fill us with its breath."
>
> Laurence Binyon (English poet, dramatist and art scholar)

When feeling depressed we are encouraged to, 'cheer up, keep busy, take up a hobby'. All platitudes which may be well meaning but miss the real point of depression. Yet it is this very point that our deeper self calls us to contemplate.

People often describe going through some sort of breakdown before seeing the meaning of their depression. Before being able to have a more honest relationship with it. The spiritual point of this process, although outwardly painful, is to encourage us to drop everything that is not serving our highest potential. To adapt old coping mechanisms, defences and habits that no longer describe who we now need to become. Yes, a form of breakdown, only one that leaves a space to break through to the authentic core of who we are.

Physical pain is the body's way of letting us know that something is amiss. That something requires our attention. The purpose of the emotional pain contained within depression calls us to consider something similar:

- ❑ *What is out of alignment in my life right now?*
- ❑ *How am I not living according to my true values?*
- ❑ *Where am I not being authentic?*

By its very nature, the journey through emotional pain is difficult and challenging. It requires facing feelings of confusion, bewilderment and anxiety. Feelings that sometimes rise up to levels of, what we term in the west, depression.

Nonetheless, coming out the other side with a renewed identity and greater self-awareness is a goal worth striving for. It is not a journey for the fainthearted. But its rewards are profound, empowering and life-changing.

The arena of depression is a huge one. Anything that refers to a concept of infinity within will always seem foreboding and overwhelming. My intention here is not to try to patronise or oversimplify this challenging and painful emotional state. Instead, I invite you to see the nature of depression through a different lens. The eyes of your deeper self.

Sadness requires us to accept change. And to integrate that change as a new reality into our everyday lives. I want to add to that by suggesting that depression, an acute type of sadness, doesn't just require us to accept some sort of outer change. It requires an inner one too.

The journey from outer to inner also describes our spiritual calling from ego to deeper self.

Perhaps depression is a challenging invitation to look more closely at the relationship we have with ego. To consider how we now want it to serve us, rather than us serving it:

> "Depression is like a woman in black. If she turns up, don't shoo her away. Invite her in, offer her a seat, treat her like a guest and listen to what she wants to say."
>
> Carl Jung (Swiss founder of analytical psychology, psychiatrist and psychotherapist)

ANXIETY

Anxiety and depression are close bedfellows. We can become depressed when we feel anxious because the emotional energy of anxiety takes us round and round in the same repeating, ultimately pointless, cycle. Finally we give up trying to work out why we feel so stuck. It just doesn't seem to make any rational sense.

Anxiety is like a heightened, focussed form of worry. And worry is a fear that something bad may happen. So being anxiousness could be described as losing a connection with the confidence in ourselves to cope with what life brings.

Periods of anxiety leave us feeling ineffective, vulnerable and hopeless. When we feel other similar emotions such as anger, angst or anguish, we still have faith that we can rise to a challenge. That an investment of the energy created by these feeling states will lead to a positive outcome, given enough persistence and resilience.

But anxiety seems to dent our trust in any hope that we can overcome. We feel pessimistic. Hence the strong association with depression. Feeling anxious means we have lost contact with our sense of security. Of self-trust. Of inner confidence.

When we lack inner confidence we put more effort into maintaining a strong outer facade. We hope that this will be a source of the security we need to get us through. Ego acts here in the only way it knows how. It seeks confirmation that our social mask will be seen to be good enough to hide the well of anxious self-doubt beneath. 'If I can just maintain an act that everything is fine, then I can keep my anxiety under control.'

The inner deal we strike.

The problem is this public facade is not a reliable source. It is conditional on the unpredictability of how others behave toward us at any given time. And on how threatening we perceive the unpredictability in our environment to be. It is this very *perception* of unpredictability which heightens anxious feelings. If we feel we cannot rely on either ourselves or the outer world, how can we feel safe?

As anxiety builds so does the sense of internal disconnect. The disconnect between what we present to the world and how we are really feeling inside. Subsequently *any* change in external circumstances feels threatening. You know that sense when your capacity bucket feels full and something you would normally take in your stride suddenly tips you over the edge? We feel like hiding away from everything and everyone. Just to maintain some semblance of internal control and external predictability.

Over time, the voice of our deeper self becomes more urgent. It wants us to be honest about what's happening inside. The ensuing battle with ego, trying to keep a lid on things, only serves to add to a crescendo of inner tension. This can culminate in panic-like attacks. Like a volcano that wants to erupt.

Our sense of internal disconnect also gets projected onto objects in our environment. We may develop phobias, fears of specific things or experiences which reflect our inner insecurities. Unpredictable animals such as spiders or snakes, air turbulence on an aircraft, sudden loud noises, heights, open spaces, closed spaces and so on. Anything that represents to us a sense of not feeling in control.

The degree of anxiousness we feel is related to the amount of blocked emotional energy waiting to be expressed by our deeper self. Ego fears that the expression of our authentic feelings would require a complete change in our self-definition. A change in our world view and how the world sees us. A change simply not worth the risk.

Have you noticed that your anxiety increases when you try to maintain an outer impression which does not match your inner feeling state?

If you can, try to experiment by sharing more of how you are really feeling. Notice what happens to your anxiety.

If we can risk coming out from behind our social masks. If we can dare to reveal more of how we are really feeling, then our inner disconnect begins to narrow. Our anxiety wanes.

Anxiety does not just come from inner disconnect, however. It also sustains itself from the fear defence ego uses to stop us believing that everything will be okay. From trusting the wisdom of our deeper self to get us through. From relinquishing control. From speaking from our heart.

Everything will be alright in the end. If it's not alright, it's not the end yet!

The overuse by ego of this defensive fear leads to a sense of latent anxiety which seems unexplainable. The 'I'm anxious but I've no idea why or what's causing it' feeling. We can become anxious of the state of anxiety. Not realising it's ego resisting to let go and trust. We fear our internal fear, not actual outside world events.

Without sufficient awareness of what ego is doing, we become strangely addicted to the fear within anxiety. To the hormone rush that gives us a fake sense of chemical aliveness. We falsely come to believe that this fear, and the associated heightened bodily state, is the *only* thing that can keep us safe. And that we need to rely on this heightened bodily state as the only source of power that can overcome what our anxiety perceives as threatening.

Where we become over-reliant, or addicted, we effectively block any hope of facing anxiety head on. Yet facing the fear is the only way to see through the ego defence mechanism. As with any addiction, we worry we may die without the object of our addiction. Without the fear 'protection' offered up by ego. (See Addiction to Things.)

How, and when, does your ego use its fear defence to suppress what you may be really feeling inside?

Could it be that unpredictable external change, which stirs the energy trapped in anxiety, is inviting you to connect with these unexpressed parts of yourself?

Amir's Story

Amir came for counselling because he continued to suffer disabling anxiety attacks. He wanted to train to become a psychotherapist and so needed some space to work through the origins of his difficult feelings.

Amir had spent a lot of his childhood living under a dictatorship in his country of birth. If he did not conform to strict religious doctrines, he lived in dread of being punished by the religious police. He had had therapy many years ago and assumed that any anxiety trigger from this experience had been fully healed.

But now that Amir wanted to help others as a therapist himself, his anxiety attacks had returned. They continued to frustrate and inhibit him. His way of dealing with them was to remain strong. To try to defeat them by building an ever greater internal resistance. It seemed like the internal battle Amir was waging was a continuation of the external governmental one that he, and his people, had fought for so long.

Through our therapy together, Amir saw that remaining rigidly defiant in the face of his inner turmoil was no longer working. It was time to try a different approach. To instead turn and surrender to his own internalised 'oppressor'. This felt like madness to Amir. His historic conditioning had taught him that to surrender meant succumbing to the very forces that took away his liberty. (See Surrender.)

Amir would have to fully face his earlier life fear of being overpowered. This was his only path to true healing. Although it meant an initial peak of anxiety, the only way out was through. His own ego now symbolised the last remnants of his governmental regime. No wonder it felt such a struggle.

Part of the original meaning of surrender is to convey. To deliver. To offer of oneself. Through a brave psychological act of surrender, Amir experienced a form of deliverance. A deliverance from the oppressive protection of his own ego. His body shook as he took his power back from it.

By facing historic fears, Amir experienced what it was like to offer himself over to a power that his ego had always feared would overwhelm him. Only to discover that it actually empowered him. He understood how it was using an old threat to continue to 'protect' him in the present. By insisting on tying him to the trauma of his past.

Any effective counsellor, healer or therapist has to be willing to trust, and be vulnerable, to offer themselves over to the healing encounter in this way. To risk getting their own ego out of the way in order to better help their clients.

The intelligence of Amir's deeper self knew how best to learn this spiritually effective therapeutic endeavour. To experience it for himself. To experience a form of his own deliverance through a surrender to his deep intrinsic fears.

This process dissolved the parts of Amir's ego which were no longer serving him. It also reduced his unexplained anxiety.

By bearing witness to his own need, and deeper propensity, to heal Amir lived this process for himself. This subsequently helped him to become a more insightful therapist on his own client's healing pathways.

In anxiety then there is a message. An unexplored potential. An unanswered question which we initially interpret only as nagging self-doubt:

> "The best use of imagination is creativity. The worst use of imagination is anxiety."
>
> Deepak Chopra (Indian-American physician, public speaker, writer and philosopher)

Sometimes we need a shake-up, a wake-up call, to get us to contemplate this process. At other times, with a degree of self-awareness and self-care we can make space. We can be kind enough to ourselves to do this before we hit an anxiety crisis point.

To check on how you relate to your anxiety contemplate this:

Recall a time that triggered some level of personal anxiety. What was it about yourself that you did not trust to be able to live through it?

What is currently the source of your own mistrust?

With sufficient reflection, we have to conclude that this mis-trusting part is the voice of ego. It is ego which talks to us as if from some critical, external observer's viewpoint.

Our inner voice, by definition, comes from within. It always speaks from a place of quiet knowing. Of trusting. It is, strictly speaking, not even a voice because an inner knowing is just that. A knowing. It communicates with us via a *felt sense* rather than verbally.

When we know and trust that ego sourced fear merely masks our ability to trust, our anxiety cannot help but transform:

When will I realise that there is nothing that I need that I don't already have, apart from my own perception that there is nothing that I need that I don't already have?

OUR LIFE SCRIPTS

Before we stand up and talk to a group of people, go for a job interview or step onto a stage, we have some idea of the words we are going to say. Of the actions we plan to take. We write, learn and rehearse a 'script' that we hope will help us shine in the eyes of others.

In the great theatre of life we rely on our scripts to get us through. Particularly the ones that appear to get us the most attention, validation, admiration and love. Our personal scripts become the stories we tell ourselves about ourselves. As well as the stories we tell others about ourselves.

Imagine you are telling a friend about the story of who you are.

Where would you begin? With qualities that you possess, things you have achieved, what you look like, your family background?

Would you focus more on how you see yourself or on how you think others see you?

We all have a unique mix of ingredients that contribute to the formation of our scripts. Many of these I have covered in the preceding chapters. They include our personality filters, our external conditioning, our internal shoulds and oughts, our drivers and our unique interpretation of our emotional wounds.

The way ego combines these sometimes complementary, but often conflicting, variables together forms our everyday sense of self. As it is ego which initially constructs this self, it could be likened to a window through which we view the world. And one through which the world views us. Just as with any window it has a frame, a boundary. A boundary within which we set the rules, and perceive the limitations, of our lives.

There is, however, another important component of limitation which we have to add to this rich mix. These are referred to psychologically as injunctions. They were first defined by Dr Eric Berne in his psychoanalytic theory called Transactional Analysis (1949).

Injunctions are similar to our drivers insofar as they are specific messages passed down to us. They consist of the fears, worries and insecurities of our parental figures and often of older generations too.

Whereas drivers tend to be conscious, explicit and well meaning messages such as 'try harder and you will get what you want', injunctions are unconscious and frequently negative in nature. We pick them up non verbally from our parents through a felt sense of their own harboured anxiety or unresolved pain. Common subliminal messages include:

- ❏ Don't be a child for too long
- ❏ Don't grow up
- ❏ Don't exist
- ❏ Don't succeed or be important
- ❏ Don't trust
- ❏ Don't belong
- ❏ Don't be who you are

These all stem from our parent's perceptions of where they felt that the world was not safe, as they experienced it. They point to the sources of their, or previous generations, core wounds. Particularly the ones that remain suppressed, unacknowledged and unhealed:

"Nothing has a stronger influence psychologically on their environment, and especially on their children, than the unlived life of the parent."

Carl Jung (Swiss founder of analytical psychology, psychoanalyst and psychiatrist)

When we are young we are deeply sensitive beings. We don't have access to the same sophisticated defences that we develop as adults. We are like emotional sponges. We have to be, in order to be able to tune into the emotional states of our parental figures. Only then can we sense their moods and respond accordingly. This vital bond forms part of the healthy, loving non-verbal attachment between carer and child.

We rely on the quality of this bond to feel secure, understood and safe. It helps us physiologically too, by ensuring an optimal environment for the development of our delicately balanced nervous systems.

But through this natural and necessary endeavour we also absorb the fears and insecurities of our caregivers. Their insecurities can be so potent that, by the age of four, we have a strong sense of their *felt* fear-based injunctions. A long while before we can learn their more affirming verbalised messages.

Put a new born baby in water and they have an instinctive reflexive ability to move their arms and legs to right themselves and stay afloat. Yet, once that same baby senses their parent's terror when they get close to a body of water, it overrides the innate trust in its natural survival capabilities.

As injunctions are mutually felt, but rarely verbally expressed, we remain confused as to their origins. Are we fearful of something that we have personally experienced? Or of something that's been passed on to us, 'second-hand?'

It is this internal confusion which adds to the challenge of trying to understand the nature of family based injunctions. We have no rational sense as to where they have come from. All we do know is that they can strangely limit us. They stop us from trusting in life. From moving forwards. From living freely.

Consider a 'don't succeed' injunction. Here, you may have unexplained feelings of guilt when you actually do well or excel at something. You may find yourself shying away from any recognition that success brings. Or inexplicably self-sabotaging opportunities in life without being consciously aware as to why, or even how, you do so.

Have you ever had a tendency to sabotage or end a relationship, job or friendship that outwardly appeared to be going well?

Was it because, at some level, you felt you didn't deserve to receive such positive things?

Do you sometimes feel guilty that you have things that others do not?

Injunctions are designed to act as defences against feeling the pain of wounds which have occurred historically somewhere in the family lineage. For example, the emotional impacts of war, famine, displacement, sexual abuse, discrimination, governmental repression, religious persecution, illegitimacy, infidelity, suppressed grief and so on. These familial stories can also be referred to as 'mythos'. They represent literal myths that describe a particular context, or emotional trauma, that has been denied or repressed. (See The Power in our Emotional Wounds.)

Mythos are carried within the group shadow of a family. They bubble up through individual family members, manifesting in a range of personal issues from addiction to anxiety and hypochondria to acrophobia.

All of these behavioural acting out reactions represent attempts by each individual to externalise, and so heal, shadow family pain or repressed trauma. Because the actual source of that pain is not always clear, it can make the manifesting behaviour of a given family member appear inexplicable and irrational.

An analogy of this would be like something going rotten in the cellar of a house. Everyone living in the house smells that something is not right, but each reacts differently. Some ignore it, some hold their nose, some spray an air freshener to disguise it, some fall ill, while others leave the house altogether. Despite the raft of different individual reactions, no one can quite work out where the smell is actually coming from.

There is always associated pain, and shame, in a mythos. The family group ego tries to suppress it with unhelpful and defensive behaviours. For example, there may be a culture of maintaining inauthentic facades, a tendency to tribal victimhood or an unconscious group 'contract' to avoid talking about anything painful.

These coping behaviours crescendo into some sort of group disharmony, the commonly quoted 'dysfunctional family'. But the spiritual nucleus of the family - the shared deeper self - knows that the pain has to be faced by someone in the tribe at some point. This is ultimately the only way for the mythos to be understood and finally healed. The only way to stop it continually being passed down from one generation to the next.

Jose's Story

Jose came into therapy because he was becoming increasingly overwhelmed by others emotional pain. He was naturally a very empathic man. This quality served him well in his job working with children with special needs. However, his gift of empathy and insight was now exhausting him. He felt the pain of others as if it were his own.

During our therapeutic journey together Jose and I discussed the history of his family. Particularly the difficult relationship that he had always had with his mother. This troubled Jose greatly. He suspected that his mother had been through some trauma when she was young. She was brought up during the Spanish civil war, but had never shared any details with her son about this period in her life.

Jose intuitively felt that something bad must have happened. What had caused his mother to be so emotionally cold towards him? He so wanted to be closer to her. To be able to understand exactly what burden she was carrying.

The 'responsibility' of his insight weighed heavily on Jose's shoulders. He instinctively felt it was down to him to heal the repressed pain of his mum. To be a good enough son. To meet his obligations he should be able to help her. Why was it he could help others in his everyday job and yet not be able to reach out to his own mother. To rescue her from the trauma of her past?

As the therapy continued, we discussed what might be the theme of the mythos hidden within Jose's family shadow. We managed to distill it down into two sentences: 'If we were to fully acknowledge our own pain, we may not survive. It might tear the family apart.'

Contemplating this mythos was difficult for Jose. But through a growing compassion for his own struggle, he realised that he had never grieved for himself. For the absence of a more loving relationship with his mother. He had never acknowledged and cried for his *own* emotional trauma.

In the presence of his family's mythos, Jose's ego had devised a unique coping mechanism. One which had made him more susceptible to other's pain. Only to avoid having to enter into his own.

The family wound had spawned an opportunity for Jose. The ability to connect with, and to understand, others more profoundly. However, now the pain caught up in this wound was suffocating him. Jose had never before taken the time to do the inner awareness work which his deeper self now required of him. He had not acknowledged the real source of the power of his empathy and insight. And, until he did so, it would continue to unconsciously drive him to heal himself solely through the vehicle of others.

As Jose began to befriend his own pain and grief, he discovered that he could be more unconditionally present for others in the face of theirs. Even the relationship with his mother gradually improved. He became less enslaved to his own egoic agenda that she must verbalise her pain directly to him, in order for him to find peace. Instead he uncovered a source of his own inner peace. A non-spoken, loving presence to his mother's buried pain that did not demand, judge or try to rationalise. An awareness that that was, and is, enough.

The inner reconciliation that Jose undertook meant that he could begin to rewrite the mythos script of his family. Just as it takes one cog in a machine to alter its direction, the rest of the machine cannot help but notice and adapt. By changing the way he acknowledged and honoured his own pain, Jose created energetic healing ripples that had a profound effect on his whole family system.

What follows is some common family mythos, as listed above, together with how they may manifest behaviourally within our personal scripts. See if you recognise any from your own experience:

'Don't Be A Child For Too Long'

This mythos injunction may arise as the result of parental divorce, death, illness or anywhere where the continuity of optimum parenting has been disrupted.

These types of experiences can lead to a need to take on greater responsibility as a child. We might feel a pressure to grow up fast, usually to help or take care of parents who have difficulty coping. We may readily adopt the rescuer ego state in later life. (See Our Inner Rescuer.)

To be appropriately creative, curious and playful, we need to to carry the qualities of our inner child into adulthood. Subject to this particular injunction we might feel ashamed of, or undervalue, this important part of our psyche. We may even develop obsessive or controlling behaviour patterns in order to try to suppress it.

As adults we're likely to feel anxious or panicky in situations where we feel that we have little control. This is because we lose faith in our natural ability to soothe ourselves through play, imagination and creativity.

'Don't Grow Up'

This is the antithesis of the last injunction. It may develop because previous generations did not feel sufficiently protected, or safe, in their own childhoods. Perhaps because of a history of extreme poverty, abuse of power or emotionally repressed parenting.

Here, parental ego attempts to compensate for this by overprotecting their offspring. By not allowing them to freely grow up. Parents endlessly try to heal their own wounds by offering their own children what they did not have. To heal themselves through the next generation.

Children subject to this mythos tend to over-rely on their victim ego state as adults. The subliminal message being that it's safer, and feels more familiar, to remain in a more infantile state. (See Our Inner Victim.)

'Don't Exist'

This may be the mythos we feel following an interruption in healthy mother/child bonding. Maybe our mother was ill, or mentally distressed, following our birth.

We may also have this sense if the pregnancy was not planned or where we came along at a time of high stress for our parents. This is not to suggest that we were not loved, simply that there may have been outside factors which inhibited quality emotional attachment.

This can manifest later as an unexplained sense of low self-esteem. And in difficulties defining who we really are, or who we want to be, as adults.

'Don't Succeed Or Be Important'

This mythos may have sourced from a family context that being of service to others is the best way to ensure security and safety. There may have been someone historically who was revered for being outwardly successful and noted, but then fell from grace in some shameful way. Or perhaps there were unexpressed talents or gifts which were unacknowledged and not given the credit that they rightfully deserved.

There is a subliminal message in this mythos that to be successful means to be exposed, open to ridicule or to risk potential failure. By remaining humble and hidden, the risk of being seen and shamed diminishes. Sadly so does the innate potential for outward success.

As adults this can result in a tendency to self-sabotage, affecting careers, relationships and self-esteem. Simply because we feel, at some level, that we don't deserve the trappings of a successful life.

'Don't Trust'

Here there may have been experiences where family members were subject to intimidation from authority figures, oppressive governmental regimes or the unpredictable attention of caregivers.

This can result in unexplained anxiety and insecurity in adulthood. We come to believe that it is not really safe to trust anyone, other than ourselves. We might prefer solitude and yet, deep down, feel lonely. We protectively assume others will let us down, if we were to become too close to them.

'Don't Belong'

This mythos is frequently felt where, historically, the family had to flee their home country or place of birth. Maybe because of war, intimidation or religious persecution. Or where individuals were ridiculed for being different, possibly due to gender identity, sexuality or cultural association.

Not knowing where we belong, where we fit in, means that we seek connection through other ways. We may become addicted or be drawn into unhealthy relationships which mirror our internal sense of isolation.

We believe that we cannot safely, and authentically, relate to others. We doubt that they would ever really understand us if we dared to do so anyway. Hence, we find more comfort and security in relating to a substance, thing or animal, as compared to another human being. (See Addiction to Things.)

'Don't Be Who You Are'

We may feel the restriction of this injunction where traditional roles within our family were confused, overlapped or strained. Perhaps if the tribal unit was disrupted through divorce, illness or bereavement and we felt obliged to be more than 'just' a son or a daughter.

We may have witnessed our father struggling to cope emotionally when our mother left or fell ill, so had to become a pseudo partner to support him. Or maybe our younger sibling had special needs, so we had to help our mother to cope.

As adults we may feel compelled to constantly adapt ourselves to meet the complex needs of another. Or we may find ourselves harbouring complex needs that we require others to sort out.

This mythos often results in some form of codependency in adult relationships. Where we become too adaptable, we lose a sense of our individuality. Of our core identity. We falsely believe that we might not truly exist, unless we can identify ourselves solely through the lens of another.

Take some time to reflect on whether you believe you may have been, or perhaps still are, subject to any of these mythos injunctions. They are revealed through patterns of behaviour which we continue to repeat, but cannot rationally explain why.

If you do locate any see if you can offer yourself (and any family members) compassion and understanding for the true source of shame, inadequacy or pain that ego-constructed injunctions were attempting to hide away.

It can be very easy to blame our parental figures or ancestors for passing down to us the legacy of a challenging mythos. But by reframing this challenge as an opportunity to heal outdated and unhelpful family script messages, we get to realise and release the power of our unique spiritual muscle.

Our personal stories

When we consider family injunctions, and all the other influences that go into forming our scripts, it is not surprising that we can come up with some unhelpful, and untrue, stories about ourselves. Just as we write our internal shoulds and oughts based on our interpretation of our generic conditioning, so we similarly reach conclusions about ourselves which assume we are not worthy of love.

The most common personal stories we tell ourselves are:

- ❏ Everyone abandons me
- ❏ Nobody cares about me
- ❏ Everyone else is better than me
- ❏ I'm to blame/it's all my fault
- ❏ I have to be useful
- ❏ It is not safe to be who I am

Do any of these seem familiar to you?

How easy is it to admit that some of these feel familiar?

In our infancy we are busy downloading our environmental and family programming. By the age of seven or so our personal scripts are well established and make up core components of our personalities. Aristotle, the ancient Greek philosopher and scientist, famously said:

> "Give me a child until he is seven and I will show you the man."

Up to the age of seven science has shown that the brainwaves of children operate at a lower frequency (delta and theta) than that of teenagers and adults (alpha and beta).

At the frequency of theta in particular, we are more connected with our intuitive awareness, vivid imagination and innate creativity. So, as younger children we are naturally less inhibited, freer to experiment and able to try out different ways of being. As adults we can still access this particular frequency of brain functioning, known as the 'flow state', through meditation and mindfulness.

Beyond seven years old our default brainwave state changes. We develop a more solid sense of who we are and the life role which works for us, based on the environmental information we have downloaded. As our personalities establish, we settle into a pattern of behaviour based around a central script theme. Because we are subject to the indoctrination of these script themes from such a young age, we falsely come to believe that they are true.

To try to escape these early negative messages ego commonly uses drivers - be perfect, be strong, try harder, hurry up, please others - as I discussed in 'Fear'. But, other than being at the mercy of our fear-based dictatorial drivers, how else can we begin to heal the negative messages we come to believe about ourselves?

Attempting to simply re-write or erase them from our minds is not going to work. They're so ingrained in our psyche, in our natural thinking state, we may not have a sense of who we are if we did not continue to define ourselves through them. The first step in understanding our scripts is to read them for *ourselves.*

For example, if you carry an 'I'm to blame/it's my fault' script, you may find that people tend to project guilt onto you. Or others might always hold you accountable when things go wrong. Even when you know you were not personally responsible.

With this type of script, we are unconsciously expressing a willingness to hold the guilt in a social interaction or situation. Out of immediate awareness we offer out our hands in readiness to do so.

This type of script forms due to something in our past that we are unable to forgive ourselves for. The resulting guilt that arises from this inability to forgive will become our 'writing on the wall'. The writing that others sense and will be powerless not to react too. (See Mistakes and Guilt.)

If you carry an 'it's not safe to be who I am' script, you may find that others frequently dictate to you what role they need you to play to suit their needs. You might feel a compulsion to constantly adapt your behaviour to fit in with other's expectations. (See Our Shadow Self and the Roles We Play.)

These are just a couple of examples of how we may gain a sense of what our real inner scripts might be, as witnessed through the way the world treats us. It is our deeper self that wants to understand and heal our own limiting scripts. It knows they are merely ego-based voices designed to keep us 'in check'.

Our Wounded Inner Child

A guided visualisation exercise follows which can help to discover where, when and why our personal scripts were first written. I suggest reading the whole text through once. Then find a quiet space where you won't be disturbed and recount the visualisation in your mind:

Sit in a comfortable supportive chair where you can keep your back straight. Plant your feet firmly on the floor and initially just notice the points where the chair is in contact with your body. Then close your eyes, relax and listen to your breathing.

Notice how cool and refreshing the air is in your nostrils. As you breathe more and more deeply, feel how the breath sweeps, cleanses and releases any anxiety you are holding in your body.

When you feel ready, visualise yourself standing outside a beautiful castle. See the tall walls and towers and the moat circling all the way around. Feel the warmth of the sun shining. Notice how it casts a shadow of the castle walls on the ground beside it. Spend some time contemplating the magnificence of this castle, until you feel the urge to go inside. The castle's drawbridge starts to creak and groan until eventually it opens, providing a bridge across the moat to access the inside of the boundary walls.

Begin to walk across the drawbridge and sense the anticipation in wanting to find out what lies inside the castle grounds. Really feel this anticipation and excitement in what you are about to discover. As you pass through the gateway you are met with the breathtaking sight of a beautiful garden. Flowers, shrubbery, lush green grass, birdsong and a magnificent cascading water fountain, dancing under a bright summer sun. Take some time reflecting and taking in the beautiful sights, sounds, smells, and sensations of this scene.

After a while you feel your eyes are drawn to a bench in one corner of the castle grounds. On this bench you can see a young child reading a book. As you focus on this child you realise that they seem strangely familiar. Start to walk over towards the bench. As you do so notice this little person looking directly back at you. You immediately sense a wonderful connection. Just like that of meeting a long lost friend.

As this child looks up into your eyes you feel this connection even more strongly. You may feel that you want to hug them. Sit down beside them on the bench. They seem so pleased, indeed relieved, to see you too.

Now allow yourself to have a conversation with this child. These can be with words or just thoughts. Without thinking too much hear, or sense, what they want to convey to you. Notice the feelings that are evoked as you listen to their story. And the strong emotional connection you have.

You now have an increasing realisation that this is not just any child, but someone who represents a deeper part of you. Your own 'inner child'. This is the inner child that has always existed, yet perhaps you have been in denial of. Unable to listen to, or understand, very well. Until now.

With this realisation, be aware of what your child wants to share with you. About the times in the past when they felt frightened, alone, rejected, abandoned or unsafe in the world. Take time now to listen and understand what conclusions you, and they, have drawn as a result of these unsettling experiences. Sense how your inner child may have been carrying these wounds, alone, for many years.

You may find that images or memories come into your mind that you had completely forgotten or pushed out of your awareness. You might feel quite emotional. Offer comfort to your child in any way that feels appropriate. It may be as simple as a hug, or a commitment to listen and understand them more in the future. What is it that they want from you now? Perhaps you want to remind them of the solidity and security of your adult support that is available to them now that was missing in the past.

Take the hand of your child and walk around the beautiful gardens. Try to become more aware of the necessary 'survival' scripts that your child had written about their world, as they perceived it at that time. They may surprise and touch you deeply.

Make time also to hear and recount happy experiences and joyful memories that come from this conversation. Recall any positive scripts that these have enabled you to conclude about life.

When you feel that you have spent sufficient time remembering, recounting and reflecting, get ready to leave your castle gardens. As you say goodbye to your child appreciate that, now this connection has been made, it can never be broken again. Feel the gratitude for all you have shared and understood from each other.

As you cross back over the drawbridge and wave goodbye, you are aware that it does not close up behind you. The path across the moat now always remains passable. The sun shines directly overhead now. There is no longer any shadow cast from your castle walls.

As you come back from this powerful and meaningful journey, you may feel quite emotional. Remember to be gentle with yourself. Share with someone you trust if you can or seek the help of a therapist if you've been considering it. Be aware that a painful experience may also be stored away from any part of your earlier adult life too. The label of 'wounded inner child' is merely meant to represent a part of you that has been left behind in the pain of a past experience.

Through this kind of visualisation exercise you can begin to take full ownership of your own script. You can start to understand how, and why, you may have written it in the first place.

When you understand that you are the author of your script, you appreciate that you have attracted people into your life who have been powerless *not* to read it back to you. After all, in the great theatre of life, they are only doing their job:

> "All the world's a stage. And all the men and women merely players; they have their exits and their entrances. And one man in his time plays many parts...."

> William Shakespeare (English poet, playwright and actor)

As other 'players' try to wake us up to how we relinquish our spiritual power to negative scripts, we start to appreciate the hidden gift in the mirroring process of their accompanying 'performance'.

Once we accept that others, through this process, are merely trying to help us to know ourselves better, it becomes increasingly difficult to continue to blame them. To hold them solely accountable for our own self-esteem woes. With this insight we can liberate ourselves through the practice of forgiveness. We come to understand that only *we* have the power to choose to release others from the madness of constantly having to read our ingrained scripts. At the same time, we free ourselves from the need to remain in a helpless, victim state. (See Our Inner Victim.)

An obvious example is if we choose to stay in a destructive relationship where our partner does not treat us very well. Then we can conveniently languish in the powerless victim state saying: 'I'm stuck here, there's nothing I can do!' Until, that is, we nurture the power of our own self-love which fundamentally knows that we are worthy and deserve to be treated better. Holistically, we can later look back at this kind of relationship and be grateful to our ex-partner for acting out their part of our negative script, giving us the opportunity to reveal, and then heal, it.

As we usually have several script themes, you may find that you want to repeat the above visualisation exercise over a period of time. Each occasion may reveal further depths and elicit different script stories. Once you can get a sense of your inner child, use that mental image to continue to understand, and love, this previously repressed part of yourself.

Be aware of life experiences, recalled through this inner journeying, which may evoke anger, resentment or fear. These emotions are symbolised by the castle walls, constructed by ego to keep your inner child safe, but effectively trapped, behind their protective qualities.

To counter the negativity of our base scripts we need to face the fear in them. If it's an 'everyone abandons me' story, it might be that you need to spend more time on your own. To discover ways to be happy in your own company. To relate to yourself better.

Take a moment to think about how and when you may have abandoned yourself in the past.

How do you currently let yourself down through negative thinking or harsh self-judgement?

If it's a 'fear of being alone' script, seek out others who would benefit from having some company too. We truly experience the potency of our silent inner power when we can offer out what it is we would like to receive. Be a model of what it is you seek.

If it's a 'nobody cares about me' script, consider how you take care of yourself. Contemplate whether it feels indulgent, or selfish, to take time out for you, in whatever form that might take. How often do you just sit and read, relax in a hot bath, get a massage, meditate, pursue hobbies?

If you are resistant to any form of self-investment, where do you choose to invest yourself instead and for what ultimate purpose?

If it's an 'everyone is better than me' story, then it's time to realistically acknowledge what successes you have had in your life. Can you congratulate yourself for them?

What benefit do you personally derive from a belief that everyone is better than you?

How does this serve your default ego state?

If it's an 'I'm to blame', or 'it's all my fault' script, where are you not allowing others to take responsibility for their own lives?

Why do you feel over-responsible?

If it's an 'I have to be useful' story, can you be at peace with yourself when you spend time doing nothing or are not being productive for the benefit of others?

If it's an 'it's not safe to be who I am' script, then contemplate what parts of yourself you have difficulty in accepting.

What is your own relationship with fear?

How does it stop you reaching your potential?

I appreciate that these concepts may be simple to say and yet much more challenging to contemplate at a deeper level. Give yourself time to consider them. It is through a process of inner enquiry, of remaining curious, that we begin to acknowledge, heal and free ourselves from limiting, fear-based scripts.

As we explore how our various stories play out in our life, we typically become aware of the base script that underpins all of the others. It is the challenging given of our human condition. The one we all grapple with:

'I'm not good enough.'

This story is at the heart of the programming of our species. But what possible good can it serve? Particularly when it leads to so much negative thinking. So much self-limiting behaviour?

If we ponder again the spiritual aspiration that we are all here to discover and understand who we really are, and to realise our creative potential, perhaps this uncomfortable base script may, in some roundabout way, be helpful. What better starting block could we have to spring from, than feeling compelled to want to fill an inner sense of lack? 'I'm not good enough' could be regarded as an opportunity. A fertile space within ourselves, inviting us to complete it. To fulfill it.

Left only to its own devices, ego will simply create additional scripts that continue to define this space as an ongoing threat. A fear-inducing, unfillable chasm. Deeper self perceives it as space to grow.

But if this basic script acts as the starting pistol for the race in our 'human race', it's also important that we don't use it to shoot ourselves in the foot! The metaphorical mountain on the horizon seduces us to climb it, to conquer it. This doesn't mean that we have to constantly climb every mountain, just to keep proving our worth. This would indicate ego script at work again. The relentless, compensatory 'must try harder' and 'be perfect' drivers.

The lesson is to realise, and to acknowledge, when we are doing our best. When we have passed a milestone on our *own* journey. And to give ourselves some recognition which is free of any compulsion to compare ourselves with others.

Each time you look at your reflection in the mirror every morning, simply repeat this powerful mantra: 'I am enough'.

This form of self-acknowledgement is both self-affirming and self-resourcing. A positive inner dialogue transforms the universal base script from something that feels threatening into a launch pad for our take off.

When we start to fill the gap inside with self-love, which knows we are good *enough,* we live a free and creative life. One which becomes valuable, not just to us, but to others as well:

> "Stories are the secret reservoir of values: change the stories individuals and nations live by and tell themselves, and you change the individuals and nations."

> Ben Okri (Nigerian poet and novelist)

CHALLENGE AND STRESS

The 'I'm not good enough' primal message we all dance with through life challenges us to prove it wrong. It either tempts us into its sticky lair or provokes us into rising up.

How we relate to this dilemma acts as the blueprint for how we engage with life's struggles. Is there then a universal plan that requires us to be challenged as a species?

Charles Darwin, the English naturalist and biologist, would probably answer in the affirmative. In his theory of evolution he concluded that in a physically challenging environment we change, adapt and grow. We evolve. In a psychologically challenging environment we have the opportunity to do the same. We get to work on our spiritual growth. Our spiritual awareness.

If we are not challenged, we are less motivated. We are less likely to know what we are capable of doing. Within the package of challenge comes its close cousin. Stress. Yet stress is something we are conditioned to believe is never helpful. Never motivating.

But life is stressful. We all have physiological, psychological and emotional needs which we strive to meet to both exist and flourish. We have to negotiate obstacles and threats - which ego only perceives as stressful - because they threaten to hinder our satisfaction of those very needs.

Contemplate a life without any stress. Nice idea? Positive aspiration? The easy life? No stress or tension means we don't have to question, to look too deeply into anything, or anyone, for that matter. Consider yourself for a moment as being like a guitar string. Too little tension and you simply go twang. Too much and you eventually snap. In perfect tension you make the pure and clear note that you were designed to do.

Perhaps stress too is a necessary part of life. To realise who we really are. Life does not go as planned or as we may have dreamed of as a child. If it did, it would mean that we were largely in control of it. Able to dictate what, and how, things happen to us. It would be eminently more predictable and computable.

However, if the truth were to be told, would you really want this?

Would this not be like living in some controlled, sanitised laboratory, where the outcomes are planned and the results already known? Carry this through to a logical conclusion, life would be like knowing how a computer game works. We would use the information to 'win' the game every time. Following the easiest path and gaining the highest score. We would never be encouraged, or persuaded, to contemplate too much, to investigate further, to discover more about ourselves in the long run. Darwin might conclude that we would even stop evolving:

> "A lifetime of happiness. No man alive could bear it. It would be hell on earth...."
>
> George Bernard Shaw (Irish playwright, polemicist and political activist)

Consider again that it's not so much the stressors (that is life events or experiences), that are stressful, but our attitudes and reactions to those events which make them feel intolerable.

Does this spring from an ego need for continual sameness in life?

Most of the time, when we feel really stressed, it's because the self that ego wants us to be has been threatened or compromised.

Naturally we blame the stressor itself. The external event that led to the crescendo of intolerable stress. We blame it for revealing a deeper, perhaps vulnerable and susceptible, part of ourselves that lies beneath. A 'weak' part that we don't want the world to see.

When was the last time that your regular, unquestioned routine was broken by something, or someone, outside of your control?

Did it change your thinking, encourage you to approach something differently or serve to break your sense of attachment to an ego-desired outcome?

When stress leads us to the point where we have little option but to reveal what ego sees as our less than perfect parts, we feel like we've failed. That we've lost the stress battle.

A build up of stress indicates that our own needs have gone unnoticed, or been ignored, for too long. When we finally reveal who is behind our superhero mask, others may not approve of the loss of their selfless saviour. If they are reacting from their ego selves, they will rebel and complain. 'Where is the person who was always there for me, selflessly serving my needs?' This reaction represents a further spiritual test. Can we maintain our resolve and relinquish a role which only added undeserved pressure to our lives? (See Our Inner Rescuer.)

This stress journey was never going to be an easy one. Particularly as the old part of us seems to have to shatter and break, before a new one can emerge. Sometimes it seems to have to get a little worse before it can get better. Keep the faith. This is a necessary part of the growth cycle. The snake has to struggle to shed its old skin in order to reveal the tender new, better fitting, one underneath.

Recent scientific research indicates that when we are faced with environmental challenges, along with the traditional stress hormone cortisol, our body releases a compensatory hormone, oxytocin.

Oxytocin is sometimes called the love or cuddle hormone. It is produced when we feel connected, and in close harmony, with the world around us. The physical closeness of another cherished human being, or the stroking of a beloved pet, releases its bonding properties.

Yet connecting with others during periods of high stress goes against ego's natural programming. Life struggles which force us to adapt, to drop our false sense of self, should make us hide away in shame, in its eyes.

So instead of merely triggering the fight or flight response, moments of peak stress give us an opportunity to reach out. To tend and befriend, rather than isolate and defend, ourselves.

Consider this acronym of STRESS:

Sustained **T**ension **R**evealing **E**very **S**oul's **S**tory.

When you feel highly stressed do you normally withdraw and isolate yourself or naturally reach out to others?

If it's the former, could you reach out and tend yourself by sharing some of your 'soul story', rather than isolate and defend yourself?

Depending on our perception, stress can be seen as anything from a gentle breeze which ruffles our feathers to a ferocious hurricane which appears to destroy everything which is familiar to us. It is not until we can muster the courage to bravely turn and open our wings to its message, that we can ever give ourselves the chance to to ascend upon its breeze:

> "Not everything that is faced can be changed, but nothing can be changed until it is faced."
>
> James Baldwin (American novelist, playwright and activist)

Stress teaches us that we do not, and cannot, know how the 'computer game' of life works. If we did, we would already know what there is to know. Existence would not be the potentially great voyage of discovery that it is. It would be a mundane repetition of predictable, familiar, well-trodden pathways.

What I have outlined up to now is an ideal response to the stimulus of stress. But sometimes the stress is just too much, too sudden. The task of navigating a way through can sometimes seem impossible.

When our stress levels are rising we frequently fall back into established ego-centred coping mechanisms. Many of these coping mechanisms take root from the superhero type ego state. If we can just stay strong enough for long enough then we will, somehow, get through.

Unhealthy coping strategies include addictive, compulsive and obsessive type behaviours. All of these represent an attempt to deny, manipulate or control the painful stressor. To silence the internal call to change that it is trying to evoke.

Where we get lost in coping, in avoiding, we block our intuitive feeling self. When we stop feeling, we start filling. We fill our lives with a preoccupation that something, or someone, 'out there' can soothe the stressful pain that we harbour.

ADDICTIVE AND COMPULSIVE BEHAVIOURS

Every one of us has had, at some point in our lives, some attachment to an addictive behaviour. An unhelpful coping strategy. When stress builds, or something around us suddenly changes, we naturally rely on these to maintain our old, familiar, sense of self. Many coping mechanisms we develop early as children or adolescents. Because we see that they have 'worked' for us before, we can become very resistant to letting them go.

In many cultures, coping mechanisms are seen to be a positive attribute. They are the vital shields we must carry to protect ourselves out on the great battlefield of life. When we see a friend going through a stressful time we typically ask: 'How are you coping?'

We immediately focus on the strength and viability of someone's defences. And less on how they are responding and adapting to any sudden change in circumstance.

Consider the question: 'How are you responding to the stress?'

This enquiry allows more space for a deeper contemplation of the inner change that may be occurring, or that needs to occur, for someone.

Try asking this next time you want to know how someone is 'coping'. See if it elicits a different response.

In a culture where there is less emphasis, and value, placed on where we can adapt to change, and more focus placed on how we can defend ourselves against it, it is clear where our societal priorities lie. It is of little wonder then that when rising stress is reshaping our personal landscapes, ego will do its utmost to appear to remain in control. Even if that involves only an *illusion* of control.

When ego senses that old coping mechanisms are no longer working, it will compensate by over-controlling some other aspect of our life. It tries to achieve this by:

- ❏ constantly repeating something
- ❏ overthinking
- ❏ becoming rigidly attached to an external 'solution'
- ❏ being addicted to a substance that changes our perceptions
- ❏ becoming obsessed with a particular task or ritual

When you are under a lot of stress be curious how, and when, ego tries to protect you. Typically, it busies our mind with everyday earthly matters. Perhaps constantly going over the same things or compelling us to check a to-do list. By keeping our conscious mind occupied, full of trivia, the painful stressor is kept at bay.

On hearing shocking or unsettling news we have all, no doubt, reacted in a way which seems to obsess with keeping busy. With doing. Especially when the thought of sitting with a new reality is just too overwhelming.

When the stress is acute, it is easy to see how an in the moment obsessive reaction can lead to a longer term over-reliance. The ego thought form which tells us that, with sufficient repetition or obsessive behaviour, we may somehow be able to regain some control back that we feel has been lost. These coping behaviours may culminate into what is commonly referred to as obsessive-compulsive disorders (OCD).

This condition develops out of, what was, a natural ego reaction. But this initially measured response sometimes goes out of balance and becomes a compulsion to complete specific obsessive type rituals. List writing, cleaning, counting, hand washing, checking and so on.

Eating disorders too fall within this category. They represent an emotional wound rooted from an inability to control what was happening to us. Maybe as a result of the behaviours of manipulative people, particularly anyone who abused their power over us.

An example might be a domineering, or emotionally suffocating, parent or caregiver. Possibly they did not allow us enough personal space to take appropriate responsibility for our own safety and security. Always trying to convince us that they knew what was 'best'.

Or we may have been brought up in a relatively predictable and secure environment which was unexpectedly shattered due to a parental divorce or death. Representing a sudden loss of personal safety and security.

Through a use of OCD type behaviours or ritualistic eating patterns, ego is actually trying to achieve something constructive. It is seeking to gain back a modicum of personal control which a life trauma has seemingly taken away.

The default obsessing tendency of ego plays out within all of us throughout life:

Remember as children when we avoided walking on the cracks in the pavements? We bargained with ourselves that to do so may bring us bad luck.

Or as adults, when we cannot relax in a room where there is a picture on the wall which is not level. Our minds craving a certain symmetry and order.

All of these types of self-talk and indoctrinating thoughts indicate how ego likes to think it has some mastery and influence in the world. A world which, fortunately or not, has its own higher order agenda. Obsessiveness is ego's way of attempting to rebel against this, seemingly intolerable, universal reality. The degree to which we seek *unnecessary* order indicates how much ego is keeping us in order. In control.

When OCD type behaviours take hold as a coping mechanism, our faith in whatever we are doing is thrown out of a healthy balance. Ego attempts to rescue us from facing historic pain by diverting our attention into avoidant, obsessive thinking acted out through repetitive tasks. Many of these compulsive rituals are therefore undertaken in an absence of full aware presence of mind.

Without a fully present and calm mind, when we carry out a task, we are later not sure if we have done it thoroughly and completely. And how can we, when our mind doesn't feel complete? Half of its thinking capability is being suppressed.

So we will go back and either check, or complete, the task again. Our mind is effectively divided between past trauma and present reality. No wonder we have difficulty trusting ourselves to be fully competent in whatever we are doing.

As such, we have all completed everyday tasks with only half our mind on the matter. Locking the front door, checking the taps are off or unplugging the iron.

The principal symptom of an OCD type behaviour is that, even when the task is repeated, there is no clear and obvious closure. There is something in our past, or coming up in our future, that we have not fully reconciled with. Something that is still stressing us out. Calling for some of our present moment attention.

Use the challenge in the following quote to help to reframe the relationship you currently have with your thoughts. Be curious about your own automatic thinking process tendency:

"Thoughts are only thoughts. They are not you. You do belong to yourself, even when your thoughts don't."

John Green (American author)

See if you can sense your continuing, fully aware, calm presence behind any obsessive or unproductive thought.

Joe's Story

Joe had suffered for many years with OCD behaviours. Despite being on anxiety medication, his condition was now affecting his personal relationship. He had run a successful furniture business with his husband for many years and some of the 'positive' traits of his OCD - extreme thoroughness and meticulous standards - had helped their business to thrive.

However, now Joe wanted to work less and spend more time travelling, enjoying the fruits of his labours. As he reduced his working hours, frustratingly, he found his OCD tendencies became increasingly unmanageable.

The more Joe described the sort of person he was, the more it occurred to me how responsible he felt for everyone else but himself. His husband had a physical disability. And there were many of his employees who, quite naturally, relied on him when difficulties arose in the business.

We spent time recounting his early family life. Joe described his mother as being very loving and supporting. While his father was much stricter and, in his words, a 'workaholic'.

Joe continually referred to his childhood as being 'idyllic'. Nothing but positive memories. Yet, this rigidly held, rose-tinted vision seemed to restrict him from acknowledging the true difficulties that he had faced growing up.

As the therapy progressed, Joe started to sense an uncomfortable rage towards his father. He had great difficulty in expressing this initially. It became clear that the repression of these challenging feelings was affecting his healthy, complete functioning as an adult.

Whilst Joe described his mother as loving him unconditionally, he admitted that he could never quite win the love and approval that he craved from his father. He felt he still really needed this. Only then could he allow himself to say that he had made a 'success' of his life.

Joe's father was frequently absent from the family home, working long hours and some weekends. So Joe invested more into the relationship with his mother. In his own words, he said that he felt guilty that his father was not available enough for his mother. He did his best to compensate by being both a son, and 'partner', to her.

The script that Joe wrote for himself growing up seemed to say: 'I have to be more than who I am.' As he matured, this manifested as a feeling of over-responsibility for those close to him. Particularly in terms of ensuring their safety, security and happiness.

Many around Joe, including his disabled partner, interpreted this as a form of selfless love. Sadly, because of his perception of his childhood experiences, this selfless love for others became the only measure by which Joe felt he could value himself.

But the stress that Joe's ego script was having on him proved unsustainable. The impulse driving his OCD became: 'I need to check everything is safe and secure around me and my loved ones. If anything bad happens to them, it's my fault!'

Because Joe had never really understood how, why, or when his compensatory ego script had been written, he was helpless to stop his obsessive checking. He had always assumed that, in order to be free of his OCD, he must defeat his repetitive thoughts and gain back control of his mind. Yet, through an understanding of why his ego had created this particular coping mechanism in the first place, he was able to see that it was doing its best to 'help' him.

Joe saw that trying to fight against his OCD only served to fuel the stress of his already obsessive thinking. Once he understood that his compulsiveness was borne out of love and concern for others, the negativity he bore towards it waned. He reframed his OCD and personified it more as a friend, rather than an enemy. This appeared to lift him out of a constant round of pointless inner conflict.

Joe devised his own, more constructive, ritual. He contracted with himself to look deep into his eyes in the mirror everyday and to simply say, 'I am enough'. Over time, he realised that it was okay for him to be 'just' a son to his mother and a partner to his husband.

With a greater sense of self-regard and tenderness, Joe released a guilt that his ego had taken on as his own. The guilt that rightly belonged at the feet of his father. It was him, not Joe, that put the needs of his career before those of his family.

By constructively channelling the emotional stress in his system, and reconciling with the residual anger towards his father, Joe's OCD became more manageable. His perception of it, and attitude towards it, changed. Its extremes were brought back under control. Back into balance. He admitted that he even developed some gratitude towards it for playing a part in helping him to become a successful businessman.

◆ ◆ ◆

Ego finds it easier to live in any moment other than the present one. It wants us to remain engaged in ruminating about events from the past or worrying about, as yet unknown, fantasies of the future. This is how it believes it maintains control.

When we are fully present in the present, or as fully present as we can be, there is less space for obsessive ego thinking. In each timeless moment we are effectively freer to observe, and absorb, the reality of our surroundings. More able to trust what we are seeing and doing. And less likely to need to constantly check what we have done:

> "The moment one gives close attention to anything, even a blade of grass, it becomes a mysterious, awesome, indescribably magnificent world in itself."
>
> Henry Miller (American writer and philosopher)

What habitual or compulsive behaviours do you use at times of heightened stress, to try to regain a sense of control that you feel has been lost?

What is it about your ability to be fully aware and present that your ego does not let you trust in at these times?

Think about ways you can soothe the stress of your insecure ego. What does it need in order to join you in full and present awareness? Your compassion? Your understanding?

MANIPULATIVE BEHAVIOURS

Unlike compulsive behaviours, which attempt to regain some sort of internal self-control, manipulative behaviours are designed to control what's on the outside. They are a projection of the obsessive nature of ego mind onto those around us.

Here, instead of obsessively controlling our world internally, we manipulate people externally. We want them to dance to our tune. To an agenda that we believe to be the best. We get to witness a sense of our own superficial power, seeing how others respond as we yield it. Can we get them to do what we want, so that we can then feel good about ourselves? (See Personal Power.)

Manipulative behaviours take on a variety of different genres, some obvious, others less so. The more common ones include:

- ❑ exaggerated displays of neediness
- ❑ overt flirtation
- ❑ controlling passive/aggressive tendencies
- ❑ attempting to intimidate/dominate
- ❑ feigning illness for sympathy or attention
- ❑ constantly criticising or persecuting
- ❑ gaslighting

Gaslighting is any underhand tactic that we use to get another person to question their own reality. Or, at the very least, their perception of reality.

Gaslighters may try to convince someone that something was their fault, when they know that it was they who were responsible. Or they swear blind to their partner that they said or did something in the past, which they know full well they did not.

The term was taken from the 1944 movie, 'Gaslight'. The plot centres around a man who manipulates and convinces his wife to the point where she thinks she is going mad.

Have you ever felt that you have been on the receiving end of someone's gaslighting or other manipulative behaviour? If so reflect on the following:

> "Sometimes people try to expose what's wrong with you because they can't handle what's right about you."
>
> Author unknown

Does this insight help you to forgive, and so release, a manipulator from your past?

Manipulative behaviours act like the conductor of an orchestra. We use them to get others to respond in specific ways and to put them into specific positions. The 'harmony' we create is music to our egoic ears. Although slightly insidious, we all employ these types of behaviours. Sometimes covertly, sometimes not.

No matter to what extent, think about how you may have used any of the above listed behaviours in the past to influence how others respond to you.

Many of us would have readily done so as children. Perhaps blaming our sibling for something we did or wildly exaggerating how much something hurt.

Can you recall what it was you were really trying to achieve at the time?

These behaviours are nothing more than coping mechanisms we use to try to control a world which does not respond in a way that we would like it to. In a way which allows us to feel as though we have some modicum of control over it.

Take a moment to consider the following:

If I consistently rely on employing manipulative behaviours, I simply reinforce my internal script message which says, 'I'm not okay'.

If I continue to believe this script, then I will attempt to control others as a way of feeling more superficially powerful. And to prevent them from seeing that it is me, actually, who feels less than okay.

Many clients coming into therapy initially spend a lot of time wondering why their partners behave in certain ways toward them. And whether this means that they really love them or not. A lot of ego fear is invested in the incessant worry: 'If only he, or she, were to act in this way or that way, *then* I would be convinced of their love for me.'

The ego insecurity rooted in this classic love dilemma frequently shifts us into adopting manipulative behaviours. The panic that someone may not love us as we want drives us to try anything to get the attention that we need to feel okay.

From the secure base of our deeper self we need to decide whether a relationship, be that a lover or a friend, reflects the respect and worth that we feel we deserve. If we personally think that we don't deserve that much, we are more likely to try to persuade others to prove us wrong. In truth, we want others to do the work of showing us the love that we feel unable to show ourselves.

Much of the influence of advertising and media in our society relies on subtle manipulation. It persuades, hypnotises and cajoles us into believing their messages or buying their products. It is not surprising that we readily resort to these techniques to meet our own insecure needs. They have become a normalised, and acceptable, societal method of covert control.

As babies and young children too, we witnessed the felt benefits of being able to manipulate our environments. By turning on the tears to smiling sweetly and innocently, we win mummy's or daddy's attention and sympathy. We quickly learn how to play our parental figures like a drum. Back then it seemed vital for our survival.

But when we over rely on these infantile manipulatory techniques as adults, we risk developing some rather challenging character traits.

Consider what is your 'go to' trait when others are not doing what you think is right, adequate or paying you enough attention?

- ❑ *Narcissism*
- ❑ *Victimhood*
- ❑ *Dominating*
- ❑ *Criticising*
- ❑ *Undermining*
- ❑ *Sexually manipulative*
- ❑ *Conceitedness*
- ❑ *Rebelliousness*

Could you instead risk sharing truer feelings of vulnerability that these traits are attempting to mask? (See Vulnerability and Shame.)

When we become obsessed with manipulating others' responses or emotional states, we act like the director of a theatrical play. We attempt to put everybody in a place where we can see, assess and direct them. We hope that this gives them little opportunity to see around the false, ultimately insecure, character that we are portraying. And the truth that we really don't feel 'okay' about ourselves.

ADDICTION TO THINGS

Whether it's shopping, food, money, work, sex, gambling, exercise, video games, hoarding, social media, eating, alcohol, smoking or some other form of drug we are all, at some point, addicted. It's part of our ego-obsessive nature. It's part of our complex, diversionary journey on the road to fulfilment. It's a road that we all tread. Sometimes thinking it's the only road. Other times realising it's not.

Our habit, addiction or craving brings us pleasure. If it didn't why would we do it? We know that it's probably not doing us much good, that things may be out of balance. But it gives us a high. A relief. For a while, at least, we don't have to face the meaninglessness, the emptiness, the pain.

We are conditioned to need to need. When we sense an inner void of pain, we look for something to fill it. When we think we have found it, we hope this thing will prove to be the answer to our dilemmas. Naturally, we place our fragile trust in it.

This external thing, or substance, often becomes personified. A 'good friend'. One who is there for us when we're hurting. When we're in need. A good friend won't let us down like others have in the past. They become a source of fascination. Of hope and security.

Yet how do we really know that we are under the spell of addiction? Ask yourself:

When I have as much of something that I physiologically or psychologically need, do I still find myself wanting more?

Think of all the things you accumulate, over and above that which you actually need, for your day to day living.

Clothes, food, money and other material possessions are everyday examples.

Does the acquisition, or consumption, of all these things give you what you really want?

When life is difficult to bear, or we feel like the rug has been pulled from under us, most of us instinctively reach out. We run our story by someone, a friend, a partner, a family member, perhaps a therapist. We need to talk about it, to share it with someone who can be solid for us; emotionally available, empathic.

Sometimes that someone is not immediately present. Or maybe they are part of our pain and so wouldn't understand anyway. When ego feels dominant it pipes up and tells us to be strong. To deal with it on our own. This makes it even harder to authentically relate to another. We go within, suffer and anaesthetise.

There is a psychological theory that says that we only feel we really exist when in relationship with someone, or something, else. So we all need to connect to know ourselves, to feel alive. When human connection feels scary or impossible, we transfer that same need onto an object. A substance or a habit. The substitute friend.

As I discussed in 'Sadness', the recognition of pain in another is one of the most powerful ways that we can feel commonly connected and empathically attuned. But when we attempt to suppress, or push down, pain through addiction, we sabotage our principle method of feeling at one. Of relating authentically to someone, rather than to something.

When these things happen to be alcohol or drugs, there

is a perceived benefit of an artificially-induced connection. Through their consumption uplifting emotions can become more accessible. We feel an affinity and a safety not so easily attainable when sober. Alcohol particularly helps us to calm any social anxiety nervousness. It gives us courage and reduces everyday inhibition.

Many recreational drugs too have the capacity to induce altered states of consciousness. They create auras of security and euphoria allowing us to be more open, and apparently authentic, whilst under their influence.

Many with a strong propensity to be addicted to substances have experienced mistrust, betrayal or disruption in early formative relationships. This makes maintaining a faith in the security of adult relationships all the more challenging. Who is really there for me? Who can I really trust?

Ironically, these people are often the most sensitive and empathic people you could ever wish to meet. Because of the need to source secure attachment that eluded them as youngsters, defence mechanisms are less well developed and employed. They provide less protection from the ravages of the adult emotional world. Hence there is a heightened sensitivity, an openness, an innocent vulnerability. Pain is harder to deal with. And deep feelings evoked through relationships frequently overwhelming.

Alcohol and drugs can offer a sense of safety, of refuge, when trying to survive in an unpredictable world. When ego remains in control we assume they provide the only doorway to the trusted security that we seek. We falsely believe that by relating *only* to this metaphorical doorway, rather than in what lies beyond it, we may eventually find the love that we need. The love that will enable us to love ourselves.

The rigid ego alone cannot see that this doorway is merely a means to an end. The 'end' being a more constructive way of relating. Of being and connecting to the world. One that is free of the need of intoxicating substances, habits or diversions.

When we are in the throws of addiction we tell ourselves that it will provide us with a way out. A way out, albeit temporarily, from the pain of isolation. From some unresolved emotional wound. From the loss of self orientation. We hand it the same responsibility that we would a compass when we are lost in the wilderness.

Anything we perceive as having the 'answer' we will naively continue to invest in. Relinquishing more and more of our power to it. Until, one day, we wake up and realise that we feel powerless over it.

It is the very act of surrendering to our sense of powerlessness, through the ascension from the futility of the battle, that finally breaks ego's unquestioned obsession with addictive habit. That's hard when its plan for easing our suffering has somehow got us through in the past. Helped us to survive the emotional ravages of youthful pain and insecurity.

Yet it is not until we can grow through ego's power that we can ever hope to tap our true power. The silent inner power which ego cannot trust. Let alone trust to deliver us from our pain by transmuting it, and us, into a higher state of spiritual awareness. (See Surrender.)

Our deeper self knows that it is only through an *authentic* relating with the world that we can facilitate a pathway to our spiritual core. It knows that it is what is on the other side of the doorway of addiction that is the real goal. And that there are other ways to get there.

The allure and confusion of intoxicating substances, and of psychological diversions, is that they also create a similar, temporary sense of liberation that the surrendering to our deeper self brings. That is why the journey through addiction is fraught with confusion and relapse. We grab this off-the-shelf compass we think is going to help, probably many times, before finally relinquishing our trust to our spiritual homing device that lies within. That was always lying within.

Unless we understand *what* our addiction is trying to achieve, and trust that there is a non egoic path to it, then it can destroy us. This is perhaps the greatest tragedy. The very coping mechanism ego employs to deal with the pain only creates more pain and suffering in the longer term. A classic case of the cure being worse than the cause.

What do you use to quell your psychological pain?

Maybe you have used alcohol or other drugs.

Or spend endless hours on social media, shopping, gambling, exercising, making more money, playing computer games, sex?

Whatever it is, be mindful how you use external stimulants. Be curious as to how easy it is to become addicted.

What is it you are trying to escape through their overuse?

Becoming curious about where, when and how we are addicted enables us to be more honest with ourselves. When we open a space for internal honesty we can be more real with others. And begin to build more authenticity into the relationships we have with others. Facilitators of alcoholics anonymous support groups know that the new participant is not ready to navigate their healing path until they can say: 'Hello, I'm Jackie/John and I'm an alcoholic.'

To heal we have to be able to get to know, to relate to, ourselves and our pain soberly. Without continuing to succumb to the allure and illusion of the false gods within earthly distraction and substance.

Too often people regarded as addicts are marginalised. Too quickly assumed to be weak and powerless. What they, we, actually need is to be understood. Loved. Accepted for the journey that they are on. The journey that we are all on. Even if we all have different ways of getting there:

> "You have succeeded in life when all you really want is only what you really need."

Vernon Howard (American spiritual teacher, author and philosopher)

BLAME

Trapped in an addictive cycle we feel powerless. Ego wants to hand over responsibility for this loss to something outside. It wants to blame.

Blaming is easy. Convenient. It easily becomes addictive because it gives us a sense of our righteousness. By default, when we are right the rest of the world has to be wrong. Of course ego is the perfect preset righteous part of us because it represents our unexamined mind. Our automatic, unquestioned thinking. If we only question others, and never ourselves, of course we get caught up in blame. It's as alluring and escaping as any drug.

When we are victim to, and caught in the throes of, an addiction we more readily blame other things, or other people, for our fate. Our parents, our ex-partner, our unjust employer. We so easily find ourselves in an ever decreasing circle that gives away the very power we need to heal. The addiction becomes entrenched as we lose our way.

Blame comes from the root of the word blaspheme. In the general religious sense, to blaspheme means to commit a sin. To blame a god or a deity for one's predicament. If things go wrong, or not as expected, then it is God's fault!

Looking back at the original definition of the word sin, it actually meant being absent. 'Without.' Not present or unconscious. It is curious that the meaning of sin is interpreted by particular Christian traditions as being a wilful wrongdoing.

The original meaning implies far less judgement or ridicule than the, now more commonly understood, religious one. It accepts that any assumed perpetrator of the sin was not fully present, or spiritually unconscious, when a given act was committed.

Step outside of the indoctrination of religious definition then and we sin when we assume little responsibility for our own actions or feelings. When we are effectively in a state of 'unconsciousness'.

That is not to imply that every time we do something unsavoury, hurtful or thoughtless, we can use the excuse of simply being unconscious. It is merely an indication that we are operating from an egocentric perspective. From a spiritually blind state.

It is ego that lives by fear and wanting. And it is these qualities which have the potential to cause the most hurt and destruction when the compensatory spiritual qualities of oneness and connectedness are absent.

The deeper self does not see separation or incompleteness. It is the source of our unencumbered, whole joint consciousness. It is therefore theoretically impossible to sin or blame when we operate from this place within us. From a place of being conscious of how we choose to perceive experience. Of being open to the higher reason we may be having that experience.

Before religious indoctrination took hold the disregard of our potential for spiritual insight was what was regarded as sinful. The term reminded us that we were still in the grip of blind ego. That we had missed the point of what an experience was trying to show us about the source of our true power. Not that we had necessarily committed any cardinal wrongdoing.

How many times have you witnessed others blaming everybody else for their 'stuckness?' Perhaps this someone else is sometimes you?

There must be the occasional ego advantage in giving away our power. Otherwise why would we do it? Ego can be quite self defeating at times. Quite masochistic even. It's happy to reap the 'benefits' of appearing helpless and irresponsible.

Do you sometimes seek sympathy by appearing powerless through blame?

Does remaining powerless enable you to stay in an angry, fearful or frustrated state?

Does this state keep you stuck in a repeating blame cycle?

There are a multitude of paths to follow to become more conscious. More enlightened. More full of 'light' energy. One way Buddhist philosophy defines enlightenment is aspiring to be *personally* responsible for how we are feeling. A tough spiritual test indeed.

As we work on not relinquishing this responsibility through blame, we see more of how we are creating circumstances which keep us unhappy. By blaming the outside less, we empower ourselves to decide how we *want* to feel. By choosing *how* we perceive life and its experiences.

Recall a life experience which you find hard to move on from or to let go of. Is it because you still harbour a good deal of blame towards somebody?

Try to assess what you know about yourself now, that you didn't know before this particular experience happened. What changed in terms of your self-awareness?

Does this new self-knowledge make it any easier to let the blame go?

It is important to be aware of the difference between taking a greater responsibility for how we are feeling, versus actually blaming ourselves. If we always blame ourselves we are likely to feel, and so remain, full of 'sin'. Unable, or unwilling, to forgive ourselves. Without self-forgiveness we root ourselves in our past and inhibit our full aliveness in the present. We remain semi-conscious. The original meaning of sin.

In a situation where we continue to blame ourselves, we sin against both ourselves and others. Where we cannot help but look to others to do the work of our own forgiveness, we give away the very power we need to achieve it.

Alison's Story

Alison came into therapy burdened by guilt. She continued to blame herself for her son's drinking problem.

My client admitted to never really being happily married. She initiated a divorce from her husband when her son, Matthew, was 12 years old. She felt that the pain that this had inflicted on her son had caused him to start drinking heavily in his late teens. Acting on her own needs meant that her son suffered.

As a devoted mother, Alison loved and cherished Matthew. She convinced herself that her lack of love for her ex-husband drove her to commit what she called a 'selfish act'. Now she deserved to be punished for not being able to stay married to him.

Alison tried to atone for this by being as selflessly supportive and loving to her son as she could. Yet their relationship remained difficult. Whenever she tried to reach out her love was rebuffed by him. Then, whenever she took a step back, he wanted her to be closer. Alison was caught in a strange dance of compensatory love and repressed self-blame. Blame that she did not know how to escape from.

Through the therapy Alison became aware of an unconscious agenda that had been playing out in the relationship with her son. She secretly desired forgiveness from Matthew. Only then could she forgive herself for the pain that she felt she had caused.

All the time the power for this forgiveness was being sought unconsciously, Alison's shadow side remained enmeshed with Matthew's. He couldn't actually give his mother what she needed. The ability to be able to forgive herself. No wonder he was at a loss as to how to act.

Much of the rest of Alison's therapy focussed on how much she honoured and valued her own needs. She realised that for her to live her life inauthentically was ultimately unfair. Not just to herself, but also to her son and her ex-husband. The short term pain she caused was necessary, she concluded. It was a necessary part of her journey to being free of self-blame and more aware of where she had historically 'sinned' against herself.

Are you waiting for someone else to grant you forgiveness for some assumed historic misdemeanour?

If they were to offer it to you now, would you then be in the position that you want to be?

And what happens when we continue to blame fate for our less than favourable personal circumstances? The short answer - anger. This kind of blame permits us to remain angry at life, at God, the Universe or whatever other personification we choose to give to fate. 'Why is life always so unfair', we hear ourselves shout.

The problem is that residual anger freezes us, closes us down, puts us into defensive mode. It is, of course, a natural initial reaction to an event which seems unfair and an important part of our emotional repertoire. Yet many of us take refuge in this place. It offers a veiled protection from further hurt.

Continuing to hold a strong emotional anger energy provides us with a superficial sense of power. Ego persuades us that it is *only* through this form of emotional energy that we can remain powerful enough to survive. To stop further 'bad' things from happening to us. It's no wonder that it regards blame as a useful weapon in its protective armoury. (See Anger.)

Do you feel that there is a strong connection between anger and blame?

What happens to your anger when you continually blame?

Who, or what, do you normally blame when you are angry?

By having an awareness of the power of our perception, of viewing events as teachers rather than takers, we can put the energy lost in the cycle of anger and blame to more constructive use. We wake up to the 'response-ability' hidden in responsibility. We can 're-greet' with spiritual insight rather than merely regret from ego. We stop investing in the power of others and start trusting in our own:

> "Take your life in your own hands, and what happens? A terrible thing: no one to blame."

> Erica Jong (American novelist, satirist and poet)

BELIEFS

Healing and growth require change. Change in how we see and define ourselves. Change in how we see and define others. Ego's job is to maintain an established and familiar world view. To ensure a semblance of control and predictability.

Ego learns that by *proactively* assessing events, experiences and people as either good or bad, pleasurable or unpleasurable, desirable or undesirable, it can continue to maintain this familiar world view. One in which it's easier to prejudge, presume and then assume.

If someone offers you a different perspective, or new way of looking at something, how open are you to at least considering it?

When we quickly judge things as either good or bad we cannot help but assign an assumed meaning. A quick superficial interpretation of what something means to us, and our world, as we have decided to see it.

As we do so we develop a set of beliefs. If things *appear* good we will ascribe them a more positive, affirming belief. If they *appear* bad we will offer up a more negative, perhaps even fearful, one.

As a simple example, one belief might be that sugar is good for because it makes you feel satisfied, gives you a burst of energy and tastes good.

Another equally valid belief is that sugar is bad for you, because it increases your weight and rots your teeth. So which one is the right belief?

Of course, it depends on how you see it, from which perspective. On whether you value your taste buds or your teeth. Our beliefs offer us an insight into our valuing system. A clue as to the value we place on what things.

If our valuing system says that our own in-the-moment satisfaction and energy levels are more important than our longer-term health, then we are likely to eat more chocolate bars than carrot sticks. But again, both beliefs are valid as they both contain their own relative truths.

Beliefs are really nothing more than emotionally charged thoughts. Emotionally charged because they are made up of a passionately held mental model of what the world should look like. And of how we should be within it.

Recalling the concept of emotions being energy-in-motion, they can act as the fuel which spark us into action. Emotionally charged thoughts give us determination and stamina at best. Stubbornness and dogma at worst. Being passionate forms of thought, beliefs can define us rigidly, enslaving us to their diktat. Or they can serve us. It all depends on how doggedly we attach to the thought forms. To ego. To our unexamined mind.

To become more aware of how your fundamental beliefs are formed, consider what your intrinsic values are. Take a few moments to reflect on the following statements. Try to establish which ones are currently the most important for you:

1. *My personal survival is more important than anything.*
2. *Assisting the survival of my tribe (or family) is more important than anything.*
3. *My immediate gratification (or pleasure) is more important than anything.*
4. *Maintaining the establishment (e.g. religion, govern-*

ment, family structure) is more important than anything.

5. *My success is more important than anything (not necessarily materially but achieving life goals).*
6. *Supporting my/the community is more important than anything.*
7. *My development/awareness is more important than anything.*
8. *Saving the planet (or humanity) from destruction is more important than anything.*

Although this list may appear haphazard, there is a natural evolutionary sequence to the various values. The ones lower down on the list (numbered 1-5) are more ego-based. That is, they lean toward an establishment in which ego can continue to thrive. They play an important part of our early development and burgeoning sense of self.

Numbers 6-8 are more altruistic in tone. They could be described as instinctive aspirations of our deeper self. They are more concerned with inclusiveness and service to others and society. With joint evolution.

However, the values which are important to us may change, even on a daily basis. Depending on whether we feel positively or negatively about the world. And depending on how we see ourselves as being an intrinsic part of it.

Pick one or two of the sentences from the list which currently seem relevant for you. Take a moment to think about how that helps to form your present belief system about life. About meaning. About purpose.

For example, if number 3 is currently relevant for you, then you might have formulated a belief that says: 'The world is about meeting my needs.'

If number 6 stands out then your overriding belief might be:

'It is important for me to make a positive difference to the lives of others.'

As we become more aware of how ego operates, and begin to take our power back from it, we will naturally move up the list to greater, more inclusive, values. We believe that our beliefs form our values. However what we value, what is true for us in this life, forms, and continues to influence, our beliefs.

Contemplate whether your beliefs today are the same as they were, say, ten years ago.

Have your values also evolved over that time?

Sadly, many get stuck in the earlier stages of this valuing system. Not necessarily because they are happy to be selfish or self-serving, but because they have not yet become aware of how their unchecked ego has *predetermined* which life values are the most important:

"It is done unto you as you believe."

Jesus Christ in The New Testament

The original founder of Transpersonal Psychotherapy, psychologist Abraham Maslow, proposed that we have a 'hierarchy of needs'. He formulated a model that he used to summarise the origins of human motivation in his 1943 paper entitled, 'A Theory of Human Motivation':

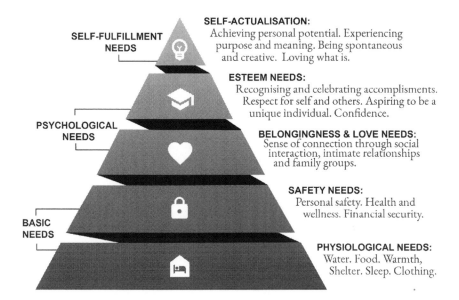

SELF-FULFILLMENT NEEDS

SELF-ACTUALISATION:
Achieving personal potential. Experiencing purpose and meaning. Being spontaneous and creative. Loving what is.

ESTEEM NEEDS:
Recognising and celebrating accomplisments. Respect for self and others. Aspiring to be a unique individual. Confidence.

PSYCHOLOGICAL NEEDS

BELONGINGNESS & LOVE NEEDS:
Sense of connection through social interaction, intimate relationships and family groups.

SAFETY NEEDS:
Personal safety. Health and wellness. Financial security.

BASIC NEEDS

PHYSIOLOGICAL NEEDS:
Water. Food. Warmth, Shelter. Sleep. Clothing.

You can see that the lower levels of this hierarchy are the basic human physiological requirements for physical survival: food, water, shelter and rest. These everyday necessities need to be in place first, as Maslow describes, for us to be able to nurture our higher needs: psychological well-being and a sense of belonging and love. In turn, these provide the platform to build a healthy sense of self and self-esteem.

The upper level of Maslow's hierarchy refers to 'self-actualisation'. The aspirational state of having an unconditional acceptance of self and others. This describes the point before a sense of self transcendence, of being enlightened as the Buddhists might say. A place free of ego, of suffering, of attachment to physical form, of the human drama.

This hierarchy of needs reflects much of the aspirational journey, and deeper message, of this book. It also similarly parallels the list of ascending values (1-8) as outlined above.

Referring to this model, what level of need are you currently trying to meet in your life?

Reflect on what levels your ego first draws you to.

An ego-centred approach to life convinces us that our belief system is the only one that will make our world better. When acting alone it creates division. Less unification and cooperation. A consequence of the false belief that we are separate from everything, and everybody, else in the world.

Our beliefs become entrenched when they act as a psychological refuge. When they provide a prescriptive safety, security, identity and predictability. Taking refuge among others with similar beliefs affirms us in our attachments to our own. Here they conveniently escape enquiry from others with different perspectives.

We are meaning-seeking, but superficially lazy, creatures. When we ally with ready made religious, political or cultural belief systems, we don't have to think too deeply. These kinds of doctrines present a seemingly sorted and complete, ready-to-go package. A prescribed formula for making immediate sense out of an, outwardly confusing, world.

By blindly following these doctrines, ego escapes the work of questioning what parts of a laid-down belief system actually reflect who we are at a deeper level. At the same time, it profits from the apparent advantages, safety and security of identifying and belonging. Literally swallowing whole the antiquated and established givens of a group belief.

So often in the allure of political and religious doctrine the individuality of each member is lost, as they identify solely with group identity. Under the spell of primal joint belief, individuals may do things they would never normally consider doing alone. The confluence of the Nazi regime, mob rule or mass riots, are obvious and dramatic examples of this.

Sadly, a dogmatic group belief system serves nothing more than to relinquish us from the individual responsibility of finding *personal* meaning in, and from, life.

Do you feel that your entrenched beliefs always serve you?

Do they keep your mind open or closed?

How 'alive' is a closed mind?

The deeper self wants to question, to make something its own, to evolve through wondering. Both within, and outside, the context of differing belief systems.

It is only through questioning, and digesting, that we can hope to unveil our individuality. Our spiritual values. Our unique calling.

Do you consider yourself a 'free thinker?' To what degree are you:

- ❏ *able to have a high degree of independence from others*
- ❏ *self-directing*
- ❏ *self-responsible*
- ❏ *non-conformist*
- ❏ *able to show flexibility in the face of change*
- ❏ *not worried about what others think*

All these characteristics describe the self-actualising stage of Maslow's hierarchy of needs.

In order to know up we have to know down. To appreciate warmth we need to feel cold. To recognise black we have to see white. We only really know ourselves when we place ourselves within a context of difference. Being amongst those far divorced from our own tribe is a great way to understand what it is about others which stimulates new thinking in ourselves. By exposing ourselves to difference, and standing out from our own crowd, we fan the flame of our self actualisation.

We are born to naturally change and grow; belief systems not so readily. It is ironic that the word 'lie' is literally hidden within the word be**lie**f.

When beliefs are more informing than defining. When we can observe rather than submerge. When we chew over rather than swallow whole, our beliefs move from masters to servants of who we are. And who we wish to become:

> "If you don't change your beliefs, your life will be like this forever. Is that good news?"

> W. Somerset Maugham (British playwright and novelist)

VULNERABILITY AND SHAME

Step away from group belief. Step out of what we have always believed about ourselves and we risk exposure. Ridicule. Rejection. Yet in that scary space, just outside the confines of our comfort zone, lies opportunity. Our greatest source of spontaneity and creativity. Our vulnerability.

Vulnerability gets a pretty bad press in today's world. We are conditioned to believe that to be vulnerable means to be weak and inadequate. Maybe to even put ourselves in danger.

As primitive man, vulnerability was experienced as just that. A very real threat of being killed by wild animals or enemy tribes. This remains part of our primal programming. Our modern day sense of psychological vulnerability feels similarly risky and frightening. Sometimes even deadly.

Since ego is more concerned with our physical, rational survival, it hides vulnerability under a defensive cloak of fear and shame. Fear that, if we were to reveal our vulnerability, we may be overpowered by some outside force (a primal response). And shame, because the world may find something out about us which would deem us unworthy of acceptance from others.

When was the last time you remember feeling ashamed?

Was there a sense that others were seeing, or knowing, something about you that you did not wish them to?

Which of these shameful fears were you most concerned about?

❏ *Others might think less of me*
❏ *They might laugh at me*

❏ *They will know something about my past that I don't want them to know*

❏ *They will change their opinion of what they think I'm capable of doing*

❏ *They will see that I'm not as clever, attractive or special as I need them to think I am*

❏ *They might no longer love and accept me*

Do you recognise the voice of ego in any of these concerns?

Appearing less powerful than others (vulnerable), or unworthy of connection with others (shame), is threatening to ego self. An inauthentic connection, built on superficiality, is more valuable to it than risking the opportunity to relate more genuinely. More openly.

Thus the fear/shame cycle perpetuates itself. Outwardly, it is more than a good enough reason to continue to defend ourselves against any perceived 'weakness'.

We rely on our primitive defences when our public sense of self is threatened or feels compromised. The more afraid we are the more vulnerable we feel. The more threatened ego becomes, the deeper it tries to bury our vulnerability. This is why ego and vulnerability were never designed to be the best of friends. (See Defences.)

The challenge for therapists working with clients who feel particularly vulnerable is to ensure a high degree of *felt* psychological safety. This is communicated through an implicit trust that the therapist will honour, respect and care for whatever the client brings.

Once this atmosphere is established, and felt by the client, they become less fearful about being judged. Less worried about bringing their assumed shameful selves into the counselling room. It takes a lot of emotional energy to suppress the parts of us that we feel ashamed of. Over time it becomes exhausting. A good therapist will help the client to redirect that same energy into forging a stronger connection to the shamed self suppressed within.

First, that connection has to occur within the client. Once they feel safe enough, they can begin to communicate internally with the different parts of themselves. Including the banished, shameful parts.

Second, the client builds enough bravery to risk sharing this inner dialogue with the therapist.

Third, they can then use this new sense of inner connected wholeness to be more complete, more rounded, more authentic in everyday relationships.

It is not until we discover the emotional energy that we so readily trap in our shame, that we can liberate the potent spiritual power hidden away in its associated vulnerability:

> "Shame is a soul eating emotion."

> Carl Jung (Swiss founder of analytical psychology, psychoanalyst and psychiatrist)

When do you feel safe enough to be vulnerable?

What sort of human qualities need to be present?

Can, or do, you ever offer these to yourself?

Jack's Story

Jack came to see me after having been the victim of a violent mugging on holiday. Whilst his physical wounds had healed, he was still suffering with flashbacks, nightmares and sweats. It was clear that there was still emotional trauma energy trapped in his body.

Jack was a tall, well built man. He was very much used to being strong for others. He described himself as always being the 'life and soul' of the party. The elder sibling who helped to care for his younger brothers and sisters growing up.

Now he appeared emotionally broken. He wanted to get back to his job and his 'old way of life' as soon as possible. He saw that as the only real way to heal, to move on. To prove to his assailant that he was not beaten.

But, on returning to work, Jack felt extreme fear and panic. It was obvious that, in his mind, he wanted to get back to work. Yet his body seemed to be saying no. It was telling him something different. That he had not yet fully integrated the emotional significance of his trauma.

Through therapy, Jack began to open up to his internal sense of shame regarding the assault. First, he had made himself physically vulnerable on the night of the attack by taking a route through an unlit area. Second, he had not been physically strong enough to fight off his assailant. And, third, that the 'old Jack' couldn't just pick himself up and get back to work.

I shared with him my sense that he was being really tough on himself. Even slightly violent, in his self chastising manner, to 'just get over it'. It seemed difficult for Jack to let in my compassion and understanding.

The presence of my care revealed a deeper level of shame for Jack. He was ashamed of being vulnerable enough to show me that it was simply care that he needed. For him, letting in care meant that he could no longer be the strong, confident man that he always was. The one he so desperately wanted to return to being.

During a profound moment of connection between us, I asked Jack if the confidence he so readily exhibited before in his life was always entirely genuine. Or was it 'manufactured' in some way? After a few moments he admitted that it was, in fact, not how he really felt inside. Shy and insecure for much of the time. His outer confidence was a 'social mask' as he described it. It had worked very well for him. It meant he could fulfill the many roles he had assigned himself in his life.

Now I knew we were getting closer to the spiritual significance of what had happened. Jack's ego assumed that the only way forward was to return to his old self as quickly as possible. Only then could he hope to move on from the effects of his trauma. His deeper self, however, seemed to be inviting him to focus elsewhere; on what sort of confidence he now really wanted to build for himself. (See Self-Confidence.)

Jack admitted that the effects of the trauma had appeared to dismantle his whole sense of who he had assumed himself to be. Of how he had always strived to define himself. But, there was a deeper opportunity in that too. The chance to rebuild himself from the ground up. And this time of a material which more closely reflected his true essence.

Over time, the new confidence that Jack built was made up of a greater authenticity. Of tenderness for himself. Just as his physical scars had healed, his emotional ones began to as well. He opened up to sense the spiritual message in his trauma. He did not really want to go back to just being the old Jack. He wanted to be more real. More at peace with his vulnerability. Less ashamed of showing the world who he really was underneath. His vulnerability proved to be the key which opened the door to genuine care. Care that diffused the potency of his toxic, limiting shame.

◆ ◆ ◆

Our deeper self knows that it is indestructible and timeless. It knows that it is outside of the illusory fear of death. If we can see through the fear in which our ego wraps our vulnerability, uncertainty becomes more acceptable. We make space for spontaneity, creativity. Aliveness. (See Fear.)

Our vulnerability opens us up spiritually. Our shame closes us down. To have a closer relationship with vulnerability means, paradoxically for ego, to get in touch with a real inner strength. A constant. A foundation from which a more authentic relationship with our deeper self can be forged.

Vulnerability is the source of our creativity, belonging, connection and love. To risk being vulnerable means to risk being human. It is often said that true love sources its energy, not from some outer flawless perfection, but from an inner, shared fragility. True love flourishes when ego boundaries dissolve.

As babies learning to walk we are hardwired to struggle. To fall down, to learn and to get back up again. We feel the pain of the failure and then use that as the fuel to try again.

At this tender age we instinctively know that we are worthy of love and belonging. That we need to fall down and get up again in order to grow. The acronym FAIL - **F**irst **A**ttempt **I**n **L**earning, sums up this optimistic infantile philosophy perfectly. Our 'unconditioned' inner child still has much to teach us, it seems.

As we grow we become conditioned to assume what success is supposed to look like. With this programming comes a harsher judgement on our 'failings'. Instead of seeing them as signposts, encouraging us to approach something in a different way or rethink our strategy, we end up only deflated and defeated by them.

The original infantile drive of continuing endeavour, despite failure, evolves into a tribal fear of feeling vulnerable because of the stigmatism of failure. This is where we have come to misinterpret the gift of vulnerability. Instead of seeing it as a necessary component of endeavour and growth, we have placed it into a box of fear and shame and tightly closed the lid. (See Mistakes and Guilt.)

Whenever we risk being vulnerable there will be others who, if acting from ego, will perceive themselves as having power over us. Where we can stay out of ego's control we know that, however others may try to dominate, it is superficial. And, from a deeper perspective, spiritually impotent.

Have you ever risked being vulnerable with someone only to have them seemingly take advantage of your position?

Maybe you denigrated yourself for sharing your vulnerability because someone made you feel small and powerless?

If you reflect back now, from a more self-aware place, where did the real spiritual strength lie in that interaction?

For every person who may try to monopolise on another's vulnerability, there will be many more who will be encouraged and inspired to open up to their own. There will be many more who will be prepared to risk more connection and understanding. Disclosure, finally, leads to disclosure.

Our vulnerability becomes a source of strength when we realise that it is from this place that we are freer to be more creative and spontaneous. To be able to plant seeds and be open to whatever grows. To connect rather than feel compelled to impress. To risk that we are enough.

Both symbolically, and literally, hidden within our vulner**ability** is the key to our greatest ability:

> "Vulnerability is the birthplace of love, belonging, joy, courage, empathy, and creativity. It is the source

of hope, empathy, accountability, and authenticity. If we want greater clarity in our purpose or deeper and more meaningful spiritual lives, vulnerability is the path."

Brene Brown (American research professor, author and keynote speaker)

MISTAKES AND GUILT

The groundbreaking journey through vulnerability offers up many qualities. One of the most fertile is a renewed source of self compassion. Compassion allows us to reframe mistakes that we feel we've made in life. And soothes associated guilt.

Any outward admittance of a mistake frequently brings guilt, regret and embarrassment in its wake. That's why it can be hard to admit to ourselves, let alone anyone else, that we've made a mistake. That we got something 'wrong'.

And yet do we feel more compassion for a politician who is brave enough to say, 'I got it wrong?' Or to a child who shows genuine remorse if they think that they've upset us? We probably do.

Owning our mistakes, our misdemeanours, requires us to face our fallibility. Our humanity. Our fear of not being perfect. So many consequences for ego. No wonder it has difficulty in beating a path towards taking responsibility.

Sadly, this means that we typically bolster our defences, our righteousness, to protect ourselves from the risk of feeling the fragility of our own humanity. Hindering the work of our deeper self which wants to contemplate *all* experience. Including that experience which may be difficult to accept.

Break the word 'mistake' into it's two syllables and we have 'mis' and 'take'. We can interpret this as 'miss-taking' the potential to demonstrate what we were capable of in a given situation. Perhaps we missed the chance to shine in front of an audience. Didn't prepare as well as we might have done for an important exam. Or made a decision which, with hindsight, we judged to be unwise.

As we dwell on our mistakes there is a natural tendency to want to go back and replay them. We wish, in our heads, that we had done something differently. Or not at all. We endlessly fantasise about a different outcome. The dense energy, contained within the associated emotion of guilt, keeps us tied to the past.

Imagine that you are sitting down to dinner with the part of you that harbours guilt.

From the source of your own compassion, what is it you want to say to that part now?

Does it want to say anything back to you, to rejoin you in the present?

To start to untangle the complex emotion of guilt we need to understand that it is rooted in fear. Fear that we are not, or were not, 'enough'. When we incessantly wish that we had done something differently, we refuse to accept that something unfolded as it did. We deny reality. Stuck in this pointless cycle, we simply continue to send mental energy into the past. All in a vain effort to change who we were then. Instead of focussing on who we want to be in the *now*.

There is opportunity to reframe the negativity trapped within guilt and use it for more constructive purposes. Guilt seems to consistently call us back to rescue its repressed emotional energy and bring it into the present, where it can be used more constructively. To do this we need to develop the art of self-forgiveness. This spiritual practice requires us to find the compassion within our vulnerability. And to use it to release our guilty self from the prison of our past. This healing process represents the deeper aspirational striving for a state of completeness. Of wholeness in the present. (See Forgiveness.)

When we choose to leave this emotional energy within the vault of guilt, we resist the opportunity for healing. We refuse to understand what drove us to behave as we did, knowing what we knew at the time. Without the capacity for self understanding, self compassion cannot flourish.

Through a greater understanding of how you acted before, can you be more at peace with who you are now?

Can you hold some compassion for that former part of yourself that did the best that it could at the time?

Growth and evolution require that today is not the same as yesterday. That we see things differently this year than last. Until we can reconcile that the past is for reference and *not* for residence, the egoic emotional energy within guilt traps us there.

This sums up both the challenge and benefit of growth. By its very nature it reminds us that we have the innate capacity, and capability, for change. We get to see and perceive things differently. Each time from a higher perspective. As we learn, and have the potential to evolve, from each experience.

By reframing past mistakes within the context of this philosophy, the trapped energy within guilt and shame is liberated. Far from being threatening, maintaining an open and compassionate stance on our mistakes allows us to grow spiritually. That is what we are really here to do, and that is ok:

> "Guilt can either hold you back from growing, or it can show you what you need to shift in your life."

> Author unknown

I am reminded of all the heartwarming stories of people who have reframed their own mistakes of the past and transmuted them into opportunities to reach out and help others. The ex-convict who shares their story with vulnerable teenagers. Genuinely wanting them not to 'mis-taking' better choices. Or the ex-alcoholic who runs a support group helping others to work through addiction. Knowing that they understand some of what they may be going through too.

We should not squander the fertile emotional energy within guilt. Instead of weighing us down, preventing us from ascending, we can release it through self-forgiveness. And use it as a medium to connect with others who are also struggling. Those in pain, but unable to open the portal to their own self-compassion. The compassion that is vital for healing and wholeness.

SELF-CONFIDENCE

As we near the end of this book, I wanted to include a chapter on self-confidence. Not only to offer a brief recap on some of the material that I have covered in the preceding pages, but also to pose a small task before you embark upon it.

As you read this chapter, try to do so from two separate mindsets. First, through the eyes of your ego-centred self. Be aware of what feelings bubble up for you.

Then, reflect on what your deeper self concludes, having navigated and contemplated the emotional journey of this book so far.

See if both 'selves' can start to build a greater compassion and understanding for each other.

What do we really mean by self-confidence or 'confidence of self?' What do we imply when we say that someone has self-confidence?

When viewed solely from the perspective of comparing ourselves with others, confidence implies that we are better at something than somebody else. Or that we feel more important than others. Crudely speaking, it's a measure of the degree of the apparent power we either take, or have bestowed upon us, from the outside world. This makes it unpredictable and dependent on whatever is happening in our immediate surroundings.

Ego confidence is principally sourced from securing external attention, adulation and credit. So the energy in a group tends to be focused on the person who appears most confident.

Where the attention goes the energy flows.

Consider the effects of an audience screaming and applauding a pop star on stage. The pop star's confidence will, with little doubt, be riding high. They gain much of their confidence power from the audience. Being at the centre of other's attention and energetic focus.

However, if the audience applause stops for long enough, the celebrity's sense of confidence wanes. The costumes, the lights, the stage and the setting are part of a facade, a platform, which naturally draws power to those centred upon it. How many celebrities seem less confident when interviewed offstage? When wearing their normal clothes and having to revert to their everyday persona.

We invest a lot of our energy into the maintenance of outer confidence. Especially when we do not feel particularly confident inside. The world is like a stage. We are expected, and conditioned, to step out with confidence.

The question for our deeper self is whether we feel we deserve to have this confidence power bestowed upon us. If our drive to seek confidence is largely motivated by an inner lack of it, we can feel like a bath full of water with a hole in one end. We need the taps of affirmation fully open at one end, just to maintain a degree of water confidence in our bath. Particularly as we witness how quickly it drains out of the other:

> "Confidence is not 'they will like me', confidence is 'I'll be fine if they don't'."
>
> Christina Grimmie (American singer, songwriter, actress and YouTuber)

We all have days when we feel vulnerable and fragile. Maybe after a shock or when someone has knocked our confidence. It is at these times that we tend to seek reassurance from others.

Ego needs these reassurances. The 'yes I still love you' or, 'you look great as you are' kind of affirmation. Initially, this makes us feel good. But unless we can *really* believe it, we will need to keep both our bath taps on full flow.

In situations where you feel lacking in confidence where, and how, do you try to acquire it?

Is it normally from an outside (others) or inside (self) source?

Earthly importance and confidence is often confused with the degree of material wealth, beauty or fame that we happen to have at any given moment. Money, in particular, is a shallow valuing system. Many use it as a measure of whether someone deserves the right to respect and confidence.

Ego tells us that if we are rich then the associated degree of status will automatically give us confidence. Perhaps the great quest for status and wealth is an illusory, misguided aspiration, masking the deeper self source of true inner confidence.

As far as we know, we are the only mammals on the planet who have the capacity to be self-conscious. Put a very young baby in front of a mirror and they will be confused as to what they see. They have not yet developed any sense of self-consciousness.

Before around six months we are not aware where we end and where the world begins. We literally still feel at one with everything around us. There is no shame, embarrassment or ego. We maintain a sense that we are still fundamentally connected with all that is.

As we grow we begin to realise that we are, in fact, a separate body. We necessarily develop an ego to help us to establish both who we are, and who we want to be, as a separate individual.

It is this sense of feeling separate that is, in itself, a test for our natural spiritual confidence. It is here that we realise we must appear to stand alone as a separate being for a period. Otherwise, how could we ever hope to have any sense of the unique power of our individual presence in the world?

It is only through standing alone that we have the ability to develop an external consciousness of self, a self-consciousness. Ego serves us by acting as our outer shell. An overcoat. Essentially dressing and identifying our sense of separateness.

This consciousness of self helps us to become the singular, insightful, contemplative and emotionally challenged person that we are. And, at the same time, offers up the responsibility to reflect on how we use this sense of separateness to positively affect the whole.

Where we use the phrase 'self-conscious', we traditionally imply that someone is shy. Possibly insecure or lacking in confidence. It is ironic that we have come to use this label to sum up someone in a rather self-limiting way.

Do you consider yourself to be a self-conscious person?

Try to contemplate this question from both its traditional meaning and from a deeper spiritual perspective.

Is there a difference?

Much of the key message of this book is to inspire you to become more conscious of your 'self'. Of who you really are beyond the limitations of your physical body.

As we have been discovering, this journey is fraught with challenges and fears. Nothing can be discovered unless fears are faced and minds opened. To do this we must develop a degree of true inner confidence. Of trust. Of faith.

The word confidence comes from the Latin verb 'confedere', meaning 'with faith'. Faith is a belief founded on some sort of authority. Self-confidence, by its very definition, involves the self. And what better authority do we have over ourselves, other than ourselves?

Yes, we can use external references, filtered through ego, to inform and bolster us. Yet an inner faith cannot be shattered when ego judges those external references to be less than positive. As inevitably it will.

A faith that our journey before us is there to be taken helps to consolidate that confidence. Trusting that we were born with the inner resources to stay with it. Even when the going gets tough:

> "One to me is loss and gain; One to me is fame and shame; One to me is pleasure and pain...."

> Ram Dass (American spiritual teacher, psychologist and author)

An inner 'one' knowing which we have the faith to have confidence in, even when nothing else makes rational sense, reminds us that we trust in the greater wisdom of the Universe. And in its unique plan for us.

A MEANINGFUL LIFE?

In the concluding chapter of this book, I invite you to momentarily reflect upon the words that you would like to see written in the concluding chapter of your own physical life journey:

Envisage yourself listening to the conversations of your friends and family as they gather to commemorate your life at your wake or funeral. What do you imagine they would be saying about you?

More importantly, what would you like them to be saying?

Whilst initially seeming slightly morose, this exercise can prove distilling and enlightening. It helps to bring into the light of everyday awareness just what sort of person you currently believe yourself to be. And to compare it with the person you would like to become.

It also enables us to consider ourselves from a more detached perspective. As following our death we can no longer be identified with, or by, our physical body. At funerals we tend to refer to the deceased less by physical characteristics and more through qualities of character.

Even when we say, 'she was such a beautiful person', we do not generally refer to physical beauty, but a deeper beauty. How she treated others. When we recall, 'he always had a good word to say about everyone', we refer to how he made us feel in his presence.

This exercise reminds us that we are capable of seeing ourselves, other people, places and things from this different perspective if, and when, we choose to. It reminds us that we are capable of coming out of our heads. Of not narrowly viewing life through the lens of a continual rational process. To free ourselves to rise up and view things more holistically. More spiritually.

So often it is not until we contemplate the end of physical life that we actually grant ourselves a vantage point to have a healthier perspective upon it. Whilst totally immersed, we frequently identify solely with mind and its constant, distracting mental chatter.

When our nose is 'pressed against the glass', all we can see, and feel, is the glass. We literally cannot focus on anything else. We rarely step back far enough to see *through*. To 'wake up to what our emotions are really telling us'.

Through this book my hope is that I have encouraged you to take that step back. To see, or at least contemplate seeing, through the glass.

All the while we view life, and its experiences, solely through the medium of our limited minds we suffer. Ego *is* our unexamined, unchecked, spiritually uninformed mind. Operating alone in the wilderness of what it sees as a chaotic, separated, threatening world. Without the soothing, reassuring presence of our deeper self, ego mind remains lost, confused, frightened....

Yet what, or who, are we if we are not our minds? Where do we place our deeper self in relation to the mind and body? How do we conceptualise this part of us that enables us to see through the glass?

It appears that there is no easy answer. It is our very mind that wants a prescriptive solution to this conundrum. To be able to appease the reductionist ego which drives it.

Perhaps, to move closer to the answer, we need to shift our thinking into a different paradigm. One that is more of a feeling, felt sense. Just as the sense that we still have of someone when we stand at their funeral. Through their presence that we continue to feel in our hearts.

If we sense the presence of our deeper self in this way, we move closer to an appreciation of how it operates and expresses itself. As pure self-aware, non-judgmental, consciousness.

Try to feel it as the space within which your very thoughts form. As the watchtower that notices all the suggestions that ego throws into it. As the truster that everything is happening to help us grow spiritually:

> "To be conscious means not simply to be, but to be reported, known, to have awareness of one's being added to that being."

> William James (American philosopher and psychologist)

We have set ego the tough task of caring for us in a world which batters and bruises us. Both emotionally and psychologically. Its reaction has been to help us prove ourselves by constantly trying to be the biggest, strongest, smartest, most powerful human being on the planet. To ward off all of our 'foes'. Paradoxically, it also tries to persuade us that we are the worst, most useless, ugly and inept thing on it too. It's no wonder that we are left so lost and confused.

As I discussed in 'Our Life Scripts', this dichotomy is created because of the underlying message that we all struggle with: 'I'm not good enough.' When we identify solely with ego, we are torn between its forces of latent inadequacy and its tireless attempt to prove this universal script message wrong.

Given the unenviable task we throw down at ego's feet, I have to hold my hands up and propose that we give it more credit for all its undoubted worldly efforts.

After all, it is only trying to do its best. Particularly when we consider the complex, confusing mission we have set before it. In this physical realm we need it and it needs us.

Throughout this book I have insinuated that it is the monster in the room. The reason why the world is in the chaotic state it is today. For now, I ask you to forgive this rather one-dimensional viewpoint and to consider its vital purpose. To provide us with the launch pad for our deeper self to take off.

Before we build a house we need to have a detailed plan on paper. An idea of the finished article. Something to act as a guide during the construction process. Without it, we would have no idea of what our house is capable of becoming.

Once we have the materials, we lay the foundations and start to build the walls of our house. When the walls get to a certain height, we need scaffolding to continue to build. We use this supportive framework to complete the upper storey and then to add the roof.

In this analogy, the scaffolding represents ego. To have a house that is strong, symmetrical and well built, we need the scaffolding to work from during the construction process. Without it our house would take much longer, be more complicated, and potentially dangerous, to build.

Once completed, we can remain safe and warm inside. Especially when we perceive the harsh weather of life approaching. This weather is symbolic of the difficult, challenging life circumstances that cause our emotional wounds.

This wounding weather shapes, forms, guides and inspires us to adapt the type and build of our house. Without it we may never have known just what type of house we were truly capable of building.

Now imagine if we were to leave the scaffolding in place after it had served its purpose. The continuing sight of all that metal containment would spoil the natural beauty and grandeur of what lies beneath.

Because we appreciate that the ego scaffolding played such a vital role, we are loathed to let it go. We fear that our house may crumble and fall without its, at one time, necessary support.

This analogy helps us to understand why we have become so over-identified with ego. We falsely believe it to be the totality of who we are. When something has served us well, and played a vital role in our formation, then of course it seems counterintuitive to let such a trusted ally go.

It has given us good advice, got us through, helped us to develop a strategy for survival. A strategy that shows us the doorway to our gifts and potential through our very ability to survive in this physical world.

Yet, if we continue to hide behind this trusted ally, and remain submerged beneath the metal, we lose something of our essence. Of our real spiritual beauty. Of our true identity.

The journey to our deeper self is fraught with complex emotions, struggles, conflicts and challenges. All of this difficulty is somehow intelligently designed to eventually break down the scaffolding structure of ego, when it no longer serves us.

Given the intrinsic fear lurking within our societal conditioning, we believe that our deeper self may not have enough strength, enough silent power, to sustain us. We continue to bolster *only* this outer structure by reinforcing an array of ego defences.

It is only through risking surrendering to our vulnerability by stepping out from behind this egoic structure; by being brave enough to enter into the core of our indoctrinating shame; that we come to discover the enduring strength, wisdom, timelessness and gifts of our deeper self.

We discover that what ego fears, our deeper self wants us to face. For us to remember, know and trust in its unconditional love and wisdom. When we connect with this love, the inner love, the inner acceptance of who we are, fear dissipates and our true confidence grows.

If we were to release a forming butterfly from its cocoon before it was ready, it would simply fall to the ground and die. It is only through the struggle to free itself from its casing that the butterfly can develop the muscles that it needs to fly.

Ego is much like this cocoon casing. It keeps us safe. It gives us the cosseted environment in which to grow. But at some point we need to struggle through it. To build the strength to spread our beautiful butterfly wings. And to take flight.

Credit ego when it appears. Acknowledge it. Then summon the courage to put it to one side. Face, and place, challenging life experiences within the wise womb of deeper self. Let them gestate from pain to insight.

With this spiritually dedicated approach we replace fear with love. In an absence of fear, and in the light of love, we embrace the spiritual consistency and growth opportunity inherent within all life on this planet. We suffer less. We live more.

Through this trust, joy and peace, we reveal the higher truth in all experience. We surrender to our true transcendent nature. Ego want in the world transforms into giving. And fear dissolves into love:

> "The privilege of a lifetime is to become who you truly are."
>
> Carl Jung (Swiss founder of analytical psychology, psychoanalyst and psychiatrist)

***

ACKNOWLEDGEMENTS

Heartfelt thanks to all the people who have helped me to bring this book into being:

My editor-in-chief Leslie Williams, for subjecting my manuscript to the utmost scrutiny with her wise eagle-eye. Not forgetting her unparalleled patience as I chopped and changed bits requiring numerous re-reads.

To gifted illustrator and digital artist Nicolas Bowley for designing and creating a great visual concept for the cover.

To talented graphic designer Eman Carballo for overseeing the formatting of the cover, internal images and logo design. (www.eman-designs.com)

To the insightful and innovative Mark Showler for his invaluable assistance with branding, website, marketing and promotions. (www.sensechi.com)

To my wonderful friends and counselling colleagues who helped me navigate through numerous drafts of my manuscript. Offering invaluable feedback, input, moral support, humour and inspiration. Couldn't have done it without you all!

Particular note going out to Gerard Egan, Debra Engle, Jonathan Izard, Sarah Richardson, Valerie McColl, Gardenia Imber, Justin Shelley, Lesley Hallows, Christopher Moyes, Steve Burchell, Graham Sharpe, Jacqui Launchbury and Tracey Ariss.

To all the inspirational workshop leaders, teachers, lecturers, group facilitators, supervisors and insightful speakers who have sparked my enthusiasm, fielded my questions and shared their wisdom whilst I navigated my own training and awareness pathway.

And last, but not least, to my counselling clients. You unceasingly inspire me with your courage, teach me through your sharing and expand me with your perspectives. Thank you all. Particular mention to those who have given me permission to share your stories here, so that others may learn and grow.

Thank you.

ABOUT THE AUTHOR

Chris Partridge

 Chris Partridge was born in London, England. He spent much of his early career travelling the world working for an international airline. Through the enlightenment of travel, meeting and working with people from many cultures, creeds and continents, he learnt that we are all, ultimately, searching for one thing. Self-fulfillment.

Witnessing the myriad of ways people universally try to fill and complete themselves, Chris became increasingly aware of how we suffer when we try to achieve this solely through external means. This led to a spiritual awakening. Persuading him to relinquish the dominance of his ego and embrace more unconditionally everything that life was showing him. To surrender to and transmute his own pain into awareness.

Since qualifying as a counsellor and psychotherapist more than 25 years ago, Chris has become increasingly fascinated by the overlap between the evolving science of quantum physics and spirituality. Particularly the basic premise of this science which states that the observer affects what is observed. Or, if we change the way we look at something, what we look at changes.

This scientific-based awareness of the innate spiritual power in how we choose to perceive something, and of the interconnectedness of all things, transformed Chris's therapeutic approach to one of holism. He realised that you cannot truly heal the mind unless you include the body and spirit.

By including a number of additional healing modalities within his practice: somatic bodywork, hypnotherapy, EFT and EMDR, Chris now likes to define himself as a holistic mind/body/spirit therapist.

'Wake Up' is Chris's first full length book. He has also written many articles for magazines and journals and contributed to the seminal text, 'Aviation Mental Health - Psychological Implications for Air Transportation' published by Routledge (2006).

He splits his time between London and Barcelona where he continues to write, facilitates workshops and trainings, and works as a supervisor of other therapists.

BECOME A PART OF THE 'NEW NORMAL' MOVEMENT

As we enter the 'new normal' together following the global 'rebooting' effects of the current world health crisis, I am passionate about continuing to integrate the deeper emotional and spiritual ramifications. Visit my website below to share how you have shifted emotionally and awoken spiritually as a result of the planetary reset. Sign up to keep in touch through newsletters and blogs. I would love to hear from you!

Lastly, thank you for purchasing, reading, and investing in, this book. If you have a moment, I would appreciate it if you could leave an honest review on my Amazon book's page. All of your comments will help me to better understand how this work has impacted you as I write more and strive to continue the momentum....

www.thenewnormalmovement.net

Printed by Amazon Italia Logistica S.r.l.
Torrazza Piemonte (TO), Italy

16539422R00190